011956434

OUR SOCIAL HERITAGE

Our Social Heritage

By

Graham Wallas

*Author of "Human Nature in Politics," 1908
and "The Great Society," 1914*

LONDON : GEORGE ALLEN & UNWIN LTD.
RUSKIN HOUSE, 40 MUSEUM STREET, W.C.1

First published in 1921

TO

MY WIFE

October, 1920

CONTENTS

SYNOPSIS

CHAPTER I (pp. 15–25)

INTRODUCTION

Our social heritage consists of that part of our " nurture " which we acquire by the social process of teaching and learning. Men have more social heritage than other animals, and are more dependent on it for existence. We have, indeed, become biologically parasitic upon our social heritage ; and, if we once forgot what we have been taught, our species might die out before it had time to acquire a new social heritage. The mass of our social heritage is rapidly increasing, and the problem of securing economy in its acquirement and use, and efficiency in its continuous criticism and improvement, is becoming more urgent.

CHAPTER II (pp. 26–54)

SOCIAL HERITAGE IN WORK AND THOUGHT

Part of our social heritage consists of the power, which we acquire by education from infancy onwards, of making sustained and conscious muscular and mental efforts. We learn to recognize the difference between will and impulse ; and are thereby enabled to make continuous use of processes which are naturally intermittent, to invent methods of compensating for the resulting nervous strain, and to avail ourselves of the " drive " of artistic impulse. Thought under modern conditions requires us to learn, not only how to stimulate artificial intellectual effort, but also how to use artificial intellectual methods. These methods have hitherto been most successful in the physical sciences ; but it seems likely that in certain respects the direction of self-conscious intellectual effort may in the future be developed more successfully by the students

9

of the moral sciences. If so, that development may produce an important effect on educational technique both in Britain and in America.

CHAPTER III (pp. 55–76)

GROUP CO-OPERATION

Group co-operation, under modern conditions, requires (like individual work and thought) a combination of socially inherited expedients with biologically inherited instincts. Men are a loosely gregarious species who instinctively used significant cries even before the invention of language ; and they naturally co-operate by a clamorous alternation of the impulse to lead with the impulse to follow. Our socially inherited expedients of group co-operation by discipline and discussion are still imperfectly worked out, and are apt at any moment to break down, and their place to be taken by the primitive instinctive process. These facts may be illustrated from the Reports of the British " Dardanelles " and " Mesopotamia " Commissions of 1917.

CHAPTER IV (pp. 77–100)

THE NATION AS IDEA AND FACT

National co-operation is more dependent on our social heritage than group co-operation. In a group, men think and feel about direct sensations and memories of their fellows ; in a nation, they must think and feel about some entity of the mind. At present we generally leave the formation of the mental " panoramas " which represent our nation for each of us, to chance, or to the scheming of professional manipulators of motive. We should try to make the formation of a trustworthy idea of our nation into a conscious process. Our idea when it is formed should remind us of the facts of the human type, of the differences between individual human beings, and of the quantitative relation between the grades and kinds of difference. Such an idea will help us to realize that a modern industrial nation is not likely to be permanently coherent unless habit is based on contentment ; and unless contentment is made possible by an approximation to social equality, by a clearer understanding of economic facts, and by a greater liking in each of us for his work. That liking will only be secured under modern conditions if our social organization and our educational methods are based more on the idea of difference than on the idea of identity.

Chapter V (pp. 101–119)

THE CONTROL OF NATIONAL CO-OPERATION

During the nineteenth century the industrial nations of the world directed their large-scale co-operative activities by two main expedients, the territorial state and capitalism. Both expedients are now widely distrusted, and progressive opinion often inclines towards vocationalism. Vocational organization is in many ways useful, but when it is proposed to make vocationalism the main source of social power we must examine its tendencies in the present and its history in the past. Does guild socialism offer us a sufficiently varied and interesting life? Will it tend to strengthen professional conservatism? Is it compatible with "integration of labour," when that process is socially desirable, or with the sufficient accumulation of capital for future work? On all these points our experience in the war indicated that the modern democratic state tends to take the more socially desirable and the modern vocational organizations the less socially desirable side.

Chapter VI (pp. 120–154)

PROFESSIONALISM

The problem of vocational organization as a socially inherited expedient can be approached with less prejudice by examining the professions than by examining the Trade Unions. The profession of the law is the most powerful of the English vocational organizations, and shows the difficulties and dangers of uncontrolled vocationalism most clearly. The organization of the medical profession is more recent, and yet reveals important intellectual and administrative defects. Military professionalism has a history as old as civilization, and its dangers are obvious. The professionalism of teachers is peculiar in its relation to the special but intermittent teaching instinct, and in the relation between the process of teaching and learning and the whole of our social heritage of new and old knowledge.

Chapter VII (pp. 155–182)

LIBERTY

The psychological facts which give political force to the idea of Liberty may be seen in the results which follow from the obstruction of human impulses. Those results depend on the nature of the obstructing cause even more than on the nature of the obstruction. Obstruction by human agents produces a different reaction to that produced by obstruction by non-human causes ; but this unfreedom-reaction is only produced when obstruction is felt to be an interference with the normal course of human relations. Pericles' conception of Liberty showed enormously more psychological insight than did that of Mill; and the loss of control by the British Liberal Party in the nineteenth century was largely due to an insufficient analysis of the principle which they shared with Mill. The Oxford metaphysical criticism of the principle of Liberty and Arnold's psychological criticism of it were ineffective as political forces. The future of Liberalism may depend on its power to apply to modern conditions the vision of Pericles.

CHAPTER VIII (pp. 183–198)

RIGHTS, HONOUR, AND INDEPENDENCE

The analysis of Liberty helps us to analyse Natural Right. That analysis will show both that Natural Rights are real things, and that it is not always good for us to receive them in full. It also will show the cause of the historical assertion and denial and conflicting interpretation of Rights. The principle of Honour is based on similar psychological facts, and can be made more useful by a similar analysis. So is the principle of Independence, in the case of judges, quasi-judicial officers, technicians, and administrators. A psychological analysis of the principle of Independence may also help us in the difficult task of adapting to modern needs the expedients of parliamentary representation and the newspaper press.

CHAPTER IX (pp. 199–217)

WORLD CO-OPERATION

The change of scale from national co-operation to world co-operation involves a change in the co-operative process. Our co-operative instincts of defence may here act as a cause of international hatred. But world co-operation is necessary if the human species is to survive ; and the chief hope of world peace lies in a recognition of that fact, leading to the effort of rational calculation and calculated action. For that purpose we must bring a new " problem-attitude " to bear on such sciences as logic, history, law, and biology, and on such principles as Liberty, Independence,

Nationality, and Equality. We must also make an effort of invention in the adaptation of national institutions to world purposes, and in the creation of new world institutions and traditions.

CHAPTER X (pp. 218–239)

CONSTITUTIONAL MONARCHY

British constitutional monarchy is described by Bagehot and other writers as a means of securing instinctive personal loyalty for a government which is in fact parliamentary and impersonal. It is also now described as the " great symbol " of that relation between Britain and the Dominions which would otherwise be " openly and frankly nothing." Queen Victoria and the other British monarchs during the nineteenth century claimed, however, that their prerogative was " limited " rather than symbolic. The limitation of British monarchical prerogative depends on the two conventions, that the monarch should not veto legislation, or retain in power a ministry without a majority in the House of Commons ; and on the presumption that the army will always obey a parliamentary government. The events of 1909–1913 left the first convention and the presumption no longer unchallenged ; and during the war, constitutional monarchy abroad became less constitutional. Constitutional monarchy as symbol represents the primitive expedient of a " specimen-symbol " rather than a " word-symbol." It has the psychological advantages of its type ; but it also has the disadvantage of providing a less penetrating working conception of the political relation which it symbolizes.

CHAPTER XI (pp. 240–252)

SCIENCE

The " world-outlook " of Science has given mankind a growing sense of power both over their environment and over their own conduct. But it still leads to the old dilemma of free will and determinism. We may some day escape from that dilemma ; but meanwhile it has, whether in its theological or its scientific form, an unfortunate effect on our conduct. Our simpler motives seem to us more " scientific " than our less simple motives. The materialist explanation of history was till 1848 a conservative, and has been since 1848 a revolutionary economic force. Darwinian determinism has made wars more likely ; and psychological determinism is apt to diminish personal initiative and responsibility in a modern democracy. We should not allow either the physical scientists or the metaphysicians to divide the facts of human motive into those which are " scientific " and those which are not.

CHAPTER XII (pp. 253–284)

THE CHURCH

What part in the control of modern long-range conduct is played by the socially inherited fact of organized Christianity, and especially by the great Catholic and Lutheran Churches ? In the case of those national actions during the war which are now most universally condemned, it would appear that there was an inverse statistical correlation between membership of the historical churches and an attitude of protest against the wrong-doing of one's nation. In the English Church such failure as exists in intellectual and humanitarian leadership may be partly due to defects in current Anglican metaphysic, and in the psychology of current sacramentalism. Sacramentalism has no necessary connection with any ethical solution of modern problems, and tends to substitute a ritual for a social conception of conduct. Sacramentalism also encourages professionalism among the clergy in its narrowest form. If the Anglican Church is disestablished, this professionalism may make it a disruptive rather than a conservative force, with an ideal not of individual initiative but of corporate and nationalist particularism. Clerical professionalism will concern itself chiefly with education, and may tend to diminish fruitful intellectual effort, either by bringing education under more effective clerical control, or by maintaining obscurantist compromises. If the twentieth century sees a new birth of intellectual energy, the part played by the organization of emotion in our social heritage may be radically changed.

OUR SOCIAL HERITAGE

CHAPTER I

INTRODUCTION

MEN, like all other animals, are enabled to exist in their present numbers by a combination of " nature " and " nurture."

Our " nature " consists of those facts of structure and instinct which are inherited by the biological process of begetting and birth. We inherit biologically, for instance, the viscera by which we digest certain kinds of food, and the instincts which make us desire them ; a skin which resists bacterial infection, and an instinct to brush away a fly before he pierces our skin ; a highly complex nervous system, and an instinctive impulse to think.

The " nature " of all animals empowers and impels them to acquire, after birth, the structural modifications and nervous and muscular habits and memories which constitute their " nurture." Men are mammalian verte-brates, and " nurture " plays a much larger part in the lives of mammals than it does in the lives of invertebrates like the insects, or of lower vertebrates like the fishes or reptiles. The " nature " of a higher mammal is, indeed, a strongly outlined sketch, the details of which are filled in after birth by his " nurture."

Our "nurture" may, again, be divided into two parts. The first part consists of that which each one of us acquires for himself, without learning it from other human beings. The second part consists of the knowledge and expedients and habits which were originally the personal acquisition of individuals, but which have been afterwards handed down from one generation to another by the social process of teaching and learning. It is this second part of our nurture which I shall call our "social heritage." [1]

Men differ widely from all other animals by the extent of their social heritage, and the degree of their dependence on it. Those insects among whom one generation dies out before another is born can obviously have no social heritage at all; nor can fishes, or any other species among whom parents do not associate with their offspring. A certain amount of social heritage apparently exists in some species of birds. Birds are long-lived, and acquire much individual experience. The young of some bird-species remain a comparatively long time with their parents; and useful expedients can be socially transmitted from one bird-generation to another by flocking and other gregarious processes. In the cold spring, for instance, of 1895, a few seagulls found that they could

[1] The term "social inheritance" is, I find, used in the sense in which I use "social heritage" by Benjamin Kidd in his *Science of Power* (1918), pp. 113–114. Baldwin (quoted by Drever, *Instinct in Man*, p. 80) uses the term "social heredity" in that sense. Watson in his *Behavior* (1914), p. 187, uses the term "phylogenetic habit" in much the same sense. Wells in his *Outline of History*, chap. vii, § 2, uses the word "tradition." Wells confines the "tradition and the nervous organization necessary to receive tradition" to the mammals. The evidence seems to me to indicate that some birds have more of it than many mammals. Sir E. Ray Lankester, in his *Encyclopædia Britannica* article on Zoology, uses the term "Record of the Past" or "Record," as related to "Educability."

easily obtain food by going up the Thames into the smoky atmosphere of London. Since then, large numbers of gulls come to London every winter, in mild weather as well as in cold. They have evolved no new biologically inherited instinct, but have acquired a new socially inherited habit, which will probably last long after the original pioneers are dead. In the annual journeys of migratory birds, it may be that, while the instinct to follow the flock or to return to the point from which it started, is biologically inherited, the actual route is socially inherited. In New Zealand the " mountain parrot " apparently hands down by social inheritance the art of attacking sheep's kidneys. Experiment, again, seems to show that, while the characteristic flight of each bird-species is biologically inherited, the characteristic song of some singing-birds is socially inherited.[1] Among mammals, seals may be guided by social inheritance to their breeding-places, and town rats may, perhaps, hand on to successive generations the habit of resorting to certain accidentally discovered stores of food. Some American naturalists claim that there is a large socially inherited element in the methods by which certain American carnivorous mammals obtain food and escape traps.

The process of social inheritance is, as far as I know, not necessary for the existence of any wild non-human species or variety. The swallows, or the London rats, might, if they forgot all that they had learnt from their

[1] " Until recent years it was supposed that the characteristic songs of birds were inherited, like instincts. Apparently this is not wholly true. It would seem from the work of Scott and Conradi that what the birds inherit is a strong tendency to sing, but that no characteristic song develops without training." J. B. Watson, *Behavior* (1914), p. 142. Watson gives an account of the experiments.

parents, sink, for a few generations, to one-half, or one-quarter, of their present numbers. But the most important and progressive varieties of the human race would probably, if social inheritance were in their case interrupted, die out altogether. If the earth were struck by one of Mr. Wells's comets, and if, in consequence, every human being now alive were to lose all the knowledge and habits which he had acquired from preceding generations (though retaining unchanged all his own powers of invention, and memory, and habituation), nine-tenths of the inhabitants of London or New York would be dead in a month, and 99 per cent. of the remaining tenth would be dead in six months. They would have no language to express their thoughts, and no thoughts but vague reverie. They could not read notices, or drive motors or horses. They would wander about, led by the inarticulate cries of a few naturally dominant individuals, drowning themselves, as thirst came on, in hundreds at the riverside landing places, looting those shops where the smell of decaying food attracted them, and perhaps at the end stumbling on the expedient of cannibalism. Even in the country districts, men could not invent, in time to preserve their lives, methods of growing food, or taming animals, or making fire, or so clothing themselves as to endure a northern winter. An attack of constipation or measles would be invariably fatal. After a few years mankind would almost certainly disappear from the northern and temperate zones. The white races would probably become extinct everywhere. A few primitive races might live on fruit and small animals in those fertile tropical regions where the human species was originally evolved, until they had slowly accumulated a new social heritage. After some

thousands of generations they would probably possess
something which we should recognize as a language, and
perhaps some art of taming animals and cultivating land.
They might or might not have created what we should
call a religion, or a few of our simpler mechanical inventions and political expedients. They probably would not
have recreated such general ideas as "Law" or "Liberty";
though they might have created other general ideas which
would be new to us.

Man has been increasingly dependent on his social
heritage since the beginning of conventional language
and of the art of flint-chipping, that is to say, for perhaps
half a million years. This fact has brought about important modifications in our biologically inherited nature.
We have become biologically more fitted to live with the
help of our social heritage, and biologically less fitted
to live without it.[1] We have become, one may say,
biologically parasitic upon our social heritage. Just as the
parasitic crustacean *Sacculina*, after living for unnumbered
thousands of generations upon the body-juices of the
crab, has evolved special organs and a special body of
instincts which fit it to obtain that food, and unfit it
to live without that food ; so man has evolved, and is
still evolving, certain modifications of structure and
instinct, which, while they increase his power of acquiring
and using social heritage, also increase his dependence
on it.

---

[1] This statement does not, of course, involve any Lamarckian
assumption of the biological inheritability of acquired characteristics. It is only necessary to assume (a) that those families
which were more able to acquire and hand down social heritage
would tend to survive, and (b) that those parts of our bodily and
nervous structure which the existence of social heritage rendered
unnecessary or less necessary for survival would tend to degenerate.

Some of these modifications are general changes in his instincts, which make him more able to learn and to teach. Man, as compared with other mammals, has a much wider and more untiring curiosity, and a greater power of responding to suggestion and of forming new muscular and nervous habits. Human beings seem also to have an instinctive impulse, intermittent and varying greatly in individuals, to teach. Even more important than these general changes is the evolution of the instinct of speech, and the corresponding structural modifications of the speech-organs in the mouth and throat and brain. Men for many thousand generations have accumulated conventional language-systems, and have been increasingly dependent on their use. We have, therefore, evolved a special instinct, impelling us to learn and use conventional words. Any one who has watched a child during its second year will see that this instinct is as definite as that which impels *Sacculina* to settle on a crab ; and that, if there were no language present for the child to learn, the speech-instinct would be as meaningless and baffled as the instinct of *Sacculina* when it finds no crab.

We can watch, to-day, certain slow tendencies in the further evolution of this parasitic relation of man to his social heritage. Families with bad teeth or very short sight are enabled to live and beget children by the socially inherited inventions of false teeth and spectacles. Women whose children would be born dead or would die for want of milk, are enabled by the arts of midwifery and artificial feeding to bring up their young ; and our natural strength of teeth, excellence of sight, and ease in bearing and suckling, are apparently beginning to decline ; though civilized man, when his health has been preserved by the art of medicine, and his sight has been corrected by the art of optics, is, on the average, much stronger, more efficient, and longer-lived than the savage.

During the last two centuries that part of the social heritage of mankind which consists of the applied industrial sciences has been multiplied many times. This process is too recent to have produced obvious biological effects within any given variety of the human species ; but it has already produced an important change in the proportionate numbers of the different human varieties. A much greater proportion of the human species than was the case two centuries ago, now belong to those European breeding-stocks whose mental elasticity and power of forming habits of sustained industry have so far enabled them to acquire most easily and exploit most fully the industrial methods which depend on mechanical energy. Perhaps, after a few more generations, the yellow races may prove themselves to be even more fitted biologically for modern industrial methods, and may be found to have increased in a still larger proportion. But the growth of the applied industrial sciences is only part of an enormous recent increase in the accumulated knowledge on which modern civilization and the size of modern populations depend. In twenty years an Encyclopedia is now obsolete ; and this increase is constantly adding to our difficulty in handing down our social heritage from one generation to the next. The difficulty has been partly met by the devices of writing and printing and cataloguing, which enable us to keep knowledge, when once acquired, ready for use, without the necessity that any one should actually remember it. It has been partly met by compulsory education, and by a constant increase in the length of the average educational course. Education, indeed, has in all civilized countries already reached a point where it is very hard to find a sufficiency of qualified teachers ; and the possibility has already to be faced that the burden of learning and teaching may prove too great to be consistent with a harmonious and happy life. But the most effective, as it is, in some respects, the most dangerous, means of dealing with the growing accumulation of our knowledge has been the division and subdivision of knowledge and function. Only one man in a million may now acquire some piece of knowledge or skill on which the safety of all the rest depends. The members of almost any profession or skilled craft can, therefore, if they agree to withhold their services, " hold up " much of the social and economic life of their nation ; and I shall discuss in a later chapter [1] the influence of this fact on the social organization of a modern industrial nation.

The problem, however, of social inheritance does not simply consist in the difficulty of handing down a steadily growing accumulation of arts and sciences, and organizing its use. Each generation, if it is to live happily and harmoniously, or even is to avoid acute suffering, must adapt to its present needs the social heritage which it received from the preceding generation. The exhaustion of an old source of supply of food or raw materials, the appearance of a new disease, or an increase of population, may, of itself, make obsolete old arts and sciences and customs, and make new discoveries necessary. A new discovery, again, like that of printing, or the compass, or steam, or gunpowder, or the microscope, or representation by election, or biblical criticism, or of such ideas as nationality or socialism, may compel the readjustment of tradition in a hundred ways. And, side

[1] Chapter V.

by side with this recurrent necessity of readjustment, is the continuous pressure of human curiosity, and of the human creative instincts, impelling the abler members of each generation to hand on to their children more than they received from their own parents. This bursting of old bottles by new wine has, in the history of mankind, usually been a slow and uncertain process. In this or that region the admitted failure of some old tradition, or a new idea put forward by some thinker or group of thinkers, leads to detailed local changes which slowly spread to other communities. But sometimes, as in the Athens of Pericles and Socrates, or in Italy of the Renaissance, or France of the Revolution, a wide and conscious effort has been made to survey the whole field of our social heritage, and to bring the old into systematic relation with the new. Such a wide and conscious effort of " reconstruction " may be found by future historians to have followed, after an interval for recovery from nervous exhaustion, the world-war of 1914–18. If reconstruction is to be successful, new knowledge, the discovery of hitherto unknown relations of cause and effect, will in some cases be required. In other cases knowledge already accumulated must be applied by newly invented expedients to new problems. Sometimes what will be needed is an alteration of the proportion of the limited learning-power of the growing generation allotted to different types of study, and of the emphasis given in education to this or that element in the past experience of mankind. Sometimes we shall have to make the painful effort of unlearning what we have been taught, and of breaking intellectual and emotional habits.

This book is an attempt to survey our relation to our social heritage in a single, though, as I believe, a very important section. I shall hardly touch, for instance, on the huge subject of the application of the physical sciences to our new world-problems. Even in the human sciences I shall refer only incidentally to the eugenic problem of restoring or improving our biological inheritance, so grievously injured by the dysgenic effects of the war. The section of our social heritage with which I shall deal will be the ideas, habits, and institutions directly concerned in the political, economic, and social organization of those modern communities which constitute that which I called in 1914 " The Great Society."

I am well aware of the difficulties and risks of the task in which I shall ask my readers to co-operate with me. Every general survey of our social heritage must start from the vision of a single human mind. But no single mind can see more than a thousandth part of the relevant facts even of a section of that heritage. A tradition which seems to any one of us useless or harmful may have causes for its existence of which we are ignorant. The social heritage of any race or people, the literature or domestic economy of China, or India, or Palestine, or Norway, or the governments or educational systems of Italy or Japan or America, may have become subtly adapted to racial or climatic facts which do not exist elsewhere. A change which in one country is easy, may, in another country, require the pulling down of firmly established institutions. We all feel, indeed, in 1920 much more humble, when approaching the problem of social and intellectual reconstruction, than did the followers of Rousseau or Adam Smith before the French Revolution, or the followers of Bentham, or Godwin, or Hegel, or Mazzini, after the world-war that ended in 1815. But the urgency of our task is greater. The new fact of modern industrial organization is spreading over the earth, and we have learnt that the dangers arising from that fact are equally universal. Unless, therefore, an attempt is now made, in many countries and by many thinkers, to see our socially inherited ways of living and thinking as a whole, the nations of the earth, confused and embittered by the events of 1914–20, may soon be compelled to witness—this time without hope or illusion —another and more destructive stage in the suicide of civilization.

CHAPTER II

SOCIAL HERITAGE IN WORK AND THOUGHT

In this chapter I shall deal with sustained muscular effort, and sustained intellectual effort. I shall argue that both these forms of human behaviour are largely dependent on the process of social inheritance ; and that we shall be most likely to increase our success in working and thinking if we clearly recognize that dependence and its consequences. Both muscular and mental effort can be studied in the individual human being, looked on as isolated from his fellows ; and I can, therefore, discuss them before I consider the various socially inherited forms of co-operation among human beings, in groups, or nations, or world-relationships.

Sustained muscular and mental effort are alike in the fact that they are dependent on the existence of the self-conscious *will*, which itself is mainly a product of social inheritance. We know little or nothing of the consciousness of non-human animals, but any one who observes the behaviour of a wild mammal may guess that it is not aware of any " self," separable from and more permanent than the impulse of the moment. Fear, or anger, or sex-love, or the hunting impulse, are, one supposes, while they prevail, inseparable parts of the animal's self. Two impulses, fear, for instance, and curiosity, may, of course, conflict. But as one watches a frightened and curious rabbit, one infers that it does not feel either that one of the two impulses is more especially its " self " than the other, or that a " self " exists apart from both of them.

Primitive man may have stood in that respect somewhere between the unself-consciousness of the higher mammals and the self-consciousness of civilized man. Civilized man is taught to separate in consciousness his " self " and his " will " from his less permanent memories and impulses by an educational process which begins even before the power of speech has developed. The youngest infant is encouraged by signs and non-linguistic sounds to make certain self-directed efforts. A more definite stage starts with the acquirement of language. As soon as a fact of consciousness can be named, it can be separated from the namer. The original invention of words like " will " or " try " must therefore have formed a new departure point in human behaviour. They made it infinitely easier to recognize the feeling of self-conscious effort, to stimulate that feeling voluntarily, and to maintain it.[1]

Now, the degree of control that can be exercised by the self-conscious will over the different factors in human behaviour varies with the earliness or lateness in biological origin of those factors. Our will exercises very little direct control over the simpler physiological reactions, heart-beat, digestion, etc., which appeared earliest in the

[1] I watched, some years ago, a small experiment in the combined process of teaching the meaning of a word and stimulating a self-conscious effort. A little girl of perhaps five years old had formed a habit of biting her hair as she went to sleep. She was told to " try " to stop it, and she asked how she was to do so. She was told that her " will " would help her. Next morning she came down and said that her " will " told her to go on biting. In a few days she apparently learnt to distinguish between " will " as conscious impulse and " will " as self-conscious effort.

evolutionary history of mankind, which are mainly subconscious, and which we share with many of the simplest
animals. Our will has more direct control over the more
conscious " instincts," and over those movements of the
sense-organs and the muscles which are the normal external
manifestations of " instinctive " behaviour. It has most
control over the highly conscious process of attention,
and over certain other factors in that behaviour of the
intellect which is the latest product of evolution.[1] And
this gradation from our " lower " and less conscious
physiological reactions up through " instinctive " behaviour to our " higher," more conscious activities, is
not only a gradation from that which is earlier to that
which is later in evolution, but also to a large extent a
gradation from that which was evolved to meet continuous
needs to that which was evolved to meet our occasional
needs. All vertebrate animals breathe water or air,
circulate their body-fluids, and digest food, by continuous
or prolonged repetitions of monotonous external or internal
movements. These movements do not soon create fatigue,
nor do the pecking or browsing movements of many birds
or mammals while obtaining food, though fatigue soon
follows the intermittent movements to which they are
impelled by the presence of danger. Hunting animals,
on the other hand, or animals, like man and the anthropoid
apes, of mixed diet, not only escape danger by the intermittent activities of flight or self-defence or puzzled
thought, but obtain their food by intermittent actions,

[1] See my *Human Nature in Politics*, Part I, chap. i. The limited
direct control of the will is, however, extended by the fact that
self-conscious effort can often produce sympathetic effects on our
subconscious processes. Voluntary muscular exercise, or the
determination to be cheerful, will improve digestion, and conscious
attention will quicken the subconscious process of remembering.

to which they feel themselves impelled " by fits and starts."

Civilized man, therefore, when he digs potatoes, or adds up figures, as his regular daily occupation, is using continuously under the direction of self-conscious will, powers which were evolved for intermittent use under the direction of impulse ; and he suffers, in consequence, daily fatigue, and at longer intervals severe nervous reactions. Habit, particularly if begun in early childhood, may diminish these effects, and even submerge them below full consciousness, but does not abolish them.[1] Sustained muscular or mental effort is, that is to say, " unnatural " to us, though it is necessary for the creation of the wealth and power without which civilized man cannot exist. It follows that progress in the arts of working and thinking requires the invention of means, not only of increasing the immediate efficiency of our work and thought, but also of economizing them and compensating for the strain which they involve. Every increase of the self-conscious exertion involved in civilized work has compelled mankind to provide for periods when self-conscious effort is suspended, and the socially inherited element in our behaviour is at a minimum. When a modern factory hand or clerk goes for a walk with his dog, the behaviour of the man is very like that of the dog, and in neither case is it greatly influenced by social inheritance. Both start with a quickened step, due to an instinctive sense of joyous exercise. Both show instinctive changes of expression and attitude on meeting an unattractive male, or an attractive female, of their own species. Both may chase a rat with similar instinctive

[1] On the relation between habit and our physiological nature see my *Great Society*, chap. v.

cries and movements. For the first mile, perhaps, both will go in a direction fixed by individual habit ; then both will stop, while the decision to take either the field path or the wood path is made. That decision may involve in both a moment of reflection ; then both will go forward with a purpose, i.e., with a conscious volition, guided in the man, and apparently also in the dog, by a more or less clear mental image of the chosen route. Thought and purpose do not here depend on social inheritance. The thought, both of man and dog, deals with individually acquired memories of past walks ; and thought and memory spontaneously produce that image of the coming walk which changes impulse into purpose. When, however, the pair come home, and the man, refreshed by an hour of natural living, returns to the unnatural effort of work or business, he enters a region of socially inherited behaviour into which the dog cannot follow him.

But, though rest and recreation, as well as sleep, have always, as a matter of fact, been necessary for the human being engaged in regular work, it is only by slow and irregular steps that the human race has included that fact in its general conception of the normal human life. This may have been partly due to the fact that regular and monotonous work was first imposed by strong men— who themselves fought and hunted and flogged by fits and starts—upon women and slaves, who could be compelled to go on pounding grain or scraping hides long beyond the point to which their own immediate inclinations or their own desires for future food and clothing, or a well-informed calculation of their own future efficiency, would have carried them. As civilization advanced, the regular labour of serfs and women, and of such slaves as were not deliberately worked to death, was made physiologically possible by interruptions due to weather, and by sabbaths, holy days, saturnalia, and other customs. But these customs, though they survived because of their physiological value, were thought of rather as religious taboos than as industrial expedients. In the Middle Ages, the conscious motive of the guildsmen in restricting working hours was at least as much a desire to prevent unfair competition as a desire to maintain the nervous and physical health of the craftsman. The British factory-owners of 1815 to 1835, when they explained their principles to the world, could still argue without insincerity, that a regular twelve hours' day was desirable in the interests of the children whom they employed.[1] But in the second half of the nineteenth century the rapid increase of machine industry made every one aware of the problem. Every European and North American nation has restricted factory hours by law, and at this moment the customary working day is by general consent being cut down everywhere, except in Eastern Asia, to forty-eight hours or less per week. At the same time, our growing knowledge of human physiology is compelling us to provide for rest-periods at short intervals within the working day, and is emphasizing the need of an intensive study both of customary working movements and of the whole environment of machine production.

Men, again, have always known that the strain involved in certain forms of work which we call " art " might be

[1] Dr. Ure, who expressed the current ideas of the factory-owners, declared in 1835 (*Philosophy of Manufactures*, p. 406) that the children discharged in consequence of the Factory Act of 1833 " from their light and profitable labour . . . are thrown out of the warm spinning-rooms upon the cold world, to exist by beggary or plunder, in idleness and vice." John Wesley made it one of the rules for the Methodist schools that the children were " neither to play nor cry " (*Dict. Nat. Biog.*).

less than that involved in the other forms, which we call
" labour." The primitive artist who painted canoes, or
carved tusks, or played the flute for ritual dances, or
improvised ballads, found in his best moments his conscious
efforts caught up by a harmonious and delightful " drive "
of his whole being, which was unknown to his fellows
who were hoeing a millet patch or clearing bushes from
a path. And many of the ablest and most imaginative
working-class leaders are now hoping that the strain of
regular work may be diminished by bringing back, without
excessive loss of efficiency, the feeling of art into forms of
modern industry in which it is at present unknown.[1]

The modern artisan is also beginning to be conscious
of other details in his own nervous system. He is beginning
to use the word " nerves." When he is tired and inattentive towards the end of the day, his " self," instead
of being identified with his fatigue, may watch it and guard
against its effect on his work or his safety. When he
returns home in the evening, he often recognizes that the
irritability of fatigue is still with him. He will, therefore,
if his wife allows him, postpone till Sunday any discussion
of their weekly expenditure ; and he will deliberately
sleep, or read, or play with his children, or go to the
moving pictures, in order to get his nervous system back
as soon as possible to its natural tone.[2]

---

[1] At the same time the creative artist has found that the " drive "
of art enables him to make efforts severer, and sometimes more
exhausting, than those of any other form of work. Dante (*Para-
diso*, XXV) speaks of " The poem which has made me thin for
many years." On the whole relation between conscious effort
and subconscious " drive " see William James, *The Energies of
Man*, in *Memories and Studies* (1911), chap. ix, and Woodworth,
Dynamic Psychology (1918), especially chap. vii.

[2] Most of the recent legislation on " social control " may be
approached from this angle. When we discuss the prohibition

The war revealed certain striking influences on military efficiency resulting from this growing consciousness of the psychology of work and recreation. It used to be assumed that civilized industry, while it increased a nation's wealth, decreased its fighting power. The hill tribes of Persia, and the forest tribes of Germany, had conquered the artisans and traders of Babylon and Egypt and Rome. Nearly the whole of the British army, and at least half of the German and American armies, consisted of industrial working-men, who went to the front after a military training far too short to create that degree of discipline which a general of the Thirty Years' War would have thought absolutely necessary for the production of reliable troops. But they stood firm through month after month, and year after year, of fighting unapproached in its intensity during the whole history of mankind. Some British officers ascribed part of this new self-control to the new fact of civilized psychological and physiological self-consciousness. A private soldier would discuss before a battle, and observe during a battle, the symptoms of his own fear, with no tendency to identify his fear with himself ; he would speak of his thudding pulse, his shaking hand, his " cold feet " ; while firing, he would remember that the frightened man, who was himself and yet not himself, would tend to aim high. His permanent self was on the watch to make a sudden severe effort of inhibition if he were suddenly seized with an impulse to run away. Therefore, in all the dull bewilderment of an intensive bombardment, or an advance through shell-

or regulation of the sale of alcohol or of betting, or the use of Sunday, or adult cultural education, or prostitution, or the planning of garden cities, we are attempting, among other objects, to invent expedients for making possible the effortless and yet harmless use of the hours between work and sleep.

fire, panic fear very seldom effectively gripped him. And the psychological self-consciousness which had transformed the modern workman-soldier, also, as the war went on, tended to transform the methods of training which some officers employed. Dr. C. S. Myers, who occupied an important medical position during the war, wrote to me in 1919, " There have been instances in this war, where psychologically acute officers have trained their men by telling them what to expect [i.e. what feelings to expect] in the trenches, with the result that their emotions have been under control." [1] In every army "rest-camps " were established (though they were not, I am told, always directed by officers who understood their purpose or their technique), and the organization of games became as important a part of the art of war as the organization of drill.

The history of sustained mental effort is roughly parallel to that of sustained muscular effort. Here also we have invented and handed down new and unnatural forms of behaviour, which we are now engaged in consciously adjusting to the facts of our nature. Perhaps the main difference between the two is that in the case of muscular work we are, for the moment, most interested in the invention of expedients for diminishing strain and fatigue, and that in the case of mental effort we are mainly concerned with expedients for increasing efficiency.

Mental activity, like muscular activity, may, as I have already said, be naturally stimulated in man, and may even, in moments of danger and bewilderment, be naturally heightened to the point of intense mental exertion. At a very early stage, indeed, in civilization, men found that thought could not be relied on for the guidance of pro-

[1] See Graham Wallas in the *British Journal of Psychology* (November 1919).

longed purposeful action, unless we learnt to start and
maintain the thought-process by a self-conscious effort of
will ; and after the invention of language, precepts were
handed down from generation to generation, like " look
before you leap," or " bide your time," or " sleep on it,"
the teaching of which was that men, before starting an
irrevocable course of action, should deliberately interpose
a period of delay during which thought, conscious or
subconscious, could take place.[1] Such traditional precepts,
however, merely inculcate delay, and take the processes
used by the thinker for granted. When, for instance, a
young English village labourer, in obedience to his mother's
advice, or the teaching of an old proverb, " bides his
time " till he has decided which of two girls he will marry,
he is unconscious of his own intellectual methods.
Thought, at this stage, is not distinguished from other
psychological processes. It may go on in unconscious
combination with fear, or hope, or jealousy, or the emotions
of leadership, or obedience, or craftsmanship, or beauty.
A man finds that when his period of waiting is over, he
has, under the joint influences of emotions and memories
and thoughts, formed, he knows not how, a new purpose.
If we ask whether the thought-process at this stage is
" natural," or " artificial," we are met with the parasitic

[1] See my *Great Society*, chap. x. The development of deliberate
thinking has probably been delayed by our slowness in inventing
words to indicate the various relations of thought to will. All
languages have pairs of words like " see " and " look," or " hear "
and " listen," by which we can distinguish between the effortless
and effortful use of certain of our senses ; though it is not easy
to find words to distinguish between the " listening " or " looking,"
which is the immediate result of an external stimulus, and that
which results from self-conscious will. But in the case of " thought "
(as in the case of " smell ") we only have the one word for the
three types, effortless, automatically effortful, and self-consciously
effortful thinking.

relation, to which I have already referred, between certain
factors in man's biological nature and his social heritage
of language. Just as man has evolved a natural instinct
to use language in speech, provided always that there is
a language there for him to learn, so he has apparently
evolved a natural tendency to use language, when he has
learnt it, in thought.[1]

But civilized man has not only learnt how to enter by
a conscious and artificial effort on the process of natural
or quasi-natural thought. He has also invented and
handed down innumerable expedients by which the
thought-process itself can be made more effective. The
most obvious of these are mathematics and the other
types of formal logic. We can guess, with the help of
the traces of early Babylonian and Greek speculation,
at some of the early steps in such inventions, and that
they must have been encouraged by the fact that individual
variation between man and man is, in respect of our
recently evolved intellectual powers, very much greater
than it is in such comparatively early facts as height,
or strength, or manual skill, and therefore the born
thinker is very widely removed from the average of his
fellows. Many men had, for instance, long before the
invention of any other logic than grammatical speech,
become interested in the heavenly bodies. During periods
of reverie at night, they thought " naturally " about
them, i.e., watched them, were anxious about them,
admired them, feared them, and wove them half-consciously
into figures of giants and animals. A few of the ablest
of them noticed, by the same natural process, that some

[1] See the evidence as to " word-blindness " and other structural
and functional disorders of those regions in the brain in which
language and thought are correlated.

of the brighter stars moved slowly about the sky ; they called them planets, and hoped and feared more from them than from the other stars. But one or two exceptional Babylonians or Greeks went much further ; they made a new use of the early and all-important invention of number ; night after night they counted the units of measurement in time and space which recorded the movements of some one star in relation to its fellows. They invented, and handed down to their disciples, new methods of arithmetic and geometry and logic, which could be used for land-surveying and architecture, as well as for astronomy. Such thought methods were often held by those who could not understand them to be so unnatural and impious that men were killed for using them. They would, perhaps, have been abandoned by the whole race, but for the fact that the new processes were found to be more efficient than the old ; the architect who used geometry built stronger temples than he who relied solely on his " eye " ; Jupiter and Venus and Mars did not always justify the old fears and hopes of victory or defeat or the deaths of kings ; but they did present themselves night after night at the points indicated by the philosophers' circles and triangles ; and the moon was eclipsed at the calculated dates.

The continuance of our present industrial civilization is now made possible by the fact that all men learn in childhood, and use during the working day, some of those logical methods which were painfully invented by philosophers and mathematicians at the beginning of civilization. A modern tenant farmer, as he stands hesitating whether to begin his harvest or not, may seem to be thinking as " naturally " as his palæolithic ancestors ; but even he will probably make a few calculations as to hours of labour per acre, market prices, and his chance of an overdraft at the bank, in which he will employ the clumsy combination of Babylonian duodecimal arithmetic and Greek decimal arithmetic which he learnt at school. A working engineer, with his case of gauges, a munition-girl at her lathe, or a chemist's assistant, lives during the working day, like Pythagoras, in a universe composed of number. Meanwhile the students of the physical sciences are rapidly inventing new and more efficient forms of thought. A modern "scientist" substitutes for the simple rules of geometry and arithmetic and logic elaborate mathematical and statistical systems, which have often been specially invented for his own branch of study, and looks on these rules as only a stage in the "scientific method" of hypothesis, experiment, and inference. He makes some use of that psychological self-consciousness which is part of the social heritage of our time, and tries to invent expedients by which certain mental attitudes may control subconscious mental processes. He inculcates, for instance, on his disciples ideals of scientific "thoroughness" and "patience" and intellectual "integrity."

Modern scientific method has hitherto won its most conspicuous successes in the sciences (astronomy, chemistry, and physics) which deal either with lifeless matter or with matter from which all qualities except the measurability which it shares with lifeless matter have been abstracted. Great, though less complete, success has attended its application to the simpler forms and qualities of living matter, in botany, zoology, and the experimental examination of such elementary facts in human psychology as sensation and perception. "Scientific method" has been least successful in dealing with the more complex forms of human behaviour. The student of human conduct cannot standardize his material, as can the chemist or metallurgist, nor isolate, like the physicist, one factor in a concrete problem from the rest. The material of his most important observations must be found, not in carefully contrived and rigorously controlled experiments, but in the observation of occurrences of daily life, each one of which is the resultant of innumerable factors which the thinker can estimate only with various degrees of uncertainty. And if he has once acquired a habit of using (as did, for instance, the early nineteenth-century economists) a logical method unsuited to his material, his subconscious, as well as his conscious thinking, may be permanently distorted. One can detect, however, during the last few decades, a slowly emerging promise that the students of the human sciences may invent logical methods specially adapted to the qualities of their subject matter, and an agreed terminology which will make it possible for those methods to be used by others as well as their original inventors. The growing accumulation, for instance, of statistical returns, and our growing caution in securing that every unit in a statistical total shall represent an answer to the same question, is making it possible to frame a special statistico-mathematical logic for the human sciences which ultimately, like arithmetic or Aristotle's formal logic, may influence the language and thought-processes of the ordinary civilized man.

But while the complexity and variability of the material dealt with by the human sciences constitute a special difficulty and require a special logic, a subtler difficulty is created by the emotional relation of that material to the thinker. The thinker about mankind, because he is a human being, is born with a number of strong instincts, jealousy, leadership, loyalty, fear, sex, etc., whose special stimulus is the presence or idea of his fellows. At what mental attitude should he aim with regard to these instincts and the emotions to which they give rise ? Should he, for instance, in order to attain to " scientific " or " philosophic " detachment, attempt, while thinking, to repress in himself all emotions concerning those about whom he thinks ? One cannot, I believe, give a useful answer to this question without distinguishing between the logical rules by which the relation of premises to conclusions are tested and the flow of associated ideas which those rules help to direct. No emotional condition of the thinker will make two and two equal to five, or turn a weak argument into a strong one, or justify the repeated claim of defenders of established political and religious faiths that an inclination to believe should be treated as sufficient evidence for any familiar dogma. But, if fertility of association without logical consistency is unsafe, logical consistency without fertility of association is barren. At every stage of sustained thought—the formation of the original hypothesis, the invention of experiments, the detection of the significance of unexpected evidence, the appreciation of all that is involved in our conclusions—we are dependent on the flow of ideas, and the flow of ideas, when we are dealing with human material, depends in large part on the richness of our emotional as well as of our reasoning processes. If, for instance, one compares Adam Smith's *Wealth of Nations* with Whately's *Lectures on Political Economy*, one sees how enormously the fertility of Adam Smith's thought has gained from his sympathy and humour, and how much he would have lost as a thinker if he had attempted to repress in himself all psychological processes which are not to be found in the text-books of formal logic. And thought accompanied by a free play of the emotions involves less strain than thought accompanied by a conscious or subconscious effort of repression.

During the last few years, the problem of the relation between our thoughts and our feelings has been further complicated by Freud and his followers, who have argued that complete inhibition of profound emotions and memories does not and cannot take place, and that such emotions and memories, if driven by an effort of will beneath the level of consciousness, are more likely to distort our thinking than if they had remained conscious. The effort of will, or nervous shock, which originally drove an idea beneath consciousness persists, they argue, as a " censor," preventing the return of the idea in its original form to consciousness, even if that return would be useful to us. The Freudian writers are mainly practising medical men, accustomed before the war to deal with patients of naturally subnormal nervous stability, whose difficulty in thinking of certain subjects might very often be diagnosed as due to some sexual or quasi-sexual event in the past. Their main remedial technique is to discover the original experience by " psycho-analysis," or some other method of " tapping " the subconscious memory, to bring it into conscious relation with the facts contained in conscious memory, and to make it the subject of consciously critical thought on the part of the patient. During the war our nerve-doctors had an enormous experience of " shell-shock " and other nervous disorders, in patients most of whom were either above or not far below normal in their original nervous health. Some of the ablest of the doctors came to the conclusion that the proportion of cases in which the " censorship " was due to a distant sexual event had been greatly exaggerated. They also abandoned the hope of finding any one technique which would fit all cases. They found that while in some cases the patient benefited by bringing his memory of a shocking war event to the surface, and talking freely about it, in other cases it was best to encourage the patient to cease to talk about the event, and to forget it as far as possible.[1]

This controversy about Freudian " psychiatry " is another of many indications that progress in thought about human behaviour may depend in the future, not only on a new relation of the thinker to his emotions, but on the invention and social inheritance of a many-sided technique, involving the conscious use by the thinker of many different expedients to secure fertility in the flow of his ideas, logical thoroughness in the process of inference, and economy of effort. At one time a thinker will suspect that he is turning himself from a man into a machine, and will attempt to smile and frown with Adam Smith, rather than imitate the cold donnishness of Whately. At another time he will suspect that he is allowing his free flow of feeling to bear him past the point where his argument calls for the severest effort of logical consistency. He will then understand what Mr. Arnold Bennett means, when he denounces the " sentimentalists " and " truth-shirkers," and pleads for " hard sustained cerebral activity and realism."[2] Sometimes the thinker will believe that his thought is being obstructed by mere habit, which can be overcome by the resolute initiation of a new habit ; sometimes he will suspect some half-forgotten experience which he had better either definitely remember or

[1] See e.g. W. H. Rivers, *Instinct and the Unconscious* (1920).
[2] *Daily News* (February 23rd, 1916).

definitely forget. Sometimes the thinker's conscious effort will be concentrated on the stimulation of subconscious mental processes. In May 1918, for instance, there appeared in many English newspapers a character sketch (from the French *Journal*) of General Foch. He was said to use two special methods of "grappling with the overwhelming problems which he has to solve." One was "the excellent method of sleeping over them. He revolves them in his mind before going to sleep, and next morning has generally found a solution." " I always think," he was represented as saying, "that my hand-mirror, when I shave before it in the morning, reflects to me the answers to the questions I had thought about the night before." General Foch's other method was that "he takes coffee and smokes an inordinate number of small dark cigars." (See *Daily Telegraph*, May 27th, 1918.) Time in war is so all-important, that if a general finds that "an inordinate number of small dark cigars" is the most immediately effective means of stimulating sub-conscious thought, it may be wise for him to use it. In peace, sleep and a walk in the woods may be a better means ; and future historians of the Peace Conferences of 1918–20 may believe that human kindliness would have had a better chance of influencing and widening French thought about the future organization of mankind if it had not been so exact a continuation of the urgent, but narrow, process of strategical invention. Again, because each part of our higher nervous structure is easily tired by continuous stimulation, and easily dis-ordered by being left long without stimulation, the thinker will find that variety of method, owing to the mere fact of its being variety, is better than uniformity. And he may also learn from music and the other fine arts that rhythmic form not only diminishes fatigue, but stimulates the still obscure instincts which cause the emotion of beauty, and, through the emotion of beauty, stimulate creative thought. We may come to learn as much about the causes which put Plato, and Dante, and Goethe, among the great thinkers of the world, from a study of Beethoven's sonatas, as from the rules of logic and mathematics.

Perhaps, in the end, the human sciences may pay back in this way something of their debt to the physical sciences. Professor A. E. Taylor may have indicated a path for future progress in the physical sciences when he wrote : " Mental facts, such as hopes and fears, fixations and relaxations of attention, accompany every physical experiment we can make, and form with it a single indivisible experience, but one may perfectly well work through a text-book of physics or chemistry or electricity without coming across the admission that there is such a thing as a feeling or an emotion in the world."[1] Sir Richard Owen, for instance, might have played a different and more helpful part in the scientific discussion of Darwin's *Origin of Species* if he had been a student of the effect of jealousy on thought. But it may be that the study of the technique of thought will be most helpful when it insists on the relation both of thought and of feeling to the whole life of the thinker. The thinker's daily activities include not only mental attitudes and methods, and mental and emotional stimuli, but also the acts of sitting down at his desk, of answering his letters, of arranging his notes, of meals and exercise, of marriage or celibacy ; and the systematic thought of the statesman, the engineer, and the financier, depends for its efficiency upon its

[1] *The Problem of Conduct* (1901), p. 23.

relation to the daily routine of administration or construction, or business. For the young official, indeed, or
business man who desires in his own case to use psychological self-consciousness as a means of attaining intellectual
efficiency I know of no more useful book than a little
manual called *The Statesman*, written in 1836 by Sir
Henry Taylor, the poet, who was also one of the ablest
of the nineteenth century officials in the British Colonial
Office. Sir Henry Taylor says that " as fast as papers
are received, the party who is to act upon them should
examine them so far as to ascertain whether any of them
relate to business which requires immediate attention,
and should then separate and arrange them. But once
so arranged . . . he should not again suffer himself to
look at a paper or handle it, except in the purpose and with
the determination to go through with it and dispatch the
affair. For the practice of looking at papers and handling
them without disposing of them not only wastes the time
so employed, but breeds an undue impression of difficulty
and trouble as connected with them ; and the repetition
of acts of postponement on any subject tends more and
more to the subjugation of the active power in relation
to it. Moreover, it will be desirable to act upon a paper
or bundle while it looks fresh ; for it will become unin-
teresting if the eye has got accustomed to it lying aside,
and absolutely repulsive if it have assumed a dusty,
obsolete, and often-postponed appearance " (pp. 82–83).
He should aim at " the statesman's powers of self-government—of intention and remission in business, of putting
the mind on and taking it off " (p. 80). The statesman,
he says, " must appeal . . . from the impulses of a per-
turbed and hurried life to the principle of order " (p. 76).
" One who should feel himself to be over-excitable in

the transaction of business, would do well to retard himself mechanically, ' and by the body's action teach the mind ' ; for the body is a handle to the mind in these as in other particulars. Thus he should never suffer himself to write in a hurried hand " (p. 78). The speculative thinker can learn from Sir Henry Taylor the value of tidiness in note-keeping,[1] and the need of over-coming by a sharp effort of will the " complex " which makes him avoid thinking about a certain branch of his subject because he has not answered a letter. But he will learn more from Sir Henry Taylor's insistence that card-catalogues and note-books cannot take the place of those silent moments in which thought and feeling, consciousness and subconsciousness, are merged in expectant contemplation. " It were to be wished," he says, that the statesman " should set apart from business not only a sabbatical day in each week, but, if it be possible, a sabbatical hour in each day " (p. 79).

Our growing consciousness, again, of the relation between our socially inherited forms of intellectual behaviour and our biological heritage of intellectual and emotional powers, should influence, not only our methods of adult mental self-direction, but also the methods of education of those who are trained in youth for a life of mental effort. School children should learn to recognize and undertake the conscious effort by which thought is made efficient, and to distinguish it, both from the automatic activity of recreative thought, and from the effortless " interest " stimulated in the members of a class by a skilled and

[1] " The arrangement, tying up and docketing of such papers as are before him, is a business which he should undertake himself, and not leave to his secretary ; for a man cannot methodize the subject-matter of his business without at the same time methodizing his mind " (p. 78).

" magnetic " teacher. Children can learn that distinction at a very early age. A little English boy, who afterwards became one of the most brilliant of the young soldiers who were killed in the war, was sent at the age of six or seven to a well-known Froebelian school in London, which aimed at obliterating the distinction between " play " and " lessons." When he returned at the end of his first week, he said to his father, " At that school, when they work they don't really work, and when they play they don't really play." In the next place, the pupil should learn to distinguish between various kinds of mental effort. In particular, he should soon be made aware of the difference between the mere concentration involved in learning by rote, and the straining expectancy, the seizing and holding to a new idea when it is only an uncomfortable premonitory feeling, which is required even in so simple a process of intellectual creation as the writing of a school essay. The teacher, again, should be conscious that while he is training his pupils in intellectual technique, he is also handing down to them the social heritage of a body of knowledge. That knowledge must be so chosen as to give his pupils the most effective intellectual equipment for adult life, and at the same time to stimulate such emotions as may increase the fertility of thought and diminish the strain of intellectual effort.

In all these respects the English educational system is now passing through a critical period. The educational renaissance started, in the eighteen twenties and thirties, at some of the older endowed " public schools," and at Oxford and Cambridge, by the writings and example of Coleridge, Thomas Arnold, and other disciples of the Prussian thinkers, had many admirable results. The student who goes from the sixth form of Winchester or

Harrow to take a first class in Oxford " Greats " or the Cambridge Mathematical Tripos, acquires a high degree of ability in what Sir Henry Taylor called " putting the mind on and taking it off." But it was never more than a very small fraction even of exceptionally able young Englishmen who were able to benefit by that renaissance ; and the need for other kinds of knowledge than Latin and Greek language and literature and pure mathematics is now so urgent that both " Greats " and the Mathematical Tripos are rapidly shrinking for want of candidates. In the new municipal secondary schools and the new universities, little Latin and hardly any Greek is taught. The newer subjects which are taking the place of the old " public school " curriculum are natural science, and history, economics, modern literature, and other forms of " modern humanities."[1] In the case of natural science, I have had no opportunity of estimating the kind of intellectual effort and emotional stimulus which accompanies school and college laboratory work. In the case of " modern culture " I sometimes fear that our present pedagogic methods may not produce the same awareness and experience of the more difficult forms of mental effort, as that produced at Rugby, or Winchester, or Balliol, or Trinity, during the second half of the nineteenth century. The writing of Latin prose, or the working of examples in analytical conics, often prepared the young public school boy of my own generation, either for a period of disgust and disillusionment, when he discovered how removed his knowledge was from the needs of his time, or for a life of contented dilettantism. But they did train him to undertake, of himself, a prolonged and severe intellectual effort which was not mere memorizing.

[1] See Stanley Leathes, *What is Education ?* (1913).

The older teaching, on the other hand, was enormously expensive, and was confined to a few richly endowed schools and universities ; a few able masters or college tutors, who had themselves gone through the experience of sustained intellectual effort, gave invaluable hints to individual boys or undergraduates in the personal interviews during which they corrected compositions or discussed essays. When we have raised the number of our secondary and university students to five or ten times the nineteenth-century number, we shall find it much more difficult to obtain teachers of high natural ability, and almost impossible to secure that any teacher should give much of his time to individual tuition. One remedy for this danger seems to me that the teacher should substitute organized class instruction in the psychological technique of intellectual work for unorganized individual hints. We should not leave instruction in mental attitudes and methods either to accident or to the " Pelman Institute," and other commercial firms. If students were taught as a body to recognize the form taken in consciousness by intellectual effort, the direction of that effort by such expedients as class-lessons, questioning, examinations, or the " looking over " of written compositions, would be made infinitely more effective.[1] The expedient of class-teaching in the psychology of mental work, both as a separate " subject," and as an integral

[1] I may perhaps be permitted to refer to an experiment which I made nearly forty years ago, when I was teaching Greek and Latin to boys of eleven and twelve who were being prepared for the " scholarships " of the big English endowed schools. I used to make them repeat a sort of catechism, in the course of which they said, " My duty as a member of this class is to acquire correct intellectual habits." Some of those boys are now grown men, and I have never had any reason to think that the effect on them of such early intellectual self-consciousness has been other than good.

part of the teaching of all subjects, will be peculiarly necessary if the political connection between Britain and India is to continue, and if British teachers are to play any part in satisfying the Indian hunger for modern knowledge. The traditions of Indian education still bear traces of the time when its main purpose was to preserve without change (in the absence of books) the socially inherited treasures of the intellect from generation to generation. The emphasis on memorizing, which was originally necessary, but is now superfluous, is increased by the mechanical system of examinations which dominates Indian higher education, and by the fact that education carried on in a foreign language must necessarily be weak in emotional stimulus.[1]

When visiting the United States as teacher and observer, I have sometimes thought that the rapidly increasing American interest in applied psychology may, in the near future, exercise a marked influence on this side of American education. An Englishman in the United States envies the universal recognition of education as desirable, and the open-handed generosity both of public grants and of private gifts to every kind of educational institution. The United States, with rather more than twice the population of the United Kingdom, has more than four times as many students in secondary schools, and more than eight times as many in universities.[2] Some of the great professional post-graduate university schools

[1] See *Report of the Calcutta University Commission* (1819), Vol. II, chaps. xvii and xviii.

[2] See P. J. Hartog in the *Journal of the Royal Society of Arts* (1919). I have used the statistics of the United Kingdom rather than of England because they are the best available. The arguments in the text apply, however, to the educational system of England. The systems of Scotland and Ireland present rather different problems.

(such as the Harvard Law School, and the Johns Hopkins Medical School) are, in equipment, number of students, and intellectual keenness, incomparably above any corresponding institution in the United Kingdom. The United States combines with these advantages the fact that her white population starts with a higher average biological inheritance of brain and body than has any other population except perhaps the few thousand free inhabitants of Athens in the fifth century B.C. or of Iceland in the tenth century A.D. And yet, in her actual production of constructive, critical, and imaginative literature, many Americans believe, with regret, that America does not now " pull her weight in the boat " of world-civilization. To a foreigner it appears as if one cause of this lies in an insufficient recognition of the need of civilized man for conscious and systematized intellectual effort. In the education of young children, successive movements for the reform of American common schools have been greatly influenced by the conception of the " natural " growth of the human mind, as expounded by Froebel and other early nineteenth-century educationalists,[1] by the coincidence of that conception with the eighteenth century political ideas of " nature " received from Rousseau by the Fathers of the American Revolution, and by the fact that the physical environment of the pioneer life of fifty years ago was sufficiently like that of primitive man to make it much safer than it is in modern New York or Chicago for him to trust to the more natural forms of thought. But Froebel seems to me to have helped to produce a

[1] Froebel goes so far as to argue in a section of his *Education of Man* that the little German develops the simpler forms of German speech by a process as free from any dependence on social inheritance as the unfolding of a flower.

dangerous neglect by current American theory of the socially inherited elements in civilization. Two very able young American physiologists, who had themselves received a post-graduate training in natural science far more thorough than anything they could have found in England, told me in 1919 that they had failed in discussion to agree on a definition of education, and asked my help. I defined education in some such words as " a process by which human beings so acquire the knowledge and habits which constitute civilization as to be fitted to live well, both individually and in co-operation." One of them replied, " That was what we wanted. We thought of education as a development of the personality and so on, but we did not manage to think of it as a process of learning things." The same intellectual tradition, combined with the practical difficulties of class-teaching, tends in the middle years of the American, as of the English municipal school system, to substitute the automatic " interest " of the class in the presence of the teacher for the conscious effort of individual attention. In the expensive private and endowed schools of the Eastern States, the tendency to avoid unnatural intellectual effort is increased by the widespread desire of the well-to-do American that his children shall have a " good time." In these schools, again, I am told that any boy who shows signs of natural athletic excellence is likely to be prevented from acquiring that consciousness of play as relief which is the necessary balance to the consciousness of thought as effort. For such a boy play means a severe specialized training of the muscles and the lower nerve-centres, carried out, often against inclination, under the pressure of school or college patriotism, of the public opinion of his fellows, and of a carefully educated instinct of combat. Such

" play " may leave the whole system as tired as does the speeded machine-tending of a modern factory, and almost compels those who have gone through it to find rest, if not recreation, during the hours of formal study.

American students have also told me that the long visits to mountain farms and forest camps, which occupy the summer months of so many well-to-do New York and New England families, are so arranged as to ignore the fact that a healthy boy or girl requires at the most only a few weeks of complete inertia before being ready to begin mental work again. No books are, I am told, taken to the summer holidays, and a student may, at the end of each September, find that the impulse of intellectual keenness has been blunted by sheer boredom. As a result, the clever boy who goes to one of the great universities of the Eastern States at eighteen, either from a public high school or from such a splendidly equipped preparatory school as Groton or St. Paul's, may be, as far as I have been able to judge, two years behind an equally clever boy from Winchester or Rugby or Manchester Grammar School in his experience of skilled and conscious intellectual effort. Childhood lasted much later into life in the England of 1910 than in the England of Anselm or the England of Milton ; and I formed the impression in 1910 that childhood among the well-to-do classes of Eastern America lasted longer than in England.[1]

[1] The fact that in certain narrow sections of education we were, in the second half of the nineteenth century, more successful than the Americans in training self-conscious intellectual effort was due very largely to quite distant historical causes. The Oxford and Cambridge colleges, and the older English endowed schools, were either monastic institutions in their origin, or were formed on the monastic tradition. The student was originally conceived of as sitting in his cell or in the scriptorium of the monastery. The American educational system developed in the main out of the

I have before me the 64th Bulletin of the American Federation for Child Study. As regards parents, the Federation state that their object is " to replace Impulse with Purpose." As regards the child, the Federation say, " the child is a developing organism, not a miniature man." It may be that twentieth-century America will realize that, though a child is a " developing organism," he is an organism which cannot attain adult well-being without the acquirement of the socially inherited accumulations of civilization ; that this acquirement will not effectively take place without conscious intellectual effort in school and college ; and that, therefore, it is in the child rather than in the parent that the " replacement of Impulse with Purpose " is most needed.

common school of the township or the training school for preachers. It is not, I think, a mere difference of phraseology which makes an American college student of the moral sciences, if you ask him how hard he is working, answer that he is taking so many courses of lectures, and not mention the reading which accompanies the lectures ; and the Oxford or Cambridge student answer that he is " reading " four or five or six hours a day and ignore the lectures which accompany and illustrate his reading.

CHAPTER III

GROUP CO-OPERATION

In the last chapter I discussed certain socially inherited expedients by which the work and thought of individual human beings can be directed. In this chapter I shall discuss certain socially inherited expedients by which human beings can direct their behaviour when co-operating in groups. I use the word "group" in a strictly quantitative sense, to mean a body of human beings numbering from three or four up to about thirty or forty. That number seems to have been the ordinary limit of co-operation by primitive mankind; and the natural range of our senses and memory makes it easy for us to see, hear, and recognize that number of our fellows. I shall postpone to later chapters the discussion of co-operation among bodies of men, like nations or associated nations, whose numbers far exceed such a limit.

Here, as in the last chapter, I shall attempt to show the relation between natural biologically inherited, and artificial socially inherited forms of behaviour. Man is a loosely and intermittently gregarious animal, who inherits instincts impelling him to certain natural forms of group co-operation in such acts as fighting, hunting, and escaping from danger. The world contains many other gregarious species, and many different forms of natural co-operation. When bees and ants, for instance, co-operate in building the nest, storing food, or tending the young, they are naturally impelled to a form of co-operation consisting of a division of labour between structurally differing classes, such as the queens and drones and workers among the bees, or the workers and soldiers among the ants. Within each class there seems to be little co-operation by leadership and obedience. Each individual in a class either goes his way in the performance of a routine task, or, as when half a dozen ants are carrying off a caterpillar, " butts in " at any point where he can lay hold. On the other hand, in the case of grazing mammals like wild cattle or deer, one male of the herd instinctively leads, and is instinctively obeyed by the rest, until he is challenged to a fight by a younger male and dethroned. In the case of some gregarious hunting mammals (such as wolves and dogs) who instinctively communicate with each other by means of significant sounds, a third and more elastic form of natural co-operation appears. There may or may not be a leading male whose general position as leader will from time to time be settled by a duel with a rival. But any one member of the pack (or many members simultaneously) may, by significant yelping, claim the lead at any particular moment of the hunt. If the older wolves are doubtful about the scent, the whole pack will follow the clamorous assertion by some younger wolf that he or she has found it, without that fact leading to an immediate fight for permanent leadership.

Man's instincts, in this as in many other respects, are comparatively varied and uncertain, perhaps because in his ancestry many minor biological variations have been combined by interbreeding. But the prevailing type of primitive human co-operation seems to have been much more like that of the hunting-pack than that either of the ants or of the cattle ; and this likeness has continued even after the substitution in man of the socially inherited fact of language for instinctive natural cries, and the evolution of a " parasitic " relation between language and some of our most important instincts. A human group is naturally led by some individual of mature age and dominating character, whose confidence in himself has been increased by past leadership, and whose fellows have formed the habit of obeying him. But his authority is never complete or unchallenged, and young human adults are subject to passionate alternations of an instinctive impulse to lead and an instinctive impulse to obey.

Natural human group co-operation consists, therefore, neither of the furious mass-industry of the beehive, nor of the blind discipline of a herd of cattle, but of a disorderly process of simultaneous clamour and action. We share common ancestors both with the baboons and the gorillas ; but our natural form of co-operation is rather the noisy bickerings of a party of baboons raiding a plantation than the gloomy tyranny of the " old man " in a group of gorillas. This form of co-operation has, when compared with that of the bees and the cattle, the great disadvantage of wasting energy and time, but the greater advantage of making co-operative action more likely to fit the changing needs of each situation. The wolf-pack, instead of having, like the cattle-herd, one leader with one pair of eyes and ears, or, like the marching ants, no leader responsible for their direction at all, has twenty potential leaders, and of these twenty the wolf whose nose comes nearest to the fresh scent-trail is likely to claim the lead most convincingly ; and a party of our primitive ancestors would be guided even more by clamour and less by discipline than a pack of wolves.[1]

[1] To some of my readers this passage may recall Mr. Kipling's contemptuous comparison, in his delightful *Jungle Books*, of the

Instinctive human group co-operation, like many other instinctive forms of human behaviour, can be more clearly observed among the half-grown young than among the adults. The best picture of it may perhaps be seen when a group of undisciplined twelve-year-old school-boys chase (with half articulate shouts of exhortation, and a vigorous but confused division of function directed by a leading boy) a stray rat in the play-ground. This natural form of human group co-operation is, however, fully effective only when three conditions are present : the co-operating group must not be too large or too scattered to hear each other's cries and see each other's movements ; the act in which they co-operate must be one which stimulates a co-operative instinct ; and the exactness or complexity required in the co-operative process must not be greater than is possible in purely instinctive behaviour. As soon as the co-operation of a larger or more scattered body is required, or the co-operative act is one that does not naturally stimulate a co-operative instinct, or precision and complexity is needed, artificial and therefore socially inherited forms of group co-operation must be used. The leader is appointed, not by his natural prominence in a noisy group of hunters or warriors, but by some artificial expedient like the lot or primogeniture or election. He utters, not inarticulate cries, but articulate commands, and may use arguments (such as demonstrations of the individual advantage which his hearers will gain from obedience) which, while they lead to co-operative action, do not necessarily stimulate any co-operative instinct.

"Bandar-log," the chattering democratic monkeys, with the un-questioning jungle discipline which is his ideal, as it is that of General Ludendorff. Even in the jungle, however, the undignified monkeys may have some advantages over the herd which follows a single obstinate and dignified leader into glorious destruction.

Or he may use an artificial form of discipline which creates a mere habit of obedience supported by fear of punishment. But beneath such artificial forms of group co-operation our natural tendency towards instinctive competition in leadership and instinctive obedience still remains, sometimes strengthening the artificial form and sometimes confusing it, or, if the artificial form has broken down, taking its place.

In natural group co-operation, as in natural individual behaviour, thought and action are not clearly distinguished. When twenty Mousterian hunters had surrounded a wounded buffalo, it would have been difficult to say whether their clamorous cries and excited gestures constituted, at any moment, a process of co-operative thought or of co-operative action. As soon, however, as artificial methods of co-operation were introduced, the thought-process which prepared a plan of action tended to become separated from the co-operative action itself. The leader of a raiding party might go apart for a period either of natural reverie, or of artificial calculation as to the number of marches required to reach a certain point. Or, before the party marched, a council might be assembled, consisting either of the whole party or of a few of the older men, to advise the leader and help in the calculations. If emotion in such a council reached a high point of intensity there may have occurred a certain amount of that " telepathic " exchange of mental impressions for the possibility of which among human beings there exists a growing, though still obscure, mass of evidence.

Thought, however, when isolated from action must have been through the early stages of human culture in the main a solitary process. The artificial organization of co-operative thought lagged, and still lags, far behind the artificial organization of co-operative action. It was not until refinement had been reached in the development of language, and until many ingenious inventions had been made of dialectical methods and of opportunities for continuous discussion, that consciously organized co-operation in thought became possible even as an ideal. And the ideal of genuine intellectual co-operation, in which men combine and compare each other's observations, follow up by logical processes each other's suggestions, and assign to each of a group of co-operating thinkers the part in a complex inquiry for which he is best fitted by his talents and training, is still very seldom realized. The most experienced statesman may still remember his most important council meetings rather as conflicts of will between the proposers of different plans than as opportunities for co-operation in building up a new plan.[1] Again, because our socially inherited forms of co-operation in act and thought are unnatural, they produce the same sort of nervous strain as do the artificial forms of individual manual and mental work. After a committee in which a man has kept his temper, restrained his loquacity, and attended closely to unwelcome arguments, he feels the need of "letting himself go" under less formal conditions.

In warfare men recognized, earlier than in the arts of peace, both the advantages and the difficulties of artificial forms of group co-operation. At the dawn of history there must have been many now forgotten chiefs, of the type of Marius or Philip, who in their individual thinking showed the military advantage of artificial logical thought based on carefully collected information and ruthlessly pushed to its conclusions, over the alternations of hope, fear, habit, reverie, quick retort, and sudden decision,

[1] See my *Great Society*, chap. xi.

by which a primitive war-leader formed his purposes. But Marlborough and Napoleon showed that success under more modern conditions required that the able leader should have the power and will deliberately to choose a group of officers of the same mental quality as himself, and by a careful process of invention with regard to their relation to each other and to himself, make it possible for them to act as a true thought-organization. By a combination of intellectual authority, intimate intercourse, and bold delegation of function, the supreme commander could then with the help of his staff think effectively of an enormously larger body of facts than he could have controlled in his own single brain. And the memoirs written after the war may show that those staffs were most successful who most consciously recognized the nature of their work, and who developed, for instance, a code of manners which combined tolerance and teachability in receiving the ideas of others, with frankness, and, if necessary, courageous persistence, in introducing one's own ideas.

The problem of the adequacy for group co-operation of our existing military expedients can be well illustrated by two comparatively simple cases in the war, as to which we happen to have unusually full and accurate information. These cases are recorded in the First Report of the British " Dardanelles Commission " (1917), and the Report of the " Mesopotamia Commission " (1917). Each of the two Reports deals with a decision (proved by the event to have been mistaken) formed during a few weeks or months by a small group of statesmen and naval and military officers. Every important member of each group (except Lord Kitchener, who had died) appeared before the Commissions. All written records were produced, and nearly every witness seems to have tried to give a frank account of his own thoughts and sayings and feelings as far as he could remember them. It is not likely that the governments of other belligerent states will publish reports of equally drastic and impartial inquiries into the higher conduct of the war ; and these two British " blue-books " may provide future students of political science with the best available account of the psychological processes by which, under the simplest conditions, a group responsible for the direction of a modern non-militarized state may form critical military decisions. They may perhaps be read by future undergraduates side by side with Mr. Maynard Keynes's description of the procedure by which the Big Four made peace in 1918.[1]

The First Dardanelles Report deals with the formation in London during January 1915 of the decision to force the Dardanelles by a naval attack, and the abandonment of that decision in March 1915. The chief figures in the Report are Lord Kitchener, Lord Fisher, Mr. Asquith, and Mr. Churchill. Lord Kitchener had proved himself in his Egyptian and South African campaigns to be a trained scientific soldier, capable of prolonged efforts of individual thought, and possessed of special knowledge and aptitude for problems of military supply. He was, however, less trained and personally less fitted to take part in the process of co-operative strategic thought, and hardly trained at all for the difficult work of co-operation between soldiers and politicians.[2] In the War Office he

[1] Keynes, *Economic Consequences of the Peace* (1919).
[2] The Final Report of the Dardanelles Commission (1917) adds that Lord Kitchener " held a strong opinion as to the necessity of secrecy in military matters, and seldom communicated his intentions or his reasons for action to anyone " (p. 5). It is also

seems to have made himself obeyed, not by argument, but by the " magnetic " effect of his instinctive impulse to lead over other men's instinctive impulse to obey. The account of Lord Kitchener in Mr. Churchill's evidence is, indeed, a picture of instinctive human co-operation which would have been as true of a Palæolithic war-party led by an exceptionally strong-willed chief as it was of the British War Council in 1915. " Scarcely any one ever ventured to argue with him. . . . All-powerful, imperturbable, reserved, he dominated absolutely our counsels " (pp. 3 and 4). Mr. Asquith had a barrister's trained faculty of coming to rapid provisional conclusions by largely subconscious methods of inference, and a barrister's trained caution in avoiding as long as possible any decision which further information or further half-conscious reflection might indicate as mistaken. He was sixty-two years old, and his personal psychological idiosyncracies probably increased his professional tendency towards procrastination. Lord Fisher was seventy-four years old. He was a sailor of genius, who, like Lord Kitchener, had been in the habit of forming his own decisions by intense individual thought, and imposing those decisions on others by the natural weight of his will to lead. Mr. Churchill, as readers of his books and speeches know, is a born literary artist, with an artist's tendency to combine

---

indicated in the First Report that he never understood the quantitative limitations of a single leader. General Murray is quoted for the statement that " Lord Kitchener acted very much as his own Chief of the Staff " (p. 6), and the Report says, " there can be no doubt that the principle of centralization was pushed to an extreme point by Lord Kitchener. . . . But it was unsuitable to a stronger force than that which Lord Kitchener commanded in the Soudan. . . . Its result was to throw into the hands of one man an amount of work with which no individual, however capable, could hope to cope successfully " (p. 13).

thought and emotion subconsciously, rather than consciously to co-ordinate them. Admiral May said, " Mr Churchill was very keen on his own views " (p. 27) Mr. Churchill will be long remembered as having called (in the House of Commons, November 15th, 1915) the Dardanelles attack a " legitimate war gamble." By this he probably meant that he had estimated the attack to have rather more than an even chance of success. If he had made a quantitative study of the working of a temperament like his own, he would have learnt not to treat any plan of his as a " legitimate gamble " unless it appeared to him to have at least a three-to-one chance of success. At elections political agents tell " keen " candidates to make an allowance about as great as that for their " personal factor." [1]

The organization of thought in the War Council consisted of little more than the acceptance by all its members of the implications (not always the same) which each of them believed to be contained in the words " expert " and " minister." Among those implications was more or less consciously included the assumption that every war-problem could be subdivided into a series of technical problems and sub-problems—naval, military, diplomatic, engineering, artillery, geographical, medical, etc. Each technical problem was to be covered by its own body of experts, and each expert could, it was assumed, be trusted so to use the methods of artificial scientific thought as to predict accurately the results on his special factor of any proposed action. The whole body was then to examine and co-ordinate the conclusions of the experts. In any large matter, all the members, with the possible exception of those who attended merely as experts, were to be

[1] See also my *Great Society*, chap. x.

responsible for forming (or advising the Cabinet to form) final decisions. Lord Kitchener, being Secretary for War, attended the Council both as minister and as expert, and was accompanied by Sir James Murray as fellow-expert. Lord Fisher and Admiral Sir Arthur Wilson attended as experts only.

The naval and military officers were accustomed to the procedure of small official " boards," composed of officers who are called on for their opinions in rotation, and where the decision is formed and announced by the presiding senior officer. Mr. Asquith and Mr. Churchill were accustomed in the Cabinet to civilian committee-procedure, where no member is called on to speak, but any member may insist on his right to speak ; and where, if a vote is taken, the decision depends on a majority of equal votes. As ministers in their own departments they were accustomed to hear or read the opinions of their expert advisers, and then to come individually to an independent and final conclusion. All the members of the Council, with the important exception of Lord Kitchener, had worked together before the war on the Cabinet Committee of Imperial Defence, which had existed since 1904. But no one of them seems to have realized that an organization, consisting of persons of such different training, and exercising powers of such terrific importance, needed a fundamental analysis of the relations between its members, leading to a scheme of rules and principles understood and explicitly agreed to by them all. The efficient formation of such a scheme might have involved a certain amount of actual invention. It might even have been necessary to invent new words or meanings for words, since an agreed terminology of the kind needed does not exist. But men, particularly if they belong to different social or official groups, are shy and awkward in talking about things of the mind ; so that no analysis or invention of methods took place, and the members of the Council came into the room each day unaware that they held completely different conceptions as to their relations to each other. Lord Fisher said in evidence, " We were not members of the War Council. . . . We were the experts there who were to open their mouths when told to " (p. 7). Mr. Churchill, on the other hand, spoke of his " naval colleagues " as having " the right, the knowledge, and the power to correct me or dissent from what I said," and as " fully cognizant of their rights " (p. 7). Mr. Balfour, when asked whether the experts " were under any obligation to initiate opinions," said that " that would depend on the view the Chairman [Mr. Asquith] took of their duties. . . . It is the business of the Chairman to see that nothing is passed over their heads on which they have an opinion until the opinion has been extracted." But " the means for letting their views be known . . . need not necessarily be an interruption of the proceedings, thrusting themselves in, as it were, in the discussion, though that would be the natural method of doing it " (pp. 7 and 8). Lord Haldane said, with regard to Lord Fisher, " We all looked on him as there to take counsel with us. . . Not one of us was asked to speak. Questions were not put round " (pp. 8 and 9). Mr. Asquith said, " I should have expected any of the experts there, if they entertained a strong personal view on their own expert authority, to express it " (p. 9). Lord Crewe and Lord Haldane agreed that " the political members of the Committee did too much of the talking and the expert members as a rule too little " (p. 9). Sir James Murray said, " I sometimes left the War Council with a very indistinct idea of any decision having been arrived at at all " (p. 9). The members of the Council, indeed, were never clear as to whether they were all and always members of a " thought-organization," or whether they, or some of them, were (since the Cabinet invariably accepted their advice) members of a final " will-organization." When they did act as a " will-organization " they seem to have reverted (except when Lord Kitchener without opposition led them) to that form of co-operation in a primitive war-party in which leadership is not complete, and a confused conflict is going on, which will be followed by the yielding of the less insistent to the more insistent clamour. Mr. Churchill, for instance, speaking in the House of Commons in the Dardanelles debate, said, " It was . . . one long, agonizing, wearying struggle to get every ship, every soldier, every gun, and every round of ammunition for the Dardanelles " (March 20th, 1917). The possible presence of further military experts meant to Mr. Churchill, not additional evidence for the formation by logical methods of an exact conclusion, but additional force behind the will of his opponents. " General Headquarters," he said, " would have sent their experts clattering over to reinforce this opinion, and no doubt General Joffre would have been called in aid to write the strongest letters of protest. After ten days' or a fortnight's discussion you would have been back to where you started " (*ibid.*) There was a moment of intense conflict on the day of the final decision, when Lord Fisher " rose from his seat with the intention . . . of intimating his intention to resign," and Lord Kitchener " at the same time rose from his seat, and, before Lord Fisher could leave the room, had some private conversation with him at the window. Eventually, according to a note made by Lord Fisher at the time, the latter reluctantly gave way to Lord Kitchener's entreaty and resumed his seat " (p. 27).

Now, when men form decisions by means of the " natural " method of a conflict of wills, followed either by an instinctive compromise or by the instinctive dominance of the stronger will, their mental processes are largely subconscious, and they are unable to give (as those often can who are co-operating in " artificial " logical thought) an account of them which can be followed by others and tested by logical rules. They are unable to explain either the steps by which their forecast of results was reached, or the relation of their final decision to their forecast of results. Lord Fisher, for instance, gave an account of his own state of mind while he was both estimating the chances of a naval attack and deciding whether he should acquiesce in the proposal to undertake it ; and other witnesses gave their own impressions of Lord Fisher's state of mind. It was, one gathers, rather one of growing emotional discomfort than one of growing clearness in thought and will. He described himself as " instinctively against " a purely naval attack (p. 50), and Mr. Churchill said, " I could see that Lord Fisher was increasingly worried about the Dardanelles situation " (p. 26). Lord Kitchener's opposition to the employment of soldiers in the attack " underwent a considerable change " (p. 31), and by March 3rd, 1915, " had apparently weakened " (p. 33). The argument about our prestige in the East " grew in importance " (p. 30), and General Callwell is quoted as saying, with regard to the later stage in the expedition, that " we drifted into the big military attack " (p. 30).

A certain amount of such " natural thought " and of

such a " natural " combination of impulse and thought is, I believe, both inevitable, and, when once the sphere of its utility is understood, useful. One can imagine a future body of soldiers and statesmen all of whom had been trained from their school-days to understand and respect the future art of rational corporate action. They might agree among themselves that the " scientific " logic of subdivided expertise was not by itself a sufficient guide in the estimation and co-ordination of such factors as the feelings of suspicious allies and inarticulate Eastern populations. They might further agree that, after allowing for differences of temperament, the fact that one member of a council felt strongly on a point at issue, and another member felt doubtfully about it, should be recognized as an important element in forming both intellectual and practical decisions. But their agreement on such points in the psychology of rational purpose would be subject to a recognition of the undiminished authority of the scientific logic of expertise within its own sphere. In the Dardanelles case, even the one principle on which the whole Council was agreed—that each expert should be responsible for all technical decisions within the sphere of his expertise—was half-consciously ignored. The decision inquired into seems to have been ultimately due to Lord Kitchener's personal and non-expert impression that a purely naval attack would succeed (p. 16). It was only when heavy losses of ships and men had occurred that the naval experts asserted their rights, and the purely naval attack was, on March 23rd, 1915, abandoned.

The Mesopotamian Report describes the co-operation of a body of ministers and officials, not gathered day by day in a Whitehall council room, but strung out along the line, Simla, Bombay, Mesopotamia, London, and mainly communicating with each other by telegraph. Those who were responsible for the calamitous first advance on Baghdad were not all, as those responsible for the Dardanelles naval attack were, men of very unusual intellectual ability and force of character. Some of them were in that respect not much above the average, though even they were professional men high in their professions. One is constantly reminded in reading the Mesopotamia Report that the professional officers of the British army before 1914 were mainly drawn from those scholars who were most influenced by the conventional traditions of the middle forms of the English " public schools," and least influenced by the intellectual stimulus which is often felt in the highest forms. According to that tradition all conscious and systematic effort in the use of the mind is apt to be treated as " bad form." The spontaneous brilliance of a clever athlete in doing a short composition is tolerated. To aim at more is to be a " smug." [1] Since leaving school and passing their military examinations most of these officers had lived " natural " intellectual lives in the presence of the unnatural facts of the modern world and modern warfare. They had given no more conscious thought to their own mental processes than a healthy boy of twelve gives to the functions of his pancreas. Many of them even seemed unaware of the need of that effort of will which alone can substitute a systematic exploration of the conditions of any proposed action for

[1] Even when the British Staff College was started after the Crimean War, " it was looked on with some disfavour by the old officers because it was a new-fangled notion, and by the young officers as a ' mug's game.' [At one time] it got about among us that no one could hope to get a good report from the Staff College, or any chance of a staff appointment in the future, unless he rode regularly with the Staff College Drag Hounds." Sir George Young-husband, *A Soldier's Memories* (1917), pp. 115 and 117.

passive dependence on the stimulus to thought given
by such facts as may casually reach the thinker. Again
and again the Commissioners call attention to the " passive
attitude " (p. 83) of officers, to their want of " prescience
and enterprise " (p. 55) and " foresight " (p. 50) ; or
say that they did not " think of definitely asking " this
(p. 31), or " were not very helpful in suggesting substitutes " for that (p. 7). The Parliamentary debates on
the Mesopotamia Report show also how difficult it is for
Englishmen to bring defects in the conduct of the mind
into their habitual moral categories of right and wrong.
It seemed to many of the members of Parliament unjust
to punish men for mistakes due to forms of mental conduct
which the offenders would not recognize as moral offences.
Lord Loreburn, the very able ex-Lord Chancellor, said
that the blundering was generally " honest blundering "
(July 13th, 1917). To Lord Islington the " paralyzing
officialdom " (July 11th, 1917) of General Duff seemed
rather a misfortune than an offence. It was easier to
form moral judgments when one thought in terms of
commercial tradition, and therefore could describe what
had happened as a want of " elementary business precautions " (Loreburn, July 7th, 1917).

If many of the officers concerned in the Mesopotamia
Expedition were untrained for the work of artificial individual thought, and unprovided with any ideals of conduct
with regard to it, they were still more untrained for the
work of co-operative thought. The most necessary rule
in that process is absolute frankness among the co-operating
thinkers. But the Report speaks of " want of frankness "
(p. 74) and quotes as " disingenuous " a letter from one
military secretary in India to another, pointing out that,
if the Indian authorities wished to get their way, it would

be better not to show their whole minds to the Home authorities (p. 41). Another necessary rule is that any one who is to take part in the give and take of thought in co-operation with others must train himself to attach no more initial weight to his own ideas than to those of others, and must strive to overcome that quasi-Freudian impulse which makes him first dislike his colleague for making a new suggestion, and then dislike the suggestion because his colleague has made it. But the Report says that " the Indian Government was at first lukewarm on a proposition which it did not originate " (p. 97), and quotes the statement that " the Mesopotamia campaign was believed to be a side-show and no man's child " (p. 96). Some of the evidence given in those sections of the Report which deal with the treatment of the wounded is specially significant. Major R. Markham Carter, for instance, was an Indian army doctor as to whom the Report says, " his sense of duty seems to be most commendable and he was fertile and resourceful in suggesting remedies " (p. 93). Major Carter insisted on seeing the Commander of the expedition in order to tell him of the breakdown of medical arrangements (p. 77), and sent to Delhi a report with a " vivid account " of the sufferings of the wounded (p. 78). Surgeon-General Hathaway said that the Army Commander ordered him to deal with Major Carter " with reference to his objectionable remarks " (p. 81), and General Cowper, the Quartermaster-General, said, " I threatened to put him under arrest, and I said that I would get his hospital ship taken away from him for a meddlesome interfering faddist " (p. 81). The Report gives these facts as instances of " an unpleasant feature in the Mesopotamia campaign, viz., the active intolerance of all criticism of defects or suggestions

of reform " (p. 81). A statement is quoted that " the
Indian system . . . allows officers to think . . . that there
is more merit to be obtained by keeping quiet and not
worrying the higher authorities than by asking for what
is necessary " (p. 105), and mention is made of " the
policy of suppressing the unpleasant " (p. 80). The
" atmosphere very unfavourable to reforming innova-
tion " (p. 74) is so much taken for granted, that men whose
good suggestions have been rejected are blamed in the
Report for not showing a degree of obstinate persistence
which would have been unnecessary among colleagues
who were accustomed to pick up each other's ideas.
General Townshend, for instance, " does not seem to
have pressed his objections hard " (p. 27). Surgeon-
General Hathaway did not urge " even his small request
. . . for an improvised hospital steamer or tug . . . per-
sistently or with sufficient emphasis " (p. 57).

The Dardanelles disaster was caused in large part by
the fact that the conditions of oral discussion between
politicians and experts were not properly analyzed. In
the Mesopotamia case the politicians were puzzled as to
the degree of final authority which they should give to
definite written or telegraphed military proposals. Mr.
Montagu (then Secretary for India) said in the House of
Commons (July 12th, 1917), " Among many things we have
never decided in this country are the relations between
politicians and soldiers." Lord Crewe said, " War is
politics, if it is not to be mere scalp-hunting " (July 7th,
1917). But Lord Hardinge was not sure of the point where
" civilian interference with military plans " (July 3rd,
1917) was permissible, and Mr. J. H. Thomas, M.P., the
direct-minded secretary of the Railwaymen's Trade Union,
said, " We are told, first, that if civilians interfere with

the military they are to be condemned, and we are told afterwards that if they do not interfere they are equally to be condemned " (July 18th, 1917).[1]

The Dardanelles Report deals almost solely with military and naval problems. Only the slightest reference is made to such " political " questions as the feelings and desires of our allies and the Greeks. The Mesopotamia Report indicates a tendency to confine the inquiry within much the same limits. This must have been partly due to a sense that it was imprudent to publish criticisms of our Russian allies, or apprehensions as to the loyalty of our Indian fellow-subjects. It may have been partly due to the fact that our intellectual atmosphere is as yet uninfluenced by the more complex forms of the art of thought, and that commissioners who were trying to produce a clear report would find it difficult to co-ordinate the comparatively " immeasurable " factors of political feeling with the comparatively " measurable " factors of military risk and advantage. In the Parliamentary debates on the Mesopotamia Report in 1917 it was urged, I think fairly, that this limitation had resulted in a certain amount of injustice to Lord Hardinge, who at the time of the Mesopotamia decision was Viceroy of India. Behind that debate one could detect not only the logical problem of treating feeling as part of the subject-matter of thought, but also the psychologico-logical problem of the function of feeling in the process of thought. The charge against Lord Hardinge was that he had not called on the people of India for the same extremity of sacrifice in men and

[1] The Mesopotamia Report incidentally mentions " the introduction by the Cabinet of political considerations into the calculations of their military advisers," and says, " we do not wish to imply that this widening of their survey is to be condemned " (p. 26)—which is not very helpful.

money as had been enforced in Britain. His answer was, in effect, that he had done as much as in the presence of the facts of Indian feeling he considered to be safe. Now, Lord Hardinge was, as was admitted throughout the debate, " the most popular Viceroy of modern times . . . a Viceroy on whose sympathy and assistance Indians could rely " (Montagu, July 12th). Lord Islington, with his long Indian experience, said that Lord Hardinge's " personal influence controlled the tendency to revolt " (July 11th) ; and Lord Montagu of Beaulieu, who had just returned from India, said, " It was largely his personal influence which held the country together " (July 12th). Lord Hardinge said, " I trusted the people of India " (July 3rd). Obviously Lord Hardinge's " sympathy " was a powerful factor in the success of the Indian Government in preventing a rising. But what was the value of that sympathy in the process by which Lord Hardinge estimated the balance of forces in the situation ? Was it positive or negative or indifferent ? Some men would expect *a priori* that Lord Hardinge's conscious sympathy with and affection for the Indian people would act as a hindrance in the intellectual process of estimating forces, and that a man like Lord Curzon, who might successfully claim to have driven below consciousness a good many of his sympathies, would have been likely to estimate the situation more correctly. Others might say that sympathy and judgment are facts so completely unrelated to each other that no one learns anything about a man's judgment by learning about his sympathy. Or, finally, one may believe that (as I have already urged),[1] in the case of two men of equal powers of logical judgment, both of whom are fully conscious of the distinction in

[1] See *ante*, p. 40.

themselves between the psychological processes of emotion
and thought,the man of the more conscious, more sensitive
and wider sympathies is the more likely, not only to
desire the right ends, but to discover the right means.
The nature of the problem becomes clearer if one thinks,
not of the Dardanelles and Mesopotamia decisions, but
of the decisions taken by the governing group in Germany
at the outbreak and during the continuance of the war.
Most Germans would now admit that the ultimatum to
Russia, the invasion of Belgium, and the acts which
brought America into the war were based upon unsound
calculations as to their probable effects. In forming
strategical military decisions the German General Staff
was an instrument of unprecedented efficiency. Those
responsible for the intellectual direction of the fighting
were chosen with the utmost care and ruthlessly replaced
in case of failure. Many of the ablest members of the
Prussian governing classes had in the generation before
the war become professional soldiers. They were trained
to aim, consciously and without British snobbery or
shyness, at intellectual integrity and thoroughness. Many
Englishmen, when they read, for instance, the report
on the Somme fighting of General Sixt von Arnim in
1916 found in it qualities which were new to their whole
conception of the military mind. The miscalculation
involved in the series of decisions in July 1914 which
made the war inevitable was not due to technical military
inefficiency, but mainly to the fact that the narrowing
of human sympathy which was consciously involved in
much of the training of individual Prussian civil or military
Realpolitiker involved also a narrowing of their thoughts,
and a lessening of the ultimate efficiency of any co-operating
group of which they formed part.

CHAPTER IV

THE NATION AS IDEA AND FACT

I NOW turn from co-operation among members of a group to co-operation among members of a nation, leaving till a later chapter (Chapter IX) the larger question of co-operation among human beings belonging to two or more or all nations. I here use the word " nation," as I used the word " group " in the last chapter, merely as a convenient term of magnitude ; by a " nation " I mean one of those organized communities of twenty million to three hundred million inhabitants which include the great majority of mankind.

The change of scale from group to nation involves a change in the form and character of the co-operative process. National co-operation is necessarily much more artificial, more dependent on socially inherited knowledge and conscious effort, than is group co-operation. In order to realise this, we must, again and again, remind ourselves of the quantitative limitations of all the factors in the human type. We are apt to think of human societies as we think of equilateral triangles. We can imagine an equilateral triangle with sides either an inch long or a hundred miles long, and in either case its qualities as an equilateral triangle will be the same. But if we imagine a heap of sand composed of sand-grains, each grain being about a hundredth of an inch in diameter, we must remember that a change of size in the heap may change the relation between the grains, and, therefore, the character of the heap. A heap of twenty grains of sand will behave differently from a heap of twenty million grains. It will, for instance, have a different " angle of repose."

In a human society the average size of the units must be taken by the social and political thinker as fixed. Unless we are prepared to wait for twenty generations of bold eugenic experiment, we cannot make the mean height of a body of Englishmen or North Americans appreciably more than 5 ft. 8 in. or the mean length of their stride more than 30 in. The natural range of our memory and the natural strength and range of our emotions are fixed by similar limits. A group of a dozen statesmen or generals assembled in one place can all, like a primitive hunting party, hear each other's voices and see each other's movements. They may find it necessary to use artificial methods of thought and con- sultation and decision. But, even when engaged in artificial forms of co-operation, they still react naturally to direct perceptions of each other ; and those who have once co-operated in such a group can, when they are separated, remember each other as clearly pictured individuals and react to that remembrance. The largest visible crowd is, however, only a tiny fraction of a modern nation. A modern civilized man can, therefore, never see or hear the nation of which he is a member, and, if he thinks or feels about it, he must do so by employing some acquired entity of the mind. I found, the other day, in a bundle of twenty-year-old notes, that I had written the words " painted box " to express my belief that each of us walks through life with his head locked within a

lighted box painted with the picture of the world by
which he guides his steps. My metaphor, however,
ignored the fact that our direct sensations form at any
moment at least the foreground of that mental picture.
It would have been better if I had referred to the panorama
of the Battle of Waterloo, which, as a child in pre-cinema
days, I saw at a country fair, with its foreground of solid
ears of corn, solid field-gun, and solid wax model of a
dead soldier, fading into a background of painted canvas.
So, when we think of our nation, the people and houses
and newspaper pages that are, as we think, within the
range of our senses, fade into a background which the
experiences of every year since first we heard our nation
named have helped to paint. And when we vote or write
a letter or telegraph an order or co-operate in any other
way in nation-wide action, we are often like an excited
rustic at the fair who should fire a gun at the painted
French army on the panorama canvas and kill a real
market woman across the square.

But the metaphor of the panorama is itself imperfect,
in that it ignores the fact that the picture before us changes
with every moment of our thought, and that, though the
first image presents itself automatically, its subsequent
changes can be consciously directed by an effort of our
will. If, as we sit in a psychological laboratory, the name
of our country is suddenly exposed on the screen, a visual
or audile image — a map or flag or bit of landscape
or the sound of a word—will automatically appear to us,
and will probably be accompanied almost simultaneously
by some emotion or impulse. If we concentrate our
attention on that image, it will rapidly develop into the
long series of associated " facts " which constitutes our
" knowledge " of our country ; and over that development

our will has much controlling power. Our accompanying emotional and impulsive reactions will also develop into a complex of feelings, due partly to the valuation and interpretation of our idea by our primitive instincts and partly to acquired association of emotion with emotion. Over that emotional complex our will has less controlling power. Our will, at the moment, has no controlling power over the automatic images and impulses which first reveal themselves when the printed card drops from the machine; but they, again, are the result of causes many of which might have been influenced by our will in the past, and may be influenced by our will in the future.

Of all this we are in our daily life only occasionally and intermittently conscious. We are sometimes vividly conscious of a sensation which starts in us the image or idea of our nation. Sometimes we are vividly conscious of the idea of our nation, and less conscious of the sensation which started it. Sometimes we are vividly conscious of an emotion or impulse arising out of our idea of our nation, and less conscious of the idea itself, or of the sensation which started it. When, for instance, on August 5th, 1914, I stood vaguely watching the incidents of mobilization outside the Admiralty and the War Office in Whitehall, I was vividly conscious of a feeling of gathering power, which was the result of a strong stimulation of my " instinct of corporate defence." My feeling was in fact preceded by the sight of a few soldiers and sailors, and accompanied by the idea of a mobilizing nation. But I was conscious rather of my feeling than of my idea or my visual sensation.

Because we are not trained to be aware of the character of this process, most of us tend to assume that there exists an objective reality corresponding exactly to those of our ideas which are accompanied by strong feelings. I can see in a walk along Whitehall a Labour M.P., an officer of the Guards, and a High Church Bishop. The sight of the long row of Government Departments with the Houses of Parliament at the end starts in each of them a half-conscious idea, which, if he were questioned, he might call " The People," or " My King and Country," or " Christian England." That idea is accompanied by feelings of pride and affection and corporate power, and these feelings are so vivid that each man is prepared to vote or fight or agitate, on the subconscious and un-examined assumption that his idea, which may be little more than a faint memory or a hundred leading articles in the *Daily Herald,* or *Morning Post,* or *Church Times,* is a trustworthy equivalent for the real England which his action will affect.

But while men are normally unaware of the process by which their idea of their nation and its accompanying emotions are produced, the practised skill of those whose business is the large-scale creation of such ideas and emotions is constantly increasing. The controllers of newspapers, especially of the sinister American or British journals whose writers are apparently encouraged to " colour the news " (as well as their comments on the news) in accordance with the will of a multi-millionaire proprietor, know pretty exactly what they are doing. The manufacturers of cinema films, though their own object may be nothing but the accumulation of money, are creating for the now growing generation of mankind an imaged world in which, against a background of Californian valleys and Chicago drawing-rooms, second-rate actors prove that luck and coincidence will always help vulgar motives to vulgar success. The ministers of

propaganda and of education in any one of the new
aggressive nations which have been created by the war
are apparently determined to leave nothing to accident
in the slow and subconscious process by which their
subjects and their neighbours form ideas of that nation.
It is perhaps fortunate that, owing to certain subtle
facts in our psychology, their deliberately created entities
do not often stir us, even in their most strident forms,
as deeply as our direct sensations of concrete facts. No
newspaper articles or posters during the war moved us
in London quite in the same way as did the low thudding
of the Messines guns, or the sight of a Zeppelin crossing
the beam of a searchlight. But the fact that the impulses
which make us vote, or invest, or dogmatize on politics
at the club are tepid and half-hearted, does nothing to
diminish the sharpness with which distant but real human
beings are affected by our decisions.[1]

How then is any of us to acquire an idea of his nation
which, with its emotional associations, will form a more
reliable guide for nation-wide action than does the
panorama-background that the accidents of past talk
and reading and travel and the ingenuities of propagandists
have painted for him ? Here, as in the whole problem of
our relation to our social heritage, we shall, I believe,
find the answer, not in a " return to nature," but in a
more resolute use of artificial expedients. The student who
is preparing himself to play a part in nation-wide co-
operation must begin with a deliberate effort of radical
scepticism. Descartes owed his influence over modern
thought to his conscious determination to substitute for
the philosophical propositions which he had accepted on

---

[1] On the relation between such " ideas " and political action
see my *Human Nature in Politics*, Part I, chap. ii.

the authority of his teachers, and the unexamined impulses which originated in what he called his "appetites," a train of reasoning every step in which it should be impossible to doubt. The modern student of the social sciences must separate from his "self" and bring under a self-conscious process of reconstruction, not only his conscious philosophy and impulses, but that idea of his nation which would automatically appear if he sat before a psychological screen, and which forms the unconscious background of his daily thinking. He must fight, for instance, against that "idol of the cave," by which the professional thinker is so often misled, his tendency to assume that all other men when he thinks about them are very like himself as he thinks. Professional thinkers about society, and the readers of their books, are unusual people—engaged on an unusual task; they have more than an average permanent interest in their subject, and at the moment of writing and reading they are devoting their whole attention on it. Because they are engaged in the effort of systematic thought or in the gathering of knowledge necessary for such thought, and because they are often convinced that the maintenance and future progress of society depends on the stimulation of thought in others, they inevitably tend to "intellectualize" their problem, by assuming that most of the actions of most men are the result of conscious, deliberate, and well-informed reasoning.

In the last chapter I was dealing with instances in which this "intellectualist" conception has a certain correspondence with the facts. The statesmen and generals and officials who made up the groups which I discussed were men carefully selected and trained, at the best age for intellectual work, and spending their whole working days in the effort to attain practical ends by the solution of intellectual problems. The majority, however, of the members of a modern nation are ordinary people, who, at any given moment, are either not concentrating their attention at all, or are concentrating it on some personal short-range purpose. The student, therefore, who is attempting slowly to create for himself a trustworthy idea of his nation, should attempt to see his fellow-nationals, not, primarily, from the inside as minds, but from the outside as moving bodies. To do so he should make as vivid and permanent a mental picture as he can of members of his nation so chosen as to be fairly typical of the mass, but not so numerous as to leave in his memory a confused crowd. If the nation which he is considering is, like Britain, mainly urban, he will be wise to watch closely for ten minutes a week, or at least imagine for two minutes a week that he is watching, the people whom he can pass in an ordinary street or see on a cinematograph film representing, not a group of denaturalized cinema-actors, but the spectators at some public event, who do not know that they are being photographed. Perhaps he is himself walking along the pavement of one of those dreary working-class streets which lie between central London and its outer suburbs. Let him fix in his memory a " moving picture " of what he sees, seeing himself if he can, not as an observing philosopher, but as a worried householder or casual holiday-maker passing with the rest.

His picture will be more fertile in starting new thoughts, if, while he is forming it, he maintains a conscious " problem-attitude," and encourages his emotions as well as his imagination to play about his problem. He should ask himself, for instance, as he watches, what is the relation between the people whom he sees in the London street and the social organization which makes it possible for them and seven million others to remain alive in the London area. How far is it true that, as an American friend said to me, the social " cement " which has so far held western civilization together is crumbling away ? The daily food of these people, and the materials of their daily work, are brought to London by a huge and precarious system of railways and steamships : their health is dependent on a complex arrangement of sewers, and watermains, and isolation hospitals, and factory inspection : the businesses which employ them are largely financed by a few great banks : the children are being educated, and the parents have nearly all been educated, in state-controlled schools : the personal security of them all depends on an elaborate state organization of justice and police. But a month hence the treasury-note in the hand of the woman across the street who is buying potatoes may be worth no more than a rouble-note in Petrograd or a krone in Vienna ; the crippled soldier may find that he cannot draw his pension, and the grey-haired cabinet-maker may be out of work. Even if no disaster befalls the central finance of the nation, a municipal election next month, or a vote at a committee this afternoon, may decide whether the boy who is turning over the "twopenny box " of the book-stall shall get a scholarship or become a carman's drudge ; and a revolutionary railway strike may at any moment set the policeman and the railway porter who are chatting at the street corner to hating and perhaps fighting each other. When he passes from this external motion-picture to the formation of an idea of the internal thoughts and feelings of his fellow-nationals, the student will find his task much more difficult. But the patient watching for little pieces of significant evidence will help to prevent him from subconsciously assuming that the "panorama" which he sees, however close it may be to the world of objective fact, is the same as that which they see.

So far he will have concentrated his attention, as did the prisoners in Plato's Cave, on the individual human beings who pass like shadows before him. But if he is watching Camden Town in London or Seventh Avenue in New York with the same intensity with which Plato watched the morning crowd in the Athenian agora, he may suddenly realize how great a sense of intellectual power comes to him, as it came to Plato, when he reminds himself that these individuals, though unique, are not unrelated—that they do all conform in varying degrees to the human physical and psychological type. Few of us now believe with Plato that that type exists, single and perfect, in "some heavenly place"; but we know enormously more than did Plato of its history and complexity, and we can estimate better than he could its relation to the moulding force of our physical and intellectual environment, and the proportion, with regard to each of its factors, between the many individuals who come near the mean, and the few who are at each extreme of excess or defect.

At this point the student may begin to use his idea of his nation as a means of judging between different forms of national co-operation. He will soon, I believe, convince himself that no national social organization can be stable which is not supported by a larger measure of general consent than is now found in any great modern industrial community. Before the war many conservative thinkers advocated national organization on the basis of mere discipline. Let each have his own place in the national system as workman, housewife, student, or administrator ; let each acquire the habit of performing his special function ; and let that habit be maintained by carefully trained policemen and soldiers and professors. No thinker in the world, except perhaps in Japan, or in the administration of the United States Steel Corporation, or the clubs of officials and soldiers in British India, would to-day be satisfied with that basis. The social organization of Prussia and Austria and Russia broke down, because, in the first place, the habituation of an individual is not reproduced in the biological inheritance of the race. The individual human beings who pass us in the street have, on the average, only some thirty years of life before them ; and every day there are born to them new human beings with all the impulses and limitations of their primitive ancestors, in whom the process of habituation must begin afresh. In the next place, the habituation of an individual human being is never perfect. At the point when training seems most complete, as, for instance, in the German navy or the Essen workshops in 1918, human nature revolts [1] ; the men become " fed-up " and the past discipline becomes a force hindering rather than helping its original purpose. Habit, like the arch in the Indian proverb, " never sleeps "; and any break in social routine or disorganization of political institutions in a country ruled by habit without conscious consent may throw out of gear the whole system of subdivided co-operation on which modern civilization, and the existence of modern populations, depend.

Nor will the classical " economic motive," the short-range calculation by each employee that if in any week he works harder his wages at the end of the week will be

[1] See my *Great Society*, chap. v (on Habit).

larger, prove a sufficient substitute for some measure of general consent. It is easy to argue that national productivity would be greatly increased if working-men, each of whom has been for eight years at school, and who are associated in huge industrial units, would confine their attention to their individual " plain interests," and leave " visionary ideas " about the justice or injustice of the organization of their nation alone. But the fact is that they do not and will not so confine their attention, and that increased production on that basis is a visionary hope.

How, then, are we to bring it about that a much larger proportion than at present of the inhabitants of the great industrial nations shall consciously consent to play their part in the process of national co-operation ? My first answer would be that we must aim at a much nearer approximation to economic and social equality than now exists in any industrial nation. The physiological arguments for greater equality are becoming every day more clear. It was, for instance, an astonishing fact that during the two years from November 1916 to November 1918, though the quantity and quality of the food consumed in London was seriously below that of the peaceful and prosperous years 1912 and 1913, yet because of comparative equality of distribution the physical well-being produced by that food was greater.[1] The proportionate reduction

[1] The School Medical Officer of the London County Council in his report for the year 1918, p. 3, gives statistics (based on the examination of more than 200,000 children) and sums up by saying, " The story is one of which London may be proud, for it is one of continuous amelioration throughout the whole period of the war. Whether judged from the state of the children's clothing, from their health as expressed by their nutritional well-being, or from the conditions found as regards cleanliness, the result is the same, practically steady improvement in each particular."

of London food-consumption during the Napoleonic wars was probably less, but because social inequality increased during those wars the physique of the whole population was, as far as one can judge from one's impressions of contemporary pictures and literature, seriously lowered.[1] But if we assume that organization on a national scale is necessary, the psychological arguments for a nearer approximation to economic equality are even stronger than the physiological arguments. At certain moments in their lives men have to decide whether they will strike or rebel or how they will vote, under circumstances where their action may weaken or help to break up the national co-operative system. At such moments they will have an idea of their own relation to that system. The feeling accompanying that idea may be anything from a burning sense of resentment, or a grudging acquiescence, to that emotion of gratitude for mutual service which is sometimes found in a well-organized and successful regiment. But resentment will not be absent, nor gratitude present, unless men and women feel that they are getting their fair share of the national product, and they will not permanently so feel unless in fact the joint product is distributed with a nearer approach to equality than industrial civilization has yet achieved. Expedients (including various forms of taxation and control) have already been invented which aim at bringing about an approximation to economic equality in advanced industrial societies. I do not purpose here to discuss these expedients in detail, but will say that I believe that, with a certain amount of patience and goodwill, these expedients, and others which might be invented, would be

[1] It would be interesting if some one would collect such evidence as exists on this point.

made to carry out their aim without loss, or without loss which was not worth while, in national wealth production.

An approach to social equality will not, however, produce social contentment, unless it is accompanied by two other conditions : firstly, a better understanding of the nature of the social co-operation created by " money-economy " ; and secondly, a greater positive liking by man and women for the work they do. Money-economy still gives rise, both among those who gain and those who lose by the present system of distribution, to fallacies which remind one of the intellectual atmosphere of the Stone Ages. Our ancestors early discovered the advantage of giving each member of a tribe a name ; but, at a period sufficiently near our own time to make it unlikely that important changes in our biological inheritance have since occurred, men still assumed that a man's name was something which, like the man himself, could be sold or captured or bewitched. So, at a later date, men discovered the advantage of naming wealth in terms of money, and we are only now beginning to abandon some of the cruder forms of thought resulting from that discovery. I thought of the *Golden Bough*, and of Messrs. Spencer and Gillen and their friends the Aruntas, when I read a speech ascribed to Miss Morgan and quoted by Professor Veblen. " Society and its ramifications depend upon the expenditure of money for their existence. We have the necessary money to spend upon entertainments and the social functions that annually give employment to thousands of tradesmen. . . . Business is kept alive by the thousands of dollars that are spent by ' high society.' "[1] In Britain we do not hear arguments about " the circulation of money " used so confidently as they were forty years

[1] Veblen, *Imperial Germany*, p. 140.

ago ; and the fallacies arising from a confusion between the money-valuation of wealth and wealth have been made to seem less real to us by the object lessons of the war, and by a partial infiltration of modern professional economic terms into current speech.   In December 1915, for instance, the Mayor of Cambridge issued an appeal drawn up by a committee containing two of the best-known Cambridge economists.   In it the public were told that " the only true saving at the present time consists in reducing our demands for goods and services " (*Times*, December 20th, 1915).   Twelve months later, the National War Savings Committee published a nation-wide appeal to women to " demand fewer services " (*Times*, December 13th, 1916), and Sir Auckland Geddes, in 1917, urged us " so to order our lives that we may make the least possible demand upon the energy of others " (November 12th, 1917).   I inferred that " F. W. H." must have been a very great lady indeed to have secured insertion in the *Times* (April 19th, 1916) for a letter advocating " a plan to help the country," which " can be done with very little effort and self-denial. Our nine household servants have agreed to give up meat of any sort for their breakfast, and the money thus saved is . . . invested in War Loan."   And the realist examination of the mining industry as a social process by the Coal Commission of 1919 made a beginning of the protection of the average coal-miner and coal-owner from the same type of thought.

The second condition, a greater zest (or a lessened dislike) in individual men and women for their work, is even more important.   Ricardo and the " classical " political economists tended to assume that all productive work must be disagreeable, and that no work would ever be undertaken except in order to secure the secondary

pleasures resulting from wages, and to avoid the secondary
evils arising from poverty.   If that were true, the elaborate
co-operative system of modern industry would be more
unstable than it now is.   If, at the Judgment of Solomon,
neither mother had desired the baby to live, except from
indirect and secondary motives, the baby would certainly
have been cut in two.   Already some men and women
for all the working day, and many for part of it, are, if
they believe themselves to be fairly well treated by the
community, carried through their work by a positive
impulse arising directly from the work itself ; a born
lover of flowers with a liking for children tends the flower
beds in a public park ; a born politician edits a local
paper ; a born wood-carver gives twenty years' work to
a new cathedral.   Sometimes a man's paid working hours
are consciously divided between those in which he feels
himself to be working for the work's sake and those in
which he is working for the wage ; a rather selfish and
ambitious man with an abnormal passion of scientific
curiosity is offered satisfaction for his intellectual cravings
if he will make, in an astronomical observatory, calculations which will lead to the improvement of navigation ;
or a man with unusual natural sensitiveness to beauty
is made a Professor of Fine Art, and is allowed to spend
his mornings in looking at seventeenth-century etchings,
on condition that he overcomes his dislike for lecturing
about them in the afternoon.   More often men make no
such conscious distinction ; a Medical Officer of Health
who is exactly the right man for his post only realizes
at long intervals that in spite of occasional fatigue and
disappointment he has much more zest in his work than
has his colleague whose only real interest in life is politics,
or the stock-exchange, or water-colour sketching.

But these cases now depend largely upon individual accident ; and the enjoyment of modern work can only be seriously increased by a widespread and conscious policy. Part of that policy (as I have indicated in Chapter II) would consist of a better adaptation of working methods to the general human type ; [1] but an even more important part would consist of a better adjustment of individual tasks to individual differences between human beings. In any million of members of a modern industrial nation it is not likely that more than one of the twenty who are best fitted to be inventors, or writers, or organisers, or explorers, or artisans, receives the necessary training and opportunity. An almost unimaginable increase of personal happiness, social contentment, and economic efficiency, would, therefore, result if the achievement of a more complete adjustment became the conscious organized and effective purpose of modern civilization. Such a purpose was proclaimed by the socialists of 1848 with their motto, " From each according to his powers ; to each according to his needs " ; but the phalanstères of Fourier and Considérant, or the self-governing productive associations of Louis Blanc and Marx and Lassalle, were contrivances wholly inadequate for their purpose, and their failure discredited any policy of bringing about adjustment between the individual and his social function by any other means than the blind competition of an individualist society. If we are to succeed where they failed, we must both understand better than they did the character of the adjustment which we desire, and be more ingenious than they were in inventing expedients for bringing it about.

The qualities of any individual at any given moment

[1] See also my *Great Society*, chap. xiii.

result from his "nurture" as well as his "nature";
so that what we need is an adjustment between three
factors : his nature at birth, his past training, and his
present way of living.   As I write Lenin and Trotsky
are attempting to make such an adjustment by wholly
ignoring the past, and are doing so at the cost of destroying
the wealth, the organization, the traditions, and to an
appalling extent the lives of the trained functionaries
of the old dispensation.   In Britain America and France
it is still possible to hope that, if time is allowed us, we
may make an approach towards a more complete adjustment at an infinitely less cost of suffering and waste.
If we are to do so, we must begin by a searching analysis
of our present educational system ; since it is to that
imperfect system that we now mainly trust for the
discovery of the individual nature of each of our future
citizens, the adjustment of his training to that nature,
and his introduction to an adult vocation.   We must,
therefore, ask ourselves whether we desire that our
educational system should be based on, and should itself
create, a general idea of our nation as consisting of identical
human beings, or of different human beings.   Our answer
to that question will affect, not only the degree of specialization which we shall deem it wise to introduce into the
schools, but much in our general pedagogic methods.
I myself believe that we ought to decide for an education
based on the conscious idea of difference, and should
direct our pedagogic methods by that decision.   Every
child, for instance, now learns arithmetic.   In most
elementary schools, he is taught as an "infant" what is
called "concrete arithmetic" ; he is shown collections
of balls or coins or sticks or cubes, any one of which is
indistinguishable from the others, and is trained to make

calculations about imaginary apples, or eggs, on the same assumption of their identity with each other. Number is apt, indeed, at this stage to seem to him a special quality possessed by such collections of identical things. He is next introduced to " abstract " arithmetic, and makes the same assumption of the identity of the units, when he multiplies the abstract number ten by the abstract number four, or when he calculates the relation between nine inches and twenty miles. I believe that it would be wise from the beginning to make a small child count and measure and weigh not only identical things, but also boxes full of such differing miscellanies as Mr. Kipling's Kim was trained to observe. Some years later he could be taught to deal with that special case which will be of such supreme importance to him as a member of an animal species who has to live by co-operating with his fellows, and by consuming the tissues of other animal and vegetable species. He could, that is to say, learn to handle the quantitative relation which the manufacturers of boots or gloves call an " assortment," i.e. a small number of certain exceptional " sizes " and " fittings " shading into larger numbers of the " sizes " and " fittings " near the mean. He could construct experimentally the normal " curve of error " by counting e.g. the number of short or long " runs " of black or white balls drawn out of a box, and compare it with the biological curve plotted from the measurement of leaves picked casually from a bush. Later on, he could compare the " curve of error" with the more complex " Mendelian " variations in the seeds of experimentally cross-bred sweet peas.

The first critical point would come, when the teacher had to decide whether his pupils should be made conscious that they themselves formed part of such a biological "assortment," that the pupils of each school year could themselves be plotted along such curves in respect of height, weight, eyesight, memory, ear for music, etc., etc., and that there were definite limits within which, and only within which, each child might expect to change his own position on each curve by self-conscious will. In this matter we are at present in a curious state of ethical confusion. In order to encourage industry and energy, boys and girls are graded by periodical competitive examinations and competitive games ; and each individual makes a rough guess as to the point at which it is worth while for him to aim in each competition. But the underlying natural and nurtural curve is a sort of guilty secret ; the local grandee who presides at the annual prize-giving hints shamefacedly at the fact that Jones minor's success in mathematics or music, and Smith major's failure, are not entirely due to moral differences ; and an hour later Jones minor vaguely envies Brown tertius, who makes fifty runs and three catches in the slips because he can see a cricket ball moving at a pace which would make it invisible to an average boy. Other factors are less clearly realized ; the scholarship-boy whose mother brought up a family on thirty shillings a week, knows with a dull pain that, because his nurture has not harmonized with his nature, he will never be equal to industrious boys from well-to-do homes of much less than his own natural ability. Little Myer Abraham, the head-boy, may be clever enough to guess that six years hence an overgrown Scotch lad in the lower fifth may have developed beyond him. A sister who at sixteen teaches her brother his lessons may fear that at twenty-one he will be teaching her.

The next critical point would be the degree to which children of different qualities should be given different courses or sent to different schools. Already at school there lies behind the haphazard consciousness of difference the subconscious malaise which comes from the want of actual adjustment between the school curriculum and the powers and impulses of the individual student; the young scientist who is kept to the study of literature, the young poet who is kept to science, the young craftsman who cannot learn from books, is often not aware of the reason why he is sulky, and disobedient, and perhaps immoral. Meanwhile the chief official of the local education committee, or the newly-elected Labour Party chairman, may be sitting before a set of official curves showing the results of unprepared " Binet " psychological tests co-ordinated with terminal examination results and the reports of the class teachers. He asks himself shall he, in order to strengthen the idea and fact of social equality, treat all children as near as may be alike ; or shall he, in order to make more exact the adjustment between the individual and his function, base his treatment of them mainly on their differences. No perfectly simple answer to this question will be possible until our powers of psychological testing are increased, and until social equality has sufficiently advanced to make the differences at any moment between children depend much more than they do at present upon " nature," and much less on the " nurture " of rich and poor, or of educated and uneducated homes. But, broadly speaking, I am convinced that social progress already lies on the line of recognized difference. On this point, when I was last in the United States, Professor Dallas Sharp started an extremely interesting and significant controversy in the *Atlantic*

Monthly (November 1919). Professor Sharp argued for the conception of identity as the main basis of education. " The true end of American Education is the knowledge and practice of democracy—whatever other personal ends our education may serve. . . . We must all go together to school, with a common language, a common course of study, a common purpose, faith, and enthusiasm for democracy." He recognized the need of special courses and even special schools for the mentally deficient ; but for him the species is divided into the deficient and the " normal," and all the " normal " are apparently treated in his thinking as identical with each other. For the normal he proposes " one common school only, for rich and poor, up to the end of the high school (i.e. sixteen years of age) ; by which time we are pretty well all we need to be for purposes of democracy." In this common school there shall be " one common course, one broad universal course, thus educating for democracy first and after that for life and living," though apparently children of exceptional ability are to be allowed to pass through that course with exceptional rapidity. " A special programme of training, vocational, business, or college, before the end of the high school, if not contrary to the Decalogue is contrary to the spirit of the Constitution, and a menace to democracy. . . . As a nation we understand the theory of democracy. . . . We can die for democracy. Yet we cannot go to school for it, we cannot *be* democratic." I was told that Professor Sharp's plea was supported by an extraordinary number of enthusiastic letters to the editor of the *Atlantic.*

I sympathize intensely with those American thinkers who fear the development of hereditary social stratification in America. And yet I am sure that if the political

organization of America is to show itself compatible with the insistent demands of modern civilization it must be based on a theory of democracy more complex than that of identity, and nearer to the formula of 1848, " From each according to his powers ; to each according to his needs." In a democracy so based the child who is called by the community to the heavy task of consciously training his exceptional intellectual or artistic talent would be much more likely to do full service as a man, and much less likely to become either a prig or a snob, than is the bewildered little " smug " who wins school prizes to-day.

In England, the idea of democracy as identity—the idea of Thomas Jefferson and Andrew Jackson—is far less powerful than in America, and in a population almost wholly occupied in commerce and manufacture is more obviously inconsistent with social fact than it is in a population more than half of which is agricultural. We are rapidly creating special schools for children of various types of mental and physical defect, and all educational authorities provide scholarships and bursaries for children of special ability. The head teachers of English city schools spend a large part of their time in recommending children for various kinds of employment. Vocational education, based on the assumption that every student should receive an education leading to the vocation for which he or she is most fitted by nature, is steadily gaining, as far as the years from fourteen to twenty-two are concerned, upon " general education." But this tendency has not yet acquired the stability which would be ensured by the general acceptance of a clear principle ; much conservative opinion in England still supports those traditions of the endowed public schools and universities which are based mainly on differentiation by hereditary class ; and much radical opinion still inclines towards the principle of ignoring as far as possible all differences whether of nurture or nature. Our official educational policy follows, however, as a rule, what I believe to be a better principle. It looks to the general progress of democratic administration to produce such a measure of social equality as to secure that the differences between school-children shall in the future be due rather to their nature than to their nurture. Meanwhile it adjusts its educational system to individual differences, partly by testing the child as nature and nurture together have made him, partly (as when a scholarship scheme favours " ability " rather than " knowledge ") by giving a preference to nature over nurture ; and it hopes that in a community educated on that principle the conception of mutual though differing service may ultimately prove itself stronger than class selfishness and class hatred, or the natural human yearning for simple ideas of complex facts.

CHAPTER V

THE CONTROL OF NATIONAL CO-OPERATION

IN the preceding chapter I argued that, since it is now necessary for us to co-operate on the scale of a modern industrial nation, and since that scale far surpasses the range of our senses, we should consciously aim at creating in our own minds and in those minds whose training we influence, such an idea of our nation as will form the most reliable stimulus to large-scale co-operative emotion and co-operative action. I said that our idea should be based on a direct observation of concrete human beings, amplified and interpreted by an understanding of the relation of each individual to the similarities and variations of the human type. An idea so formed might, I hoped, lead on to a conception of mutual service which might stimulate the emotion of mutual gratitude ; but that conception and emotion would not be permanent unless we achieved in fact a much nearer approach than at present to equality in the distribution of wealth, and a more effective adjustment between the nature, nurture, and way of living of the individual members of our nation.

There still remains the problem which is the subject of this chapter—by what social machinery should the members of a modern industrial nation direct their large-scale co-operative activities ? That problem is complicated by the fact that sufficient equality and adjustment do not now exist, and that it will be no light task to create them without wasting much that is good in the traditions, the accumulated wealth, and even the breeding stock of the present generation. Our controlling mechanism must therefore perform the double function of directing social transformation and organizing social co-operation. For this double function the industrial nations of the world adopted during the nineteenth century two main expedients. The first was the democratic state, based on the convention of majority rule, and using the machinery of a "territorial" franchise, an elected parliament, and, in the case of America, an elected president. The second was joint-stock capitalism ; those persons who desired to carry on any economic process too large for individual action associated themselves in self-governing corporations which accumulated capital, hired service, and divided gains.

The development of the democratic state was found to involve the formation of great national parties, the specialization and professionalizing of political work, and the political and economic influence of widely circulated newspapers controlled by ambitious financiers. From this has resulted a widespread disgust with modern democratic politics. An intelligent workman during an election often feels something of the angry impotence of a bull in a Spanish bull-ring. His eyes and ears and thoughts are confused by placards and newspaper articles and speeches paid for by men whom he believes to be calculating his impulses and tempting him to exhaust himself by charging at shadows. The German Foreign Office official, who told Mr. Curtin early in the war, " Public opinion. . . . Why, we create it ! " [1] was preparing the

[1] Curtin, *The Land of Deepening Shadow* (1917), p. 83.

way for the present weakness of German parliamentarism. The skill and psychological insight with which Mr. Lloyd George's election campaign of December 1918 was managed has left in the minds of tens of thousands of British working men and women a conviction that, as many of them now complain, they were " had," and that at the next election they will be unable to prevent themselves from being " had " again.

On the other hand, the free association of capitalist adventurers in joint-stock companies was found to lead to hereditary and often idle ownership of wealth by an investing class. Working-men who were dissatisfied with the national railway system or mining system or land system could not hope by their weekly savings to buy out the existing owners : their only chance was to coerce or dispossess them. Up till the end of the nineteenth century, most thoughtful working-men had proposed to do this by using their political power ; and a large part of the present working-class disgust with democracy has come from the discovery that a class of owners and managers controlling most of the means of publicity, and monopolizing many of the higher forms of education, were able to baffle any attempt to bring about economic equality by the use of the vote.

More and more, therefore, all over the industrialized world the " class-conscious " workmen, and those " intellectuals " and " professionals " who sympathize with them are turning to some form of " Guild Socialism " or " Sovietism," or " Functional " or " Vocational " society, as a substitute both for territorial democracy and for capitalism. Opposition to this tendency is weakened by the fact that the experienced politicians, who have hitherto formed the human machinery of the existing system of majority rule, are often weary of the nervous strain, the sense of unreality, the suspicion and ill-will which that system is apt to create ; and are themselves tempted to choose between military reaction and a vocational social system. In Britain we have so far had neither a violent social revolution nor any important attempt to bring one about. But the tendency towards vocational organization has in certain essential respects gone further in Britain than in any other nation with a continuous social history. Britain is the only great nation in which the industrial and intellectual employees form a clear majority over any combination of the agricultural population and the non-employed class. Therefore in Britain, though a class-conscious Labour Party has never formed a government, the vocational tendency among manual and intellectual workers has exercised an effective pressure on the policy of both the traditional political parties.

The Trade Unions and the old and new professional organizations include each year a larger proportion of the British population. In 1890 about 20 per cent of the adult male manual workers of Great Britain were members of Trade Unions, and in 1920 more than 60 per cent.[1] In 1920 the National Union of Teachers had over 102,000 members, the Union of Post Office Workers 90,000, and the National Union of Clerks 55,000.[2] Some of these organizations are, like the Trade Unions, independent of the state, though they possess strong parliamentary influence,[3] receive many statutory rights, and, by the

[1] Webb, *History of Trade Unionism* (revised edition, 1920), p. 472.

[2] *Ibid.*, pp. 505, 506, 508.

[3] Sidney Webb, in his preface to the new edition of *Fabian Essays*, says, with reference to the increase of the power of the

threat of " direct action," constantly compel the government to negotiate with them. Sometimes they are voluntary organizations of state or municipal officials, which, like the Postmen's Union and the National Union of Teachers, are more or less "recognized" by their official employers. Sometimes a profession closely organized (like law, medicine, the army and navy, and the Church) is so related to the state that it is difficult to decide whether it should be called a profession entrusted by the state with certain functions, or a professionalized department of the state. These bodies have, from the point of view of their members, the great advantage over parliamentary democracy that the pressure which an individual member may hope to exercise over the actions of the community is continuous. When the miner thinks of his Federation, or the teacher of his Union, he does not feel, as Rousseau said of the British voter, a slave from one election to another.[1]

This continual movement of feeling and of fact towards vocational organization has been accompanied in Britain, as elsewhere, by a marked change in conscious social theory. That change has taken two main forms. In the first place, the democratic convention that " the majority shall rule " is being repudiated by those who argue that a vigorous minority must in any case rule, and that it is better for society that it should rule by openly coercing the inert majority than by secretly deceiving it. In the second place, the convention that a territorial district should be the unit on which political

Labour Party, that for a socialist party " the only practical basis " is " the wage-earning class " and " the only available machinery . . . the Trade Union organization " (p. 14).

[1] *Contrat Social*, Bk. III, chap. xv.

power is based is attacked as having been made obsolete and harmful by the development of scientific methods of manufacture and transport.

The problem of the relation of vocationalism to territorial democracy will probably, in the end, be seen to be rather one of degree in the co-ordination of several expedients than of a choice between mutually exclusive principles. The organization of persons employed in a common occupation is not only inevitable, but in many ways socially valuable. The postman, or hotel waiter, or sailor, or teacher, or dock-labourer, when he has joined his union, finds his own life at once more dignified and more happy, because, like a lawyer or a doctor or a landowner or stockbroker, he can " have his say " about the conditions under which he lives. I have been for some years an elected representative of my fellow-teachers on the governing body of my University, and I am convinced that my life and theirs is made better by the arrangement that representatives of the teaching staff shall influence university administration. I am also convinced that this benefit is not confined to the members of the particular occupation in which such a vocational element exists. I am more likely, as the world now is, to receive my letters and my coal regularly and conveniently if the Unions of the postmen and the miners play a part in postal and mining administration ; and the students of any university will receive better instruction if the organized teachers of the university help to govern it. Any one who has worked in the hitherto unorganized occupation of journalism will feel that not only the personal happiness of the journalist, but the public good would be increased if journalists belonged to a profession sufficiently organized to enable them to assert their self-respect against a bullying or corrupt proprietor. The feeling of human solidarity is so difficult to create under modern conditions that we cannot afford to leave unused for the purposes of social co-operation the unforced knowledge of each other, and the direct goodwill which may arise as an incident of common occupation. When my fellow-teachers and myself meet to elect a representative, we have a knowledge of each other and a co-operative feeling for each other, which, if we were only related as inhabitants of a town " ward," would either not be produced at all, or only be produced by weeks of distasteful and perhaps insincere electioneering. There may even be certain cases where the members of a trade or profession, freely associated in self-governing bodies, can, as in the case of the proposed Building Guild, contract with the state for the performance, with the help of state-provided capital, of industrial work. This is an economic problem which future experience will decide, though past experience is not very encouraging.

The most serious difficulty of the problem of vocational organization shows itself when the members of a vocational body claim not merely to influence the conditions of their employment, or to associate freely for wealth-production, but to decide, as against any other body or person, the demarcation of their function, the terms of entry to and expulsion from their body, and the price at which their services shall be rendered to the community. This difficulty becomes more acute when the vocational bodies as a whole make it their policy to support each other's claims ; and with this purpose attempt to weaken or abolish the ultimate controlling power of the parliamentary state. In facing this difficulty we must not assume that any completely satisfactory solution is possible. It may be that mankind will never discover how to enjoy the advantages of large-scale industrial organization without the disadvantages of social friction and political confusion. But we can at least hope that men will some day invent a better solution than the existing combination in Britain and America and France of " machine politics," professional selfishness, and trade union " ca' canny."

The Guild Socialists claim that their solution is already complete and satisfactory ; and before judging that claim the student should attempt to make for himself an objective panorama of the society of the future, similar to that which I recommended him, in the last chapter, to make of the society of the present. If he assumes that men retain their present biological type, live in their present or greater numbers, and use machinery, railways and other means of large-scale production and distribution, he may feel as he contemplates the future that the first evil to be avoided is the unwilling and joyless toil of men and women who are kept at work by the discipline of mere habit or by the fear of starvation. As large a proportion of the future population for as large a part of the day as possible should have zest in their work. Zest, again, requires variety of work, for different men in adjustment to their natural differences, and for each man from year to year. But our need for variety must be co-ordinated with our need for security, and for a sufficient supply of material wealth ; and security and wealth require that variety of training and occupation should result, not solely from the following of casual impulse, but also from organized and to some extent disciplined purpose. If he co-ordinates all these factors of the problem, he will picture to himself a population trained both to expect a good deal of hard, and at times distasteful, work, and also consciously to value change and adventure. Men and women in such a population would be encouraged to enjoy, as producers, the acquirement of new forms of skill, and, as consumers, the development of new personal needs. Painters would not always paint over and over again the same picture, nor authors write the same book, nor professors give the same courses of lectures, nor machine-tenders work always on the same pattern, or the same machine, or even on the same raw material. Old men would not be expected to live the same lives as young men, nor women as men, nor people of weak health as people of robust health.[1] Men with few desires and weak wills would not ask or receive the same opportunities of enjoyment as men of many desires who were willing to undertake intense exertions. Society would demand special efforts and offer special opportunities to those whose natural powers were specially valuable to their fellows. All would understand that short hours of work, interesting leisure, and the satisfaction of material needs, require successful wealth-production : and men and women would in general be as glad if a new way of spinning wool made it possible in fewer hours to produce cheaper and better yarn, as they would be if a new composer made opera music more delightful, or a new way of building theatres made it

[1] A very able physician once said to me, "More than half the work of the world is done by the neurasthenics," i.e. men who are easily fatigued can do, if allowed, as Darwin was, to take their own time about it, an astonishing amount of useful work. This is largely true among the middle and professional classes. On the other hand, in nearly all decently paid manual occupations, a man must either do a full day's work or none at all ; and some of the most tragic figures I have known have been intelligent and public-spirited men of the type well known in revolutionary clubs and societies who would have done quite well as part-time journalists or poets or professors, but for whom as " work-shy " labourers no self-respecting way of life was possible.

possible for a larger audience to hear an opera in comfort, or a new way of fixing nitrogen diminished the toil of agricultural ploughing and sowing. In such a society, it might be possible within each trade to get rid of the grudging attitude to increased production as such, the "ca' canny" policy which diminishes both the wealth created by work, and the happiness of the worker as he creates it

The student would then ask himself whether the creation of a "blackleg-proof" vocationalized society, and the destruction or serious weakening of territorial democracy, would be likely to help in creating and maintaining such a way of life. Vocations, of course, differ widely from each other, and the limits of power, and forms of organization which are suitable for the vocational organization of fishermen or architects or teachers may not be suitable for engine-drivers or doctors or soldiers. But we can, I think, discover certain elements in the problem which are common to all kinds of vocationalism. Mr. Lloyd George, for instance, who is a member of the ancient and closely organized profession of the Law, said in the House of Commons on June 23rd, 1915, "The professional mind is essentially a very conservative mind." This conservatism is largely due to a psychological tendency which men share with the whole animal world. All animals, and apparently some plants, form habits, and shrinking from the breach of habit is only the negative side of our positive inclination to maintain habit. This shrinking may in man be accompanied by an expectation of future pain in the process of rehabituation; but it is no more due to that expectation than the closing of an eyelid is due to an expectation of the pain which will be inflicted by an approaching finger. The shrinking may indeed exist under conditions where the change of habit when it comes is felt as a pleasant relief, or as a relief accompanied only by intermittent and rapidly diminishing feelings of discomfort. Shrinking from change of habit is especially important in vocational organization, because, like the fear instinct, it is increased in force when it is experienced by a body of human beings assembled in one place, or otherwise made aware of a common impulse. The shrinking also increases with age, and is much stronger after twenty-five years of age, when the power of rehabituation tends to diminish, than in a child. There is, indeed, hardly any departure from established custom, however necessary and rational, against which a practised agitator cannot hope to infuriate a large proportion of any body of middle-aged men and women, belonging to the same occupation, who can be made aware of their common instinctive shrinking from change. Shrinking from change in a vocation is, again, greatly strengthened by the tendency to attach æsthetic feeling, and indeed something like personal affection, to any traditional act. Gothic architecture, classical education, canon law, navigation by sails, become personalities loved for themselves and defended with passionate loyalty. I shall never forget the emotion of an old Chelsea bricklayer to whom five and thirty years ago I described the methods of rapid construction which I had seen in use on the piers of the new Battersea Bridge. " It isn't bricklaying," he shouted, " it's bloody paving." Shrinking from change is further strengthened under modern conditions by our instinctive resentment to human interference from outside with the normal course of our impulses.[1] A man who might have willingly and joyfully changed his methods if left alone will show irrational anger if an attempt is made to compel him to do so ; and yet in large-scale production he must either change with his fellows or not at all.

[1] See later, Chapter VII.

There are, of course, other psychological factors which act positively in encouraging change of habit, the consciousness of relief from monotony, the joy of invention, the calculated expectation of gain or fame, the love of one's fellow-men, the immediate pleasantness of certain changes in method which are the " natural " development of an ancient art. But these factors are likely to be enormously stronger in exceptional individuals than in the majority of those present and voting at a meeting of members of a vocation.

Vocational conservatism has become more important in our own time owing to the unexpected effect of modern applied science on the principle of " the Division of Labour." When Adam Smith began the first chapter of his *Wealth of Nations* with the statement that " The greatest improvements in the productive powers of labour . . . seem to have been the effects of the division of labour," he was thinking, as his instance of the pin-makers shows, of the manual dexterity acquired by the constant repetition of an identical process. But machinery can now perform, with a greater exactness than the most delicate manual skill, almost all " repetition work " ; and it is therefore increasingly easy for any one who has learnt one kind of machine-tending to learn another. In the efficiency of manual work to-day the two main factors of productivity are the willingness of the workman to use the power of the machine to the full, and the transferability of labour from one machine or process to another in accordance with changes in demand. Both factors need rather increased " integration of labour " (if one may coin that term) than increased division of labour. A workman who can shift from one process to another is more likely, *ceteris paribus*, to feel zest in his work (and to escape the feeling of being " fed up "), and also more likely to do that work which is most needed, than one who can only superintend one process. Observers of eastern economic development, for instance, seem to be agreed as to the advantage which the comparatively transferable Chinese workman had over the comparatively non-transferable Hindoo. The same is true of many of the simpler forms of intellectual work. A Government Department in which routine officials are from time to time shifted to new duties gains more in twenty years from their increased zest and transferability than it loses from their decreased skill in the few weeks following each change. In the more complex forms of intellectual work, the question whether more integration or more division of labour is required depends on the peculiar conditions of each occupation, or even the powers and interests of each individual. It may be better for society that the trade of " engineer " should be broken up into separate professions of electrical, mechanical, and civil engineering; while it may also be better that classical tutors should acquire other forms of skill and knowledge in addition to their " exact scholarship "; and different engineers and tutors may do their best work, one in a wider and another in a narrower field.

This last consideration leads at once to the relation between vocational organization and that idea of human variation which I described in the last chapter. Does the use of vocational organization as the main basis of social organization help us to conceive of our fellows as varied individuals fitted for varied ways of living and not as identical replicas of a uniform type? On this point Mr. G. H. D. Cole in his book *Social Theory* (1920) founds his chief argument for the superiority of vocational organization over the existing state. " It [the State]," he says, " ignores the differences between men because it is con-

cerned not with their differences, but with their identity,
and its function and interest are concerned with men's
identity and not with their differences " (p. 96). " Let
us try," he says, " to see clearly what are the effects of
this principle. It excludes from the primary functions
of the State . . . those spheres of social action which
affect different members of it in different degrees and in
various ways " (p. 96).   " Many vital industries and
services . . . affect almost everybody in very much the
same way. We must all eat and drink, be clothed, housed
and warmed, be tended in sickness and educated in childhood and youth, and our common needs in these and
other respects give rise to a common relation, that of
consumers. . . ." (pp. 97 and 98). " Coal-mining affects
the coal-miner in quite a different way from that in which
it affects the rest of the people, and so through the whole
list of trades and vocations " (p. 97). " The economic
sphere thus falls at once into two separable parts—
production and consumption, in one of which all interests
tend to be identical, while in the other, production, they
tend to be different. Consumption is thus marked out
as falling, *prima facie*, within the sphere of the State,
while production is no less clearly marked off as falling
outside it " (p. 98). In all this, Mr. Cole, it seems
to me, precisely transposes the actual tendencies of the
modern state and of modern organized vocations. The
great advantage of the present state is its insistence on
the " differences " rather than the " identity " of men.
We must all, as Mr. Cole says, " be tended in sickness and
educated in childhood and youth," but the essence of
modern educational and public-health administration is
the refusal in those respects " to ignore the differences
between men " ; and it is the same with law and police
and taxation. " Identity," on the other hand, dominates

the whole habit of Trade Union and professional thought. The policy by which the Trade Unions have improved their position, and the professions have maintained theirs, against the whole body of employers and consumers has been based on the more or less conscious conception of an identical standard of work and reward. Every one, according to the half-formulated ideas of the average trade unionist or " profession-conscious " doctor or member of the National Union of Teachers, should work the same hours with the same intensity, and for the same wage ; and all promotion to directing posts should go by seniority ; and it is just this habit of thought and feeling which makes it so easy for a working-man to think in terms of Marx's " abstract labour."

The good life, again, under modern large-scale conditions, requires not only willingness to change, and adjustment between the individual and his social function, but also the accumulation of capital, or, what is the same thing, the ability of a community to organize prolonged and, for a time, unproductive labour, in order to make future labour more productive. Would a predominantly voca-tional British nation have been able, for instance, to create the British railway system ? That railway system was built by the voluntarily invested accumulations of rich men. If there are only few rich men, but a high general average of comfort, a creation of capital on such a scale must be brought about by taxation ; but, as the experience of countries with large peasant populations shows, it is extremely difficult to raise heavy taxation from an economically equal population. The main practical source of taxation in such a population is the " rent " which comes from differential advantages in production. However high the wages of miners are, and however hard it is to tax wages, the coal produced

per miner by those mines which are better than the
" marginal " mine (which it just pays to work) will
remain as a possible source of public revenue. But it
is just this source which the present " guild-socialist "
policy of the Miners' Federation aims at absorbing into
wages. The railway servants, the Liverpool dockers,
the doctors and professors will in the same way tend to
claim for wages and salaries " whatever the traffic will
bear " ; and it will need a powerful state to maintain
or increase revenue against this tendency.

All these problems are, of course, particular cases of
the general problem whether the members of a community
in which vocational organization is predominant, or of
one in which state organization is predominant, will be
more likely to direct their large-scale action by a calculation of its effect on all those other members of the
community (including the members of future generations)
whose lives that action will influence. The history of
urban civilization in Europe offers on this point a mass
of evidence ; the interpretation of that evidence is not
easy, owing to the changes that have taken place in the
scale and methods of industrial life ; and the work of
interpretation has not yet, so far as I know, been undertaken by a competent and impartial social historian. I
gather, however, without first-hand knowledge of the
historical sources, that in the fourteenth and fifteenth
centuries European urban civilization was mainly based
on the vocational organization of the guilds. I gather
also that from the sixteenth to the eighteenth centuries
the power of the guilds declined, and that by the beginning
of the nineteenth century the guilds, with the important
exceptions of the law and the Church, had been almost
completely swept away. The guild socialists of to-day
never seem to me to allow sufficient weight to this historical

fact of the failure of mediæval guild organization; Mr. G. H. D. Cole, for instance, in his *Social Theory* (1920), says, " functional association . . . has a pedigree to the full as long and as honourable as that of the State itself, and indeed longer and more honourable " (p. 11). Mr. Cole's statement is only an instance of a tendency, which any one who has argued with guild socialists will have noticed, to see the history and existing facts of their own form of organization in a haze of romanticism, and then to compare it with a savagely realist presentation of the territorial democracy which constitutes the present " state."

There seem, it is true, in the Middle Ages to have been cases, mainly in architecture and the arts of painting, sculpture and jewellery, where uncontrolled vocational organization produced excellent results. Small groups of men, organized locally as painters' or builders' or jewellers' guilds, encouraged each other to develop their art under the impulse of the sheer delight of creation and often under the leadership of some dominant personality. Perhaps the groups of jurists who at Bologna and elsewhere developed the reconstruction of Roman law could have been described as guilds. But the guilds generally were destroyed by their tendency to form hereditary monopolies, and their inability either to make new inventions themselves, or to adapt themselves to the new conditions resulting from the inventions of outsiders, or to combine effectively for the general purposes of good government. The rise of natural science in the seventeenth century was accomplished by individuals, or by free associations of inquirers (like the Royal Society or the Academy of Science) sometimes patronized by a monarchical state and opposed by the guild organizations of the Universities and the Church. The introduction of machine-industry in the eighteenth century was accomplished by individuals or free associations of capitalists, usually working in places chosen because they were outside the range of guild jurisdiction, and was opposed, broadly speaking, both by such relics of guild organization as remained, and by the new Trade Unions.

The problem of the proper function of vocational organization was definitely raised in Britain during the war. At the risk of national defeat we were forced to consider how a particular group of manual industries—those concerned with the production of munitions, food and clothing—should be carried on so as to produce the maximum result. We were forced to practise economy in the selection and use of natural ability and in the creation and use of acquired skill. We sought for persons of both sexes possessing special ability, and tried to secure that they should be freed from all work which persons of less ability could perform, and given posts which offered full scope for their powers. We decided what proportion of specially able persons could be most economically assigned to the army and navy, and what proportion to industry. In particular, we looked for the kind of natural ability which produces inventions, and tried to secure that every inventor should be encouraged to develop his ideas, and that every successful invention should be exploited as immediately and as widely as possible. In training men and women for each industry —whether they were persons of exceptional ability or not—we aimed at producing the maximum amount of personal skill in the minimum time and with the minimum of teaching effort. We gave the name of " dilution " to the whole process of economizing natural ability by the grading of work, and of economizing skill by its rapid production and organized distribution. As a result, in spite of many blunders, we were able both to maintain a huge army in the field and to multiply by perhaps two or three our national production of certain forms of wealth. And, in spite of universal anxiety, insufficiency of food, and long hours, most of those who worked under the new conditions seem to have felt something more like zest in their work than was common in British working-class life before the war.[1] Most of the Trade Unions submitted to this process because they shared the general recognition of the national crisis ; but it was clear that the effective force which brought it about came rather from the political organization of the nation than from its vocational organization.

After the war we were faced by two needs, both urgent, though less urgent than the avoidance of defeat in war. One was the reabsorption of the mobilized men into industry, and speed and economy in teaching them the necessary skill ; and the other was the provision of houses, in presence of an admitted shortage in the supply of workmen for the building trades, and the admitted fact that such inventions as the "fountain trowel" and "spray painting" made possible an immediate and enormous economy of labour in building. In both cases the state pressed forward, and the vocational organizations hesitated or resisted. If the state had been abolished, or if its place as final arbiter had been taken, as Mr. Cole suggests,[2] by a federation of vocational bodies, no power would, I am convinced, have existed powerful enough to overcome, even to the degree which was actually achieved, that hesitation and resistance.

[1] See my *Great Society*, chap. xiii.
[2] *Social Theory* (1920), p. 136.

CHAPTER VI

PROFESSIONALISM

In the last chapter I approached the relation between vocationalism and other forms of social control by taking the problem as a whole ; in this chapter I shall approach the same problem by choosing certain particular vocations —law, medicine, the army, and teaching. I have chosen " professions " rather than Trade Unions, because the history of trade unionism among British manual workers during the nineteenth and twentieth centuries has been, not merely the development of a form of social organization, but also a struggle between the masses and the classes for the possession of the national means of production. I shall so be enabled to avoid some of the confusion arising from that struggle ; since most of the members of the professions which I have chosen are either above or near the economic average of the nation, and since the means of production are not owned in these cases by a propertied class.

I will begin with the ancient and closely organized profession of the law. In 1916, when it was still doubtful whether the national need for munitions would overcome the average Trade Unionist's shrinking from change of habit and his difficulty in preferring national to vocational interests, the *Law Times* (the organ of the solicitors) wrote (on January 8th) that " The growing sense of responsibility in trade union circles should make it possible to arrive at a satisfactory solution . . . with regard to the dilution of labour. Public opinion is sufficiently strong nowadays to ensure that the trade unionists here will be as patriotic as their confrères in France and Germany." It obviously never occurred to the Editor of the *Law Times* that the same appeal and the same threat could ever be addressed to his own profession. During the war no attempt was made to introduce " dilution " into the two privileged sections (solicitors and barristers) of the legal profession ; more women and boys were used in the subordinate work of the " lawyers' clerks " who do not belong to the " profession " ; but women were not introduced into the profession itself until Parliament, women having been enfranchised, passed after the war a statute forbidding their exclusion.[1] Neither during nor after the war has anything, as far as I know, been done to throw either branch of the profession open to able members of hitherto excluded social classes, or (except to a minor extent in the case of young men who have done military service) to shorten and economize the process of training, or to secure by any method of dilution that no member of the profession should at any moment be performing functions either below or above his powers. If such proposals had been made during the war, it would have been at least doubtful whether the " sense of responsibility " in the profession, or the pressure of " public opinion " from outside, would have secured

[1] On this point the opposition of interest and feeling between the middle-class professions and the working-class Trade Unions creates a real though hitherto insufficient force on the side of the public good. Mrs. Alderton at the 1920 meeting of the Women's Liberal Federation said, " The Labour Party was doing its utmost to open the professions to women, and the professional classes were doing their utmost to see that the trades were open to women " (*Westminster Gazette*, May 12th, 1920).

their acceptance. As things are, the legal profession in England exemplifies in the most extreme form all those defects of vocational organization which are most injurious to the community. Lawyers do, of course, much very useful work ; but a layman who asks himself what effect the professional organization of lawyers has on that work is often driven to the same conclusion as Mr. Arnold Bennett when he says, " I come of a family of lawyers and . . . I consider that their two great Trade Unions are among the most vicious opponents of social progress in Britain to-day " (*Daily News*, August 4th, 1915).

The absence of any serious attempt to introduce an improved organization of legal work does not merely result in excessive profits to lawyers. Some lawyers do make wastefully large incomes ; but the main loss to the community comes from the way in which the profession is organized from top to bottom ; the policy of " make-work " is carried far beyond the dreams of the worst unions of plumbers or bricklayers : the force which maintains the rigid division between barrister and solicitor is the fact that it causes an enormous amount of legal work to be done and paid for twice over : the whole legal profession opposes the formation of a " land-registry " which would shorten the process of transferring real property as the power-loom shortened the process of weaving cloth : the assize system and the monopoly of higher judicial work by the London Courts creates the greatest possible amount of labour for the least possible result in judicial decisions : the vacations close nearly all the courts for a third of the year. The lawyers themselves practically decide what shall or shall not be " legal " work ; and just as the mediæval Church tried to make reading and

writing a monopoly of the clerical profession, so the
English lawyers try to secure that the mechanical filling
up of forms, which could be done by a girl typist in a
business office or government department, shall be " professional " work, to be done wastefully and paid for
extravagantly. The barristers fix their own prices for
work of which they have obtained a legal monopoly.
The conditions of entrance to the profession are in effect
controlled by the existing members. In both branches
of the law every attempt is made, by the exaction of large
fees for admission, to secure that entrance to the profession
shall be confined to young " gentlemen " ; and, in the
case of the solicitors, the system of " articled " apprentice-
ship, with a fee of £450, is deliberately intended to give
an advantage to the son or nephew of a solicitor over
all the other competitors. An essential condition of all
vocational organization should be that all those whose
work is controlled by any vocational body are given a
voice in the direction of that control. The professional
organization of the law in England offends throughout
against that principle. The main body of the barristers
themselves have no effective power against the little
clique of elderly " benchers " of the Inns of Court who
rule the bar : the solicitors have no effective voice in
arrangements made by the bar and affecting their interests :
the whole organization of the solicitors is carefully contrived
to prevent the skilled " Managing Clerks," who often,
as they did in Dickens's time, carry on the whole serious
work of an office for the profit of senile or idle or incapable
solicitors, from acquiring any influence over the conditions
of their work.

Any one who is familiar with the passionate affection
of most lawyers for the existing system will recognize that,

although individual calculation of pecuniary profit plays a large part in maintaining that system, lawyers are not necessarily more consciously selfish than other men. If the study of psychology formed part of the training of a lawyer, it might be possible, for instance, for lawyers to understand their own shrinking from the changes of habit involved in legal reform, and to see that shrinking in its relation to some general theory of human conduct. As it is, the lawyer surrenders himself as completely to his hatred of the " faddists " and " bounders " who propose change, as a dog does to the sensation of fear. Law reform was, a century ago, supported by a large body of British legal opinion. That in our own time has ceased to be the case. If legal reconstruction is now to take place it must be carried out by Parliament without the help of the profession ; and Parliament will not undertake that task except as a result of a general recognition of the urgency of the whole problem of vocational organization.

One of the most important functions of any vocational body is the continuous revision and increase of the heritage of knowledge and thought which comes within its sphere. In the case of law this function is peculiarly important. Law is the framework of the social machine ; and if a sufficient number of instructed, free, and fertile thinkers could set themselves to ask in the light of our modern knowledge of history, politics, and psychology, what are the purposes of law, and by what means those purposes can be attained, an incalculable improvement in human relations might result. But a report of the Fabian Research Committee, which had access to a great deal of professional knowledge, spoke in 1917 of " the undisguised contempt in which both solicitors and barristers, notably those who have attained success in their profession and control its organiza-

tion, hold, and have always held, not only all scholarship
or academic learning of a professional kind, but also any
theoretic or philosophic or scientific treatment of law." [1]
Any one who has interested himself from outside the
profession in the possible improvement of any point in
the science of law can confirm this statement. I myself,
for instance, was working a few years ago at the problem
of human " purpose " ; and it occurred to me that I
might get help from the current literature of jurisprudence.
Lawyers, on and off the Bench, spend part of their lives
in examining instances of human conduct, and in arguing
whether acts are or are not " intentional " or " wilful " or
malicious, or whether the doer is or is not " responsible "
for them. Their text-books might, I thought, contain
a stock of carefully analysed experience as to human
motive. I therefore wrote to the ablest and most learned
professor of law whom I know, one of the very few who
have preserved freshness of mind throughout an English
legal training. He replied that I would find " the generally
accepted views as to intention and motive " in Stephen,
" but," he added, " I don't think that you will find that
the English lawyers have realized that there are any

[1] Special Supplement of *The New Statesman* on Professional
Associations (April 21st, 1917). The four supplements (September 25th, and October 2nd, 1916, on Teachers, April 21st, 1917,
on Doctors, Lawyers and Artists, April 28th, 1917, on Officials,
etc) are by far the best source of information on professional organization in England. It is a pity that they have not yet been published in book form.

Progressive American lawyers complain of similar defects in the
traditions of the American profession. Professor Roscoe Pound,
for instance, is quoted in the *New Republic* of March 11th, 1916,
as saying, " So long as the one object is to train practitioners who
can make money at the Bar, and so long as schools are judged
chiefly by their success in affording such training, we may expect
nothing better."

serious psychological difficulties ; and they don't need to, as you can generally shunt really difficult questions on to the jury." I understood my friend's statement when I looked up Stephen's *History of the Criminal Law of England*. In Chapter XVIII, Stephen divides all acts of sane human beings into " involuntary " and " voluntary." The only involuntary acts which he recognizes as performed by a normal " person of full age " are such purely automatic reactions as heart-beating, coughing, efforts to avoid falling, etc. All other acts of such a person are " voluntary " ; and a voluntary act " is a motion or group of motions accompanied or preceded by volition and directed towards some object. Every such action comprises the following elements—knowledge, motive, choice, volition, intention ; and thoughts, feelings, and motions, adapted to execute the intention. These elements occur in the order in which I have enumerated them " (Vol. II, p. 100). And again (p. 84), " Human beings love and hate each other because every man can mentally compare his neighbour's actions, thoughts, and feelings with his own." This is a rather confused way of stating Bentham's doctrine that every voluntary human act is the result of an intellectual choice of means for attaining a preconceived end. About a century ago Bentham forced that doctrine on the English lawyers of his time, who would have been happier without any doctrine at all. Our modern lawyers, finding that Benthamism as expounded and simplified by Austin and Stephen is both easy to learn, and easy to reproduce at professional examinations or in court, have been satisfied with it ever since.

But the question of criminal responsibility is only a tiny subdivision of the problem of the function of law.

We have to ask what, in view of our modern knowledge, should be the relation of law to habit, to " public spirit," to the psychology of inference and classification as part of the psychology of thought, to the variations between human beings, and to the relation between variety and uniformity in the co-operation of a large-scale society. Any inquiry, however, into any of these questions must, as things now are, be started either by some " crank " of independent means, who, like Bentham, is prepared to face the hostility of his profession, or by some university or state organization which represents interests external to that of the profession. Perhaps progress may some day result from the concentration of the public control over the profession in the hands of a Minister of Justice responsible to Parliament, and assisted by a sufficient administrative and educational staff.

The one point, and that is, of course, a very important one, in which the traditions of the British legal profession agree to some extent with the public interest is the creation and maintenance of a high standard of professional " honour." I shall deal later [1] with the problem resulting from the fact that practitioners in the learned professions have to perform services which their clients are from ignorance unable to judge in detail, and with the valuable tradition of responsibility which has been created to meet that problem. In countries where legal practitioners are less closely organized than in England the public are in many respects less protected against individual sharp practice. But the standard of legal honour, as long as it is maintained as practically a professional secret, is apt to take curious forms, and to be at least as much concerned with the protection of lawyers in

[1] Chapter VIII.

general against the public desire that they should do more
work for less money, as with the protection of the public
against the fraudulent conduct of individual lawyers.

While the organization of the English legal profession
has remained in essentials unchanged since the seventeenth
century, the present organization of our medical profession
was created during the nineteenth century ; and owing
to the Health Insurance Act (1911), the growth of a state
and municipal medical service, and the passing of the
Ministry of Health Act (1919), it will certainly be further
changed in the near future. But these changes will only
conform to the public interest if the few medical reformers
are supported by an organized and instructed lay opinion ;
just as the obviously desirable admission of women to
the medical profession was only carried by Parliament
and the non-professional university bodies against the
violent and in many cases unscrupulous opposition of the
great majority of the profession.[1]

In some respects the professional spirit of the doctors
in England is much better than that of the lawyers. A
body of doctors do not talk of the progress of their science
with the same rampant philistinism which is heard in a
body of lawyers. The training and work of a doctor
makes an appeal to the instincts both of scientific curiosity
and of human compassion which is not made by that
memorizing of English case-law, or that advocacy of
whatever side has hired you, which form so large a part
of the work of an English lawyer. So, though the science
of law has stood still in England since Bentham, the
science of medicine is transformed every decade. But the
instinctive shrinking of every profession from the effort of

[1] See e.g. the history of the struggle in *The Life of Sophia Jex-Blake*, by M. G. Todd (1918).

rehabituation, combined with a narrow calculation of individual advantage, prevents the community from receiving the full benefit of that transformation. The use of an enormous and increasing body of applied science requires a complex and constantly changing relation between various forms of specialized skill, and between the man of unusual and the man of average mental ability. But the professional ideal of the " general practitioner " is based on the principle which Mr. Cole calls " identity." He aims at securing that every practitioner shall enjoy a local monopoly, made effective by an organized boycott of all pushing intruders : that within the area of his monopoly he shall carry out any treatment which he deems proper, without the necessity of keeping his knowledge up to date, or the possibility of expert criticism or discipline : and that when he retires he shall be able to sell his " practice " to the highest bidder.[1] He knows, uneasily, that he is

[1] This ideal can be attained with some success under the system set up by the Insurance Act of 1911. See an article by the Medical Correspondent of the *Times* (December 29th, 1916) on the position of " the young war-doctor without money." " Nor need he hope that in time one of the older men in the district will retire and so release patients to come to him. This will never happen, because on retiring the older man will sell his panel practice to any doctor who likes to pay for it. . . . The sick workman in actual fact, if not in theory, has to be treated by the doctor into whose hands he was sold by the outgoing panel practitioner. Doctors with ready money, not necessarily doctors with brains, or of special qualifications or experience, are now able to secure and keep in their own hands the care of the health of thousands of their fellow-citizens." As to the possible actual working of the boycott see the judgment of Mr. Justice McCardie in the action brought by four doctors connected with a Coventry dispensary against members of the Coventry branch of the British Medical Association (October 15th, 1918). As to the effect of the present system on the knowledge of the doctors, see an article by the Medical Correspondent of the *Times* (June 16th, 1916) on the annual report of the Medical Officer of Health for the Isle of Wight. " The report then goes on to show how impossible it is for doctors to keep up

fighting a losing battle, and that he cannot do justice to his patients without the help of the microscope of the pathologist, the experience of the nurse, and the special ability and training of the consultant. He gives that help to his richer patients, and tries to prevent himself from thinking too much about what his poorer patients get for their shilling fees or the stamps on their insurance cards.

Another form of the same distrust of specialist knowledge is shown in the professional opposition to the direction of medical teaching by men who are primarily scientists and teachers rather than practitioners. The medical schools of England have grown out of voluntary private-adventure combinations of doctors who opened classes at the hospitals. They were paid, partly by tuition fees, and partly by the established custom that the young practitioner should send his more difficult cases, if the patient could afford to pay, to his former teacher as consultant. It is only slowly that the professional scientist has gained any chance of appointment to hospital teaching posts. Meanwhile in the " public health " services of the larger cities, in the research departments of certain hospitals, here and there in the medical faculty of a university, or in the offices of the Ministry of Health,

their knowledge by attending hospital, except in a few cases, and how the public suffer thereby." On the whole subject of medical professional organization see the special supplement of the *New Statesman* (April 21st, 1917), based on ample inside professional information, e.g. (p. 13), " The British Medical Association . . . has always . . . vehemently objected to any ' dilution ' of the practitioner's labour by the wider use of midwives, nurses, and health visitors. It has objected that any salaried hierarchy of professionals is inconsistent with the personal dignity and individual freedom of the practitioners ; that the creation of any specialism whatever inevitably diminishes by so much the sphere of the general practitioner."

the whole question of the organization of the profession in its relation to the general good is being thought of from a larger than the professional point of view. A small minority of progressive-minded doctors, for instance, believe that the medical profession should now be divided into two bodies with different training and functions. While many other occupations need "integration of labour," the medical profession at this moment needs, they argue, "division of labour." Economy and efficiency would result from a combination of barristers and solicitors into one profession, and economy and efficiency in the same way resulted when in 1858 the obsolete separation between the rival professions of physician, surgeon, and apothecary was broken down by Parliament ; but the growth of science has now, it is contended, made it impossible for a man even of rather unusual ability to acquire and remember the knowledge necessary both for the prevention and for the detection and cure of disease. The profession of preventive medicine, with its subordinate or co-ordinate professions of analyst, inspector, sanitary engineer, etc., should, therefore, be separated from the profession of curative medicine, with its subordinate occupations of nurse, midwife, masseur, dispenser, hospital attendant, etc. ; though a free interchange from one branch to another of persons willing to qualify themselves should be encouraged ; and though certain co-ordinate professions such as that of bacteriologist should serve both branches alike. If, however, such a division of labour is to be made it can only be brought about by lay pressure and parliamentary action.

The present position, again, of medicine in Britain shows, like that of the law, how necessary it is that as soon as a vocation acquires social power, whether by statute or in fact, the state (or some other organization larger than a single vocational body and less biassed than a federation of such bodies) should control the internal vocational organization, and, in particular, the franchise and regulations under which elections and referenda within the vocation take place. When a ballot is being taken by the coal-miners on a strike which will check every kind of national industry, the whole community is concerned in the question whether boys are allowed to vote, or whether adequate precautions are carried out to secure correctness in the collecting and counting of votes. Some, though by no means all of the worst faults of legal professionalism, would be diminished by the substitution of an internal democracy of barristers for the oligarchy of the Benchers, and by giving the solicitors a real voice in the election of the persons who control the conditions of their work. In the same way nurses and chemists and dental assistants should be able to influence in some degree any body which in fact controls the whole of their work. The relation, again, of a purely voluntary professional body, like the British Medical Association or the Amalgamated Society of Engineers, to its local branches, concerns the whole community as long as the branches can set in action the machinery of a professional boycott, or a strike backed by the funds of the whole body.

The interest of a modern democratic state in the professional organization of the army is even greater than its interest in the professional organization of law and medicine. Control of law and medicine concerns the efficient and economical performance of certain necessary social functions; the control of the army concerns the existence of democracy itself. Modern applied science has made a civilian population, however numerous and united, absolutely helpless in actual fighting against even a small body of trained and equipped soldiers. Therefore, as soon as a Parliament without military support finds itself opposed to a united army, the whole convention of majority rule disappears like a dream. And the will of a modern army is rather that of the long-service officer than that of the short-service soldier. As Professor Delbrück wrote in 1913, " The decisive question for the inner character of any state is, to whom does the army belong," [1] and again, " An army which has once been disciplined remains in the hands of the officer-corps, whether the Parliament passes mutiny acts or not." [2] The revolutions of 1848 were carried out by civilians, hastily armed with weapons from gun-shops and chimney-pieces, firing bullets cast at home by boys and girls. Revolution in the twentieth century can only be carried out by mutinous troops, who have retained their artillery and ammunition and some of their officers, against an executive government that has lost all or nearly all its military support. The only civilian weapon which is even partially effective is the dislocation of all production and distribution by a general strike ; and that weapon injures the rest of the population as much or more than it injures the soldiers.

Though scientific progress has made more urgent the problem of the relation between the fact of military force and the convention of majority rule, that problem is, of course, as old as civilization. In Britain, for more than a century after the military rule of Cromwell's major-generals, the royalist pronunciamento of 1660, and the Whig pronunciamento of 1688, every English politician was acutely conscious of the political power of a professional

[1] *Regierung und Volkswille* (1913), p. 133.   [2] *Ibid.*, p. 134.

army. Blackstone, the great Tory jurist, wrote in 1765 of soldiers under a Mutiny Act as " reduced to a state of servitude in the midst of a nation of freemen " and warned his fellow-countrymen " not to intrust slaves with arms." [1] But throughout the nineteenth century (in spite of conflicts behind the scenes between the Cabinet and Queen Victoria over the position of the royal Commander-in-Chief) almost every British voter assumed as a matter of course that the army would obey the Ministers, that the Ministers would obey any parliamentary majority ; and that no considerable parliamentary minority would support the political action of the army. The danger, however, was always there, and was accentuated by the fact that nineteen officers out of twenty were intensely class-conscious members of one social class, and adherents of one political party. In the spring of 1914 the British nation was suddenly reminded of that fact. The convention of majority rule has never existed in Ireland, and in the winter of 1913–14 the Ulster minority had openly armed themselves for resistance to Home Rule, and were supported by the almost unanimous sympathy and encouragement of English " Society " and the Conservative Party. Mr. Bonar Law the leader, of the Conservative Party, said at Dublin (November 28th, 1913), " I ask him [Mr. Asquith] to turn his mind to the history of the great Revolution. Then the country rose against a tyranny. It was the tyranny of a King, but other people besides Kings can exercise tyranny and other people besides Kings can be treated in the same way. . . . There was a revolution and the King disappeared. Why ? Because his own army refused to fight for him." On September 20th, 1913, at Antrim, Sir Edward Carson declared that he and his

[1] *Commentaries*, Vol. I (1765), p. 416.

associates had " pledges and promises from some of the greatest generals in the army, that when the time comes, and if it is necessary, they will come over to help us to keep the old flag flying, and to defy those who would dare invade our liberties." Mr. F. E. Smith (since Lord Chancellor) was a "galloper" in Sir Edward Carson's force, and on February 11th, 1914, said in his speech at the Hotel Cecil that " He welcomed the Ulster movement because it enabled them to challenge the Parliament Act," which had rendered it possible to pass legislation over the veto of the House of Lords. On March 21st, 1914, the officers at the Curragh camp let it be known that they were unwilling to march into Ulster. On March 23rd, Mr. Bonar Law declared that "any officer who refuses is only doing his duty." On March 25th, the *Morning Post* announced that " The army has killed the Home Rule Bill." The other Conservative papers followed suit, and openly rejoiced in the fact that the army officers and their friends seemed to have put Mr. Asquith into a position in which he could neither enforce discipline without civil war, nor yield without political annihilation. On March 24th, Lord Northcliffe's *Daily Mail* placarded all London with a contents-bill saying, " Bullies are Cowards," and in the afternoon of that day Mr. Astor's *Pall Mall Gazette* printed " Their Death Blow " on its contents-bill. The Secretary for War negotiated with the army ; and after his agreement had been repudiated by the Cabinet he, and Lord French and the other military members of the Army Council, resigned. In the end, the government were undoubtedly influenced in their Irish policy by the necessity of considering the opinion of the army. The army did, in fact, kill the Home Rule Bill.

As I write, the problem of military force and constitutional government dominates all others throughout the continent of Europe. From Siberia to the eastern frontiers of Germany, and in Austria and Hungary, troops are wandering about fighting and destroying, and often not knowing whether they represent a constitutional government or a rebellion. In France, Italy and Spain, every statesman in forming his plans has to think about the feeling of the army ; and no one in any of those countries knows what would happen if a general election returned an anti-militarist majority, or if the private soldiers refused to obey their officers when ordered to put down a national strike. An army, if it is to be efficient, must consist of men who can be relied on to kill and be killed ; and killing and being killed is so tremendous a fact that to those who are trained for it all other human relationships seem poor and superficial. In particular, the professional soldier, with his experience of a definite hierarchy of personal command, loathes the whole electioneering process of modern democracy. A letter in the *Morning Post* of July 17th, 1917 (signed General Officer B.E.F.) was typical of this feeling. It says, " We care not one jot or tittle about politics or politicians. We abhor the former and mistrust the latter. We receive our orders from our superiors : the pledged word (so often broken when convenient) of Ministers does not concern us in the very slightest." The war has left in Britain an army much larger than that of 1913. Among the professional officers in our army attempts will certainly be made in some regiments to get rid of the " temporary gentlemen " of the war and to restore the regimental messes to their old caste type.[1]   We have also an enormous

---

[1] The Duke of Wellington said that in the Peninsula he gave commissions to volunteers and non-commissioned officers, but

body of officers and men trained to war, either in the reserve or discharged, but still more or less organized in such bodies as "The Comrades of the Great War," and here as in America, contempt for majority politics will exist among them and will often be encouraged. In the army, as in law and medicine, professional habits of thought not only create opposition to political rule but injure military efficiency itself. Promotion by seniority, routine thought, and routine administration, may come to be loved as the "real soldiering," to which one can return after the strain of invention and rehabituation and the irritating contact with the civilian mind which were forced on the professional officers by the necessities of the war of 1914–18.

One can suggest expedients for lessening the dangers of this position, though one cannot convince oneself that those expedients will secure a very high degree of safety. Democracy, for instance, in a nation with a great army will not be safe unless there is a far nearer approximation to social equality than now exists in Britain, and unless the identification of the officer-corps with a small social class is somehow prevented. It may be possible also to alter the relation between officer and private, and perhaps to lessen the professionalism and increase the intellectual elasticity and thereby the military value of the officers, by seconding them, as engineer officers are seconded in the United States, during part of their career, to civilian employment. I myself believe that a great increase of military efficiency and of the

that few of them remained in the army. "They are not persons that can be borne in the society of the officers of the Army." *Report of Commission on Military Punishment*, p. 329, quoted by M. Elie Halévy in his admirable *Histoire du Peuple Anglais*, Vol. I, p. 73.

fighting man's zest in his life-long preparation for an occasional crisis, would result from a much wider " integration of labour " in military organization. If some of the abler young military officers received part of their training on the sea and in the air as well as on land, and some naval and air officers received part of their training on land, it might be possible greatly to increase the value of the various sections of a mixed British Expeditionary Force by putting it under a staff trained to think in terms of all three elements. Such an arrangement would help us to avoid some of the conflicts of tradition and discipline which, as long as war remains as a recognized factor in world-organization, add so enormously to the difficulty of those combined land and sea operations which must always be characteristic of British warfare.

In any case, if the world is to be safe for democracy, the relation between the state and the army must be widely and clearly understood and its dangers frankly realized. And the state must be strong ; Mr. S. G. Hobson in his *National Guilds* (1914), after disparaging the state in every mood and tense, admits his belief that " The State with its Government, its Parliament and its civil and military machinery must remain independent of the guild congress. Certainly independent, probably even supreme " (p. 263). The history of the last three thousand years of civilization goes to show that, unless the ultimate supremacy of the constitutional body which controls the army is a good deal more than " probable," the army will not be effectively controlled.

But it may be that the permanent interests of mankind are more deeply concerned with the professional organization of teachers than even with the professional organization of soldiers. Modern large-scale civilization cannot

continue to exist unless every member of each generation
acquires a definite minimum of reading, writing, arithmetic,
language, history and science, combined with a minimum
of training in the conscious effort of thought and in habits
of social co-operation ; and unless a considerable percentage
of those boys and girls who are fitted to receive it are
given a course of higher education. Only in exceptional
cases can any large proportion of this formal instruction
be given by parents at home. If, therefore, a nation
of fifty millions is to be adequately instructed, about
eight million scholars should at any moment be attending
school or college, under, say, three hundred thousand
teachers. No community, however rich, can carry out
this tremendous task without the utmost economy of
effort. Every school or college building must be occupied
to the limits of its accommodation. Because general
education is a necessity for large-scale co-operation, and
because economy of teaching power requires regularity
of attendance, attendance must be compulsory. Every
teacher must find daily before him the largest class
that he can effectively teach ; and the training colleges
and university departments in which teachers receive
their professional training must be filled and used with
the same economy as the schools.

Among a body of teachers so trained and employed
vocational organization is certain to appear ; although
it may be delayed by the counter-influence of religious
division, or by the class-struggle between the " gentleman "
and the " elementary teacher." In England,[1] where
these causes of delay have been stronger than in some

[1] I speak in this section of " England " (including Wales), rather
than of " The United Kingdom " or " Britain," because the educational organization of Ireland, and, to a less degree, of Scotland
is very different from that of England.

other countries, vocational organization of teachers appeared late, but has during the last few decades advanced rapidly in numbers, political power and statutory recognition.[1] The demand of the organized teachers for a still larger control of national education has meanwhile grown in force. As early as 1861 the College of Preceptors urged that a Scholastic Council should be formed analogous to the General Medical Council (which had been created three years before) with the power to draw up and control a register of qualified teachers. But at that time the "College" consisted only of a few enthusiasts who were thinking of reform in middle class private-adventure schools.[2] When in 1919 the Annual Conference of the National Union of Teachers passed a resolution demanding "direct control of education by the teaching profession, in partnership with the representatives of the public," [3] the Union was already one of the most powerful political

[1] The tentative Teachers' Registration Council of 1902 was succeeded in 1907 by an Act providing for the Registration Council (representative of the Teaching Profession) which came into existence in 1912, and whose present small powers will probably soon be added to. The Education Act of 1902 provided for the co-optation of teachers on the local education committees ; and Mr. Fisher's Education Act of 1918 provided for the representation of teachers, and of universities, on the larger provincial bodies which it aimed at creating. In 1920 the state and many of the larger local education authorities negotiated with the teachers on salaries through Whitley Councils, half of which consisted of representatives of teachers.

[2] See the admirable "special supplements" of the *New Statesman* (September 25th and October 2nd, 1915) on English Teachers and their Professional Organization, chap. iii, p. 15.

[3] *New Statesman* (April 3rd, 1920). In 1920 a motion in similar words was put on the conference agenda by the N.U.T. executive, but was withdrawn, apparently for tactical reasons, after a motion in favour of Whitley Councils (composed of representatives of teachers and their employers) had been carried (see the debate, reported in *The Schoolmaster* of April 10th, 1920).

forces of the country, and its demand was likely to be supported by the sympathy of the great Trade Unions. Mr. S. G. Hobson in his *National Guilds* (1914) voices the "left wing" policy both of the Trade Unionists and of the organized teachers, when he argues that general education (as opposed to the technical education to be controlled by the Trade Guilds) "might be best assured by the State charging the National Union of Teachers with the powers necessary and the consequent responsibility to society for carrying it out" (p. 268).

Any one who has been, as I have been, a professional teacher in England for forty years, or who has studied the position of English teachers for the last century, must recognize the enormous benefits which the teachers and the community have gained from the recent growth of professional organization. The private-school "usher," clinging to the rags of his gentility with the wages and independence of a footman, has a chance of becoming a man when he joins the Association of Assistant Masters; the sweated schoolmistresses have successfully claimed the wages of a skilled occupation; some "public school" masters have been drawn out of their atmosphere of elderly boyhood; the whole profession has gained in intellectual independence, as against clerical "managers," capitalist governors, and the politicians on the local education authority. But the vocational organization of teachers brings with it the same dangers as the organization of other vocations. The majority of an organized body is apt to be hostile to any change which involves the effort of rehabituation. Teachers, like bricklayers, cling with passionate loyalty to their existing methods of work; they personify the subjects or groups of subjects which they teach and the institutions in which they teach, and stimulate with regard to them their primitive instincts of corporate defence.[1]

Every new scientific discovery, every new movement of human thought, every change in the relation between states or races or classes, brings with it the need of a new distribution of the time and effort of teaching and learning. If mankind are to maintain and improve their social heritage, the community must always be on the watch to discover gaps in its educational system.[2] The provision of teaching in new subjects must be accompanied by a constant process of re-division and reintegration of labour. Modern philosophy, for instance, will remain sterile unless it is brought into relation with modern history, logic unless it becomes conscious of mathematics, biology unless it learns from psychology to watch behaviour as well as structure—just as chemistry remained unprogressive in the second half of the nineteenth century until it came into contact with physics. The

[1] The President of St. John's College, Oxford, speaking to the Congregation of Oxford teachers during the debate on compulsory Greek in 1910, appealed successfully to the sympathy of his fellow-professionals on the ground that " Science, like the cuckoo, was trying to oust from the common nest subjects which had a longer prescriptive right to it than herself " (*Oxford Magazine*, December 1st, 1910).

[2] It is argued that the supply of teaching of any subject must depend on the supply of thoroughly trained teachers ; and that it is better to teach a less urgently needed subject quite thoroughly than a more urgently needed subject less thoroughly. But, even from the point of view of efficient instruction, the sense that a particular piece of thought or knowledge is urgently needed is an invaluable stimulus both to teacher and taught. Thoroughness exists for man, not man for thoroughness ; and, if no other teaching of American history is available, an able young lecturer in England may do better work by guiding his class with frank humility through a good American text-book than by communicating the latest results of his own researches into thrice-conned fourteenth-century documents in the British Record Office.

philistinism of English legal training will not be diminished until law comes into contact with history and psychology.

But in those English universities where no educational change can take place except on the initiation of the majority of a body of professional teachers, the introduction of new subjects or the regrouping of old subjects is steadily opposed and only with difficulty achieved. No undergraduate, for instance, at Oxford may, as I write, offer as part of a single Honours degree course either philosophy or psychology without a serious amount of Greek and Latin philology: he may not offer philosophy or psychology either with modern history or without ancient history : he may not combine in one course mathematics and logic, or modern history and a modern language, or history and geography, or biology and psychology. It is only because a Royal Commission on the older universities is actually sitting that there is any chance of defeating this kind of professional conservatism. In the newer universities less harm, but very real harm, is done by the maintenance of a meaningless distinction between " Arts " and " Science " ; I remember that a very able member of the London University Senate argued in my hearing against a proposal to allow a man who had taken medical and law degrees to proceed to a doctorate in letters with a treatise on the philosophy of punishment ; he told us that such a proceeding would break down the " natural " divisions between subjects. It is not necessary to introduce the extreme liberty of combination existing in some American universities ; but a rational and coherent analysis and reconstruction of university courses would, I believe, add 10 per cent. to the efficiency of university instruction in London, and perhaps 30 per cent. in Oxford and Cambridge. No expense or disadvantage of any kind would result, except a momentarily uncomfortable change of habit on the part of a few teachers and perhaps a diminution of a few vested pecuniary interests, compensated for by the aggrandisement of a few others.

Educational professionalism strengthens, and is strengthened by, educational "institutionalism," the school or college "patriotism" which conceives of an institution as having, like a "subject," rights against the individual student or the nation as a whole. This institutionalism is in England and America intensified by the deliberate stimulation of competitive passion in games. It has happened to me on several occasions to suggest that a clever "public school" boy who has won a university scholarship in the December term should leave school and work under new conditions before he goes to Oxford or Cambridge in the following October. His parents, when they passed on my suggestion, were in each case reproached by the Headmaster for disloyalty to the school as an institution.

Now that railways have been invented, there is nothing to prevent a successful university teacher or a willing student from teaching or learning during a single year or week in more than one English university town. The fact that an English university had specialized with success in the study of Chinese literature or higher optics would then be a reason why other universities should send students to it rather than themselves start rival and less efficient courses. There might even be a conscious and deliberate allocation of subjects for student research. Among those English universities where post-graduate work is encouraged there may now at any one time be four or five students preparing theses on some one subject of research while fifty kindred and equally important subjects remain untouched. If once our university system could take the great step which is represented in biological evolution by the transition from the single-celled protozoon to the many-celled metazoon, it would be possible to establish a general " clearing-house " of subjects and suggested subjects of research. But all such changes would be opposed by the traditions of English educational institutionalism.

Teachers, again, like the members of other professions, tend to think of their work as an isolated process co-extensive with their profession. But the function of teaching cannot be confined to professional teachers ; civilization, although it is dependent on the economically organized work of the " qualified " teacher, is also dependent on the fact that the whole race are, and must be, " unqualified " teachers. We could not continue to exist in our present numbers, unless mothers taught their babies from the moment of birth, unless brothers and sisters, and husbands and wives, and neighbours and friends, taught each other. Every employer and fore-man, every housekeeping woman, every writer, thinker, artist, preacher, politician, doctor, and policeman spends much of his time in teaching. In newspaper offices, theatres, cinemas, debating societies, government depart-ments, churches and chapels, libraries, ships, barracks, and factories much more effective intellectual stimulus and instruction may at any moment be going on than in the brick and stone buildings which are called schools and colleges.

The decisive point in the education of boys and girls may come when they are neglecting the school lessons to argue with a friend, or read a book, or when an elder who never dreamed of himself as a teacher drops in

10

their mind a shattering criticism of some accepted
convention.

In the debate at the 1920 Conference of the National
Union of Teachers on " Professional Self-Government,"
Mr. Hill, who seconded, said, " They were under external
control from the beginning to the end ; they were a
subject profession. . . . The right of the doctors to
practise depended upon their own professional compatriots ;
they did not depend upon an external authority " ; and
Mr. Cove (of the Executive) who moved, said, " Did
they want the power to give advice ? No, they wanted
the power to construct. . . . They wanted the right to
appoint their leaders, their inspectors, and their directors.
. . . The doctors and the lawyers had self-government,
and what they had got the school teachers surely ought
to get." [1] But the teaching profession, if it is to carry
out efficiently its work of handing down its share of our
social heritage, must always like other professions be
a " subject profession," if it is to do its work efficiently.
The knowledge, for instance, which the teacher hands down
is in the main created by non-teachers. When, twenty
years ago, I was chairman of the School Management
Committee of the London School Board, and was talking,
perhaps rather complacently, of my duties, a careful
young writer of English prose said to me, " You people
are spreading the butter which we make." The teacher
spreads the butter which the scientist, the explorer,
the poet, and the historian make, even if he finds time
to make a little butter himself. The daily class-room
lessons, again, of the teacher cannot take place without
the active co-operation of many who are not teachers,
scholars and their parents, tax-payers and tax-collectors :

[1] *The Schoolmaster* (April 10th, 1920).

and that co-operation will not be efficient unless those who are concerned are given a voice in the common work.

All these problems are very similar to those found in other professions. But there are certain respects in which the psychology of the teaching profession is peculiar. Mankind, like some birds, and some non-human mammalian species in which social inheritance is important,[1] have a specific teaching instinct. That instinct can be observed in many " born " male teachers, and in a rather larger proportion of women teachers, and particularly of women who, at the age of early motherhood, are teaching very young children. But the teaching instinct was evolved under conditions where men and women taught during only part of their lives. The professional teacher now teaches every day ; he forms, indeed, the habit of teaching ; but habit, when it overrides nature, produces severe nervous reaction. All regular work, as I have already said,[2] is unnatural to us, but regular teaching produces a kind of disgust which is more profound than that produced by any other kind of work. Habituation is more easy for the teacher, and his ultimate disgust is more profound, because he is dealing with a quickly changing series of immature minds. After every year, or at most every three years, he begins with a new class, and tends to repeat his most successful sayings, and to emphasize, without the sense of humour and proportion which comes from adult criticism, his pet ideas. When the medieval Italian laity turned the word " pedagogue " into " pedant," the word and its meaning was understood and adopted from one end of Europe to the other. The teacher, again, largely depends for the maintenance of discipline on the relationship of his own " leadership "

[1] See Chapter I, p. 20.   [2] See Chapter II, p. 29.

instinct to the " following " instinct of his pupils. But
the leadership and following instincts are also intermittent,
and the teacher who tries to use them continuously is
apt to harden into a bully. In spite, therefore, of the
technical advantages of long experience, most men and
women are better teachers from twenty to forty than
they are from forty to sixty.[1]

It is this special factor in the problem which makes
the organization of the teaching profession the most interesting as well as the most important field for that effort
of invention which is necessary if we are to co-ordinate
our need for national co-operation with our need for
zest in our individual lives. Teaching and learning are
necessary for the continuance of human existence ; but
because a certain quantity of teaching and learning are
delightful to most human beings, and because a much
larger quantity leads to the teacher becoming bored and

---

[1] In a modern educational system the psychological effects of
continuous teaching are in part disguised by the fact that a large
percentage of the more ambitious and articulate teachers become
Head Masters or Mistresses at about the age of forty, and are
transferred from work which is mainly teaching to work which is
mainly organizing. The nervous deterioration of many life-long
assistant teachers is apt to be explained as due to their disappointment at failing to gain headships. For the pathological psychology
of the assistant master see the novel *Mr. Perrin and Mr. Traill*
(Hugh Walpole). American readers will notice that I speak of
the teacher as " he." Elementary teaching in England is still
to a considerable extent a male profession ; secondary, higher
and technical teachers are with us preponderatingly male, and my
own personal experience has been mainly with male teachers. I
have had no opportunities of watching the psychology of a body
of teachers preponderatingly, as in America, female, unmarried,
organized professionally and politically enfranchised. I gather
that their nervous reaction against their work is not quite so profound as that found among a body of middle-aged male assistant
teachers, and that it does not occur quite so early in life, but that
in other respects the dangers I have referred to above do show
themselves among them.

soured and the scholar being " fed up," we must be always on the look-out to diminish the amount of teaching which is required for a given amount of education. Large-scale government has, since the days when slave-scribes piled up their stacks of clay tablets at Babylon or Cnossus, depended on the production and preservation of copies of administrative documents. The dreary process of copying dominated the atmosphere of the British Exchequer in the fourteenth century, and destroyed the morals and happiness of hundreds of " Vacher's clerks " in the White-hall departments of the mid-nineteenth century.[1] The invention of the copying press and the typewriting machine has already diminished this labour to a fraction of what it was, and a little ingenuity in the use of photography would diminish it so much more, that a share of it may be a not unpleasant incident in an official life. In the same way we may be able by the use of study-libraries, laboratories, school journeys, and a hundred other expedients, to reduce our present burden both of daily teaching and of daily learning. The burden that remains should be so distributed as to cause the minimum of weariness, and the maximum of zest in teaching. Some people can enjoy teaching all their lives, but it should be no more necessary that any one should be a life-long teacher for all the hours of every working-day than that he should be a life-long copyist, or a life-long soldier. We should contrive means to allow the teacher to alternate

---

[1] See the experiences of Hoccleve (contemporary of Chaucer) in T. F. Tout, *The English Civil Service in the Fourteenth Century* (1916), pp. 30, 31. " After twenty-three years of such work Hoccleve's whole body was smarting with aches and pains and his eyesight was utterly ruined." For the type to which " Vacher's clerks " belonged, see Dickens's account of the man whose death starts the tragedy of *Bleak House*.

teaching with research, or with literary production, or with any form of work which will give his instincts of teaching and discipline a rest. It is fortunate that the process of being taught, itself gives nervous relief when exchanged for that of teaching. One realizes one of the causes which lent zest to medieval university life, when one reads Chaucer's description of the Clerk of Oxenford, " and gladly would he lerne and gladly teche."

Educational authorities, at present, with the support of the teachers' organizations, generally dismiss girl-teachers on marriage. They ought to welcome the opportunity of " seconding " them for motherhood, and receiving them back, not only with wider experience but with renewed zest for their work. All classes of teachers, again, are now being brought under state super-annuation schemes, and that fact, useful as it is in lessening the insecurity of the teacher's life, is already making it more difficult for a teacher who desires to leave his pro-fession to do so without serious loss, or for an outsider, who feels a genuine desire to teach, to become a teacher. There is obviously no reason why men or women, earning pension rights from the state in different capacities should not exchange functions without loss, if the state thinks that such an exchange will be useful. When pension rights are given both to Treasury Clerks and to Professors of Economics, the Professor of Economics who becomes a Treasury Clerk, and the Treasury Clerk who becomes a Professor of Economics, should equally carry their pension rights with them. And if quite ordinary secondary or elementary masters or mistresses find themselves " fed up with teaching " at thirty-five, it may be the best policy for the community to allow them to carry their pension rights through a spell of pensionable work,

as clerks, or as minor superintending officials, and perhaps
to return to teaching if they recover their zest for that.
An administrator or scientist who is teaching " part-
time " should be proportionately pensionable both for
that time and for any pensionable work done during the
remainder of the day or week or year. But professional
opinion among teachers will steadily oppose this policy.

In the analogous profession of journalism, the future
of the intellectual organization of democracy depends
in large part on a free interchange between the life of
journalism and the life of action or research or creative
literature. But the professional policy of the National
Union of Journalists is steadily opposed to a free interchange between journalism and any other form of intellectual work. In January 1920 a series of letters
appeared in the *Westminister Gazette* from members
of the National Union of Journalists, protesting against
Labour M.P.'s being allowed to earn salaries as journalists.
The writers said : " The National Union of Journalists
has adopted as a plank in its platform the principle of
journalism for journalists . . . doctors and lawyers have
statutory protection, but the body politic of journalism
is open to attack by any dabbler or amateur who thinks
he can write. . . . It is a matter between trade unionist
and trade unionist. . . . Nearly all the Labour M.P.'s
are writing newspaper articles now. When we have a
Labour Government are they going to continue ? As to
any man ' doing two jobs ' to which you say you have
no objection, may I recall, from memory, Mr. Smillie's
definition of a blackleg . . . it was a man who took on
another man's job."[1]

[1] Letters in *Westminster Gazette* (January 14th and January 17th,
1920). It is interesting to note the way in which the fact that the

Any attempt to adapt the organization of the teachers to the special characteristics of the teaching instinct will, of course, involve an examination of the system of training teachers. All organized vocations have for many centuries used training, not only as a means of creating skill, but also as a means of restricting access to their vocation ; and professional policy among teachers will always insist upon the longer, the severer, and the more technical, of any alternative training schemes. But it is clearly to the interest of the community that the art of teaching, and the psychological and other knowledge necessary for that art, should be obtained as rapidly as possible by those who desire to teach, and that training should always be open to men and women of any age who are otherwise fitted for the work.[1] It will be objected that to make the teaching profession one that is easily entered and easily left involves the destruction of any possibility of that professional organization whose advantages I have already urged ; but I myself believe that there is nothing in this objection which cannot be overcome by an effort of invention. If ever it were felt to be desirable that soldiers on service should freely elect committees to represent their opinions and interests, there is no reason why all who were in fact serving at any moment, whether life-long professionals or temporary volunteers or conscripts should not vote for those committees.

nation tolerates the existing indefensible privileges of the legal profession leads so many other professions to claim the same privileges.

[1] The great Teachers' College in connection with Columbia University, New York, is an admirable instance of the way in which the stimulus of contact with new pedagogic knowledge and methods can be given to teachers of all ages. Such an institution might also be open to those non-teachers who, having the necessary knowledge of some subject, desire rapidly to acquire skill in imparting it.

But the peculiarities of the work of teaching, and the fact that in modern industrial communities almost all teaching is paid for from taxes or endowments, make it desirable that the part played in the control of their work by the teaching profession should be somewhat different from that played by other professional organizations. From the point of view of the community, the first object to be secured by the organization of teachers is that every teacher should have sufficient scope for his positive teaching instinct. The teacher's work will turn into mechanical routine, and lose its power of stimulating his scholars, unless the teacher retains self-respect and a due degree of intellectual liberty. This is best secured by the influence on national, local, and institutional educational administration of freely elected representatives of the teachers concerned ; and such a representation would also be a fertile source of educational invention and initiative. But neither the individual teacher nor any body of professional representatives should have a final voice in the choice of the subjects to be taught to any scholar. In that decision the scholar himself (acting either by a system of individual options or through elected representatives) and his parents, as well as the representatives of the community, should have a voice. Representatives of the community should be given, subject in some cases to an advisory voice from the teachers, the decisive voice in the choice of teachers, the allocation of public funds to various sections of education, and general administrative arrangements.

How should these " representatives of the community " be constituted ? In the older British and American universities they are largely constituted by the mass-vote or elective vote of the graduates of the institution concerned

—the *alumni* as they are called in America. That expedient was derived from the mass-meetings of resident teachers in the medieval universities, and has, I believe, now ceased to have any but bad effects. The *alumnus* as such has neither the knowledge and interest of the teacher, nor the knowledge and interest of a well-chosen representative of the community. Mr. S. G. Hobson and Mr. Cole would apparently desire that the community should for that purpose be represented by persons responsible to a congress of Guilds. As things now are in England I myself should prefer that it should be represented by persons elected, as the present local authorities are, by some system of national or local democracy, and officials responsible to such persons. I should expect to find such democratically appointed bodies and officials more patient and more careful of the future intellectual interests of the nation than a congress of all sorts of Guilds. Democratic bodies can, it is true, become narrow and corrupt ; but so, on the evidence of medieval history, can congresses of Guilds.

CHAPTER VII

LIBERTY

THE political part of our social heritage normally reaches us in the form of large, vague words which are used for the names of political parties, or as rallying-cries during an election. A boy finds as he grows up that he is a Liberal, or a Conservative, or a Democrat, or a Socialist, or that he " believes in " Liberty, or Equality, or Patriotism. Behind these words there may be preferences for certain political expedients, conceptions of the men and things outside the range of our senses, generalizations as to human psychology, or the acceptance of certain rules of conduct. When a man calls himself a Democrat, he is probably more or less conscious of several of those " meanings " of the term ; but he may chiefly " mean " Democracy as a form of government, or as a way of thinking and feeling about his fellow citizens, or as a belief about human nature, or as a rule of political conduct.

So far, in analysing political terms, I have dealt mainly with institutions—committee-organization, parliamentary or professional government, etc. But it is convenient to analyse certain political terms as " principles " and rules of conduct. Of these " principles " the most important historically is Liberty or Freedom. Liberty, as a dictionary word, means a condition in which human impulses are not obstructed ; and as a rule of political conduct the doctrine that such obstruction should not take place. The psychological facts, therefore, on which the usefulness of the principle of Liberty depends consist of the results which follow from the obstruction of human impulses. Obstruction in a modern society does not, of course, always, or generally, mean the physical impossibility of satisfaction ; I use it here as a quantitative term, meaning such a degree of interference as in fact prevents a man from acting on any particular impulse at any particular moment. The results of obstruction may be divided into immediate psychological reactions, such as anger or humiliation ; and more permanent effects, such as changes of a man's character by the strengthening of some impulses and the weakening of others.

The most important fact about our immediate reaction to the obstruction of our impulses is that the reaction depends more on the nature of the obstructing cause or agent, than on the nature of the obstruction. This fact is not as a rule indicated in the definitions of Liberty given in books on politics. Mr. Sidney Webb, for instance, defines personal liberty as " the practical opportunity that we have of exercising our faculties and fulfilling our desires." [1] Mr. Webb's use of the word is for many non-political purposes both legitimate and convenient. When a man says, " I shall be at liberty to see you next Thursday," one does nor need to inquire whether it is a person or a thing which prevents him from seeing you earlier. But this use does not help to explain the enormous force of Liberty as a political principle. Common usage refuses to say that the liberty of a Syrian peasant is equally violated if half his crops are destroyed by hail or locusts, half his income is taken by a Turkish tax-gatherer, or

[1] Webb, *Towards Social Democracy* (1916), p. 7.

half his working hours are taken for road-construction by a German or French commander ; because human obstruction of our impulses produces in us, under certain conditions, reactions which are not produced by obstruction due to non-human events. The reactions to human obstruction take the form, first of anger and an impulse to resist, and then, if resistance is found to be, or felt to be, useless, of an exquisitely painful feeling of unfreedom ; and similar reactions do not follow non-human obstruction. Wounded self-respect, helpless hatred, and thwarted affections, are, that is to say, different psychological states from hunger and fatigue, though all are the results of obstructions to the carrying out of our impulses. When Shakespeare wishes to describe the ills which drive men to suicide he gives,

> The oppressor's wrong, the proud man's contumely,
> The pangs of despised love, the law's delay,
> The insolence of office, and the spurns
> That patient merit of the unworthy takes,

and does not mention the want of food and clothing from which he must himself have suffered during his first wanderings from Stratford.

Common usage, again, does not treat all human hindrances to our impulses as being, in the same sense, violations of liberty ; and here also common usage is based on important psychological facts. The special feeling of unfreedom only arises when the hindrance is felt to be inconsistent with those normal human relationships, to which, in the environment of primitive society, our instincts correspond. If a man is prevented, either by the woman herself or by some other human being, from possessing a woman who does not love him, he does not feel unfree in the same sense that a man does who is denied

access to a woman who loves him, or from whom a faithful
wife is taken by force or fraud.   When Ahab tries to rob
Naboth of the vineyard which he has planted, and Naboth
resists, Ahab may fail, or Naboth may fail ; but the resentment of Naboth or any of his early-human or anthropoid ancestors is different from that of Ahab ; Naboth
will feel, and Ahab will not feel, the " oppressor's wrong."
Mr. Webb's definition does not explain why, when certain
Germans pleaded, on the strength of their text-books,
that in " exercising their faculties and fulfilling their
desires " by invading Belgium they were realizing their
nation's liberty, and that the Belgians in defending themselves were doing no more, the world treated their plea
as either paradoxical or hypocritical.[1] Even in the
highly artificial economic environment of modern society,
a propertyless workman only feels " unfree " or " en-
slaved " when he believes that his want of property is
due to the deliberate action of men who are thereby
violating the normal conditions of human society.   The
inhabitants of a country where (as in America fifty years
ago) private property in land or railways is taken as a
matter of course, do not feel unfree if they are, in respect
of land or railways, propertyless.   As soon as they begin
to ascribe their exclusion from any particular kind of
property in the means of production and distribution to
" capitalism," or " exploitation," or " robbery," they do
feel unfree ; and the control of that kind of property
then becomes a question of political and social liberty.
But the fact that the same kind of economic disadvantage
may be felt at one time to be due to our normal environ-

[1] " We claim only the free development of our individuality,
and are only fighting against the attempt to throttle it " (*Deutsche
Reden in schwerer Zeit*, Pastor Troeltsch, p. 27).

ment, and at another time to be due to the abnormal action of our fellow human beings, does not mean that the presence or absence of the feeling of unfreedom is not important. The socialist who argues that freedom of speech or religion is of no value in an economically unequal community, and the authoritarian who argues that an increase of material comfort outweighs any degree of deprivation of political liberty, both make the same psychological mistake ; and the world has during the years 1914–1920 paid heavily for that mistake.

This connection between the principle of Liberty and the normal course of human instinctive behaviour under primitive conditions is especially important when the feeling that our liberty has been infringed arises out of the obstruction of those co-operative instincts which among men and some other gregarious mammals regulate common decision and common action. A man does not instinctively feel unfree if he finds himself following another in urgent co-operative action after having had a fair chance of himself claiming the lead, any more than a hunting dog, who has vainly called on the pack to turn to the left, feels any lasting resentment when he is following a more dominant leader to the right. Where the need of co-operative action is recognized, both common speech and psychological analysis treat the essence of unfreedom as consisting in the denial of " free speech " and a fair hearing in discussion or a vote in decision. " Patient merit " suffers the agony of humiliation if spurned by " the unworthy." If the meritorious man had a half-belief that the competitor for whom he was rejected was fairly chosen he would find it difficult to work himself up even into a sham-passion of humiliation.

It must be remembered, again, that human beings are

not a gregarious species in the same way, or to the same degree, as are the ants or the bees ; our normal instinctive course leads to intermittent co-operation for certain special needs, and not to constant co-operation for all needs. The conditions under which co-operative action takes place without creating the feeling of unfreedom are, therefore, both qualitative and quantitative ; the stimulus must be such as normally to arouse the instinct of co-operation ; and the co-operation must not last so long as either to tire that instinct, or to leave other unco-operative instincts too long unsatisfied. If, owing to a generally-believed danger of invasion, the inhabitants of a democratic community are required for a year or two to submit to a " state of siege," they do not feel unfree. If they are required to do so, even by a majority of their fellows, when they do not believe that there is danger they do feel unfree. Or if the foreign or domestic policy of their country is so managed that, like the noble families in ancient Sparta, or the ordinary inhabitants of pre-war Germany, they always believe themselves to be in danger, and are always required to live in a state of siege, they will nevertheless in time come to feel " fed up " and unfree, from the excess of co-operation and absence of individual action. Friedrich Naumann, in the early weeks of the war, wrote that the Western nations " call us [the Germans] unfree . . . because they dislike the habit of order (*Ordnung*) which has become a second nature to us," and claimed that German *Ordnung* is freedom because it results from the deliberate and unfettered choice of the German people.[1] Events in Germany in 1918 demonstrated the defects of this argument, and

[1] *Die Hilfe* (September 24th, 1914). For habit as " second nature " see my *Great Society*, chap. v.

showed that a people may voluntarily choose a way of living which afterwards produces the feeling of unfreedom, just as easily as a boy may voluntarily take a bite from a green apple which afterwards produces the feeling of sourness. Mr. Lloyd George, speaking at Conway on May 6th, 1916, said, " Compulsion simply means that a nation is organizing itself." In the crisis of 1916–17 compulsory military service was not, either in England or America, felt by more than a small minority of the population to be a violation of liberty. When compulsion was proposed for Ireland, to a people who thought that they had no voice in the decision, or when in 1919 and 1920 war-restrictions were continued in America during peace, those affected felt unfree.

The immediate reaction-feeling of unfreedom is, therefore, a definite psychological state produced by facts in our biological inheritance which can, by observation and experiment, be ascertained and measured with some degree of accuracy. This makes it possible for statesmen both to explain the explosive effects of the idea of Liberty (or rather of the sudden prevalence of the feeling of unfreedom) and to guard against those effects. But it does not follow that a complete absence of the feeling of unfreedom is either possible or desirable for mankind. The instinct of resentment, though it came into existence because we needed protection from obstruction to our normal impulses, is nevertheless now part of our nature ; and an occasional satisfaction for it may be necessary for our normal life and health.[1] And it is still more important to remember that our primitive environment is gone, and that our instincts have been to some extent modified by many thousands of years of parasitic relation

[1] See my *Great Society*, chap. ix.

to our social heritage. Our instincts to-day are not perfectly adapted either to our present environment, or, if it could be reconstructed, to our primitive environment. No way of living, therefore, can now be so " natural " to us as never to involve the obstruction of impulse ; the principle of Liberty can never be absolute, and in the organization of our society we must ask, not merely how we are to prevent the occurrence of the feeling of unfreedom, but how we are to live the good life. And in answering that question, we must consider not only our immediate reactions to the obstruction of our impulses, but also the more permanent effects of that obstruction upon our efficiency and happiness.

All these complex facts may be illustrated by the history of Liberty as a political idea in Europe. The beginning of that history can be assigned with unusual exactness to the efforts of a few statesmen, historians, and philosophers in the city of Athens during the fifth century B.C. Herodotus describes how the Athenians in 480 B.C. answered the offer of the Persian King's agent to make them the richest and most powerful state in Greece, provided that they would accept Persian suzerainty. " We know as well as you do that the power of the King of Persia is many times greater than ours. . . . Nevertheless, because we love liberty, we shall fight as best we can." [1] Liberty here means little more than absence of foreign tyranny. Fifty years later Pericles delivered that Funeral Speech over the Athenian dead in the Peloponesian War which Thucydides reported and dramatized, and extracts from which were pasted on the windows of the London omnibuses in 1915. Pericles tells his hearers, some of whom must have fought at Salamis, that " the secret of happiness is Liberty, and the secret of Liberty

[1] *Herodotus*, viii, 143.

is courage." But, to Pericles, Liberty is no longer the merely negative fact of the absence of foreign tyranny. It is a many-sided positive conception, both of a type of political and social organization already in part realized in Athens, and of the conscious moral and intellectual efforts which alone could make the continued existence of that type possible. "As we manage our public life in accordance with the principle of Liberty, so we carry the same spirit into our daily relations with each other. . . . Our constitution is named a democracy, because it is in the hands not of the few but of the many. But our laws secure equal justice for all in their private disputes, and our public opinion welcomes and honours talent in every branch of achievement, not for any partisan reason but on grounds of excellence alone. . . . We have no black looks or angry words for our neighbour if he does anything merely because he finds pleasure in it, and we abstain from the petty acts of churlishness which, though they do no actual harm, yet cause annoyance to those who note them. Open and friendly in our private inter-course, in our public acts we keep strictly within the control of law. We acknowledge the restraint of rever-ence ; we are obedient to whosoever is set in authority, and to the laws, more especially to those which offer protection to the oppressed and those unwritten ordinances whose transgression brings admitted shame. . . . Let us draw strength . . . from the busy spectacle of our great city's life . . . falling in love with her as we see her, and remembering that she owes all this greatness to men with the fighter's daring, the wise man's understanding of his duty, and the good man's self-discipline in its per-formance. . . ." [1]

[1] I here use, with a few verbal changes, my friend Mr. A. E. Zimmern's translation of the Funeral Speech (*The Greek Common-*

Pericles and Thucydides understood the explosive mine of resentment which may lie beneath the surface of a community that ignores, as Sparta then did, the inevitable reaction which follows petty meddling with personal life, or executive arrogance, or judicial partisanship ; but they realized also that free government meant something more subtle and more difficult than the mere avoidance of that reaction. What neither of them understood was that the slaves of Periclean Athens were human beings also, and that a time would come, two thousand years later, when the descendants of Athenian citizens and Athenian slaves would together be called on to organize a free democracy.

No modern thinker has expressed, for the purposes of modern national democracy, a conception of Liberty approaching in psychological insight the ideal which Pericles offered to the ancient City-state. I have already argued that the definition of Liberty used by Mr. Webb is insufficient, because it does not recognize that the unfreedom-reaction depends more on the cause of obstruction to impulse than on the mere fact of obstruction. J. S. Mill and the mid-nineteenth-century Liberals who followed him spoilt their definition in another way. Mill, in his celebrated essay on Liberty (1859) starts from the basis, with which every one can agree, that Liberty means the due satisfaction of the natural impulses of man. He takes as the motto of his essay a sentence from Humboldt's

wealth, pp. 201–205). It is difficult to bring out in English the psychological sharpness and even audacity of the original. The word, for instance, translated " reverence " means frankly " fear." " Falling in love " is an even stronger term in Greek than in English. In the last phrase of my quotation the Greek present participles insist on the continuity of the moral effort which alone can preserve liberty—" ever-learning what their duty is, and ever-sensitive to shame in its performance."

book on *The Sphere and Duties of Government :* " The grand leading principle, towards which every argument unfolded in these pages directly converges, is the absolute and essential importance of human development in its richest diversity." Mill further emphasizes two important facts as to the satisfaction of human impulse. The first is that the energy of impulse can be strengthened by action, and can be weakened by hindrance to action. He describes the men whose impulses are hindered by Calvinism and other forms of repression, " until by dint of not following their own nature they have no nature to follow ; their human capacities are withered and starved ; they become incapable of any strong wishes or native pleasures " (p. 119).[1] The second fact is that individual men differ in their natural impulses, and that therefore the greatest general satisfaction of impulse in any community must come not from uniform but from varied behaviour. " Such are the differences among human beings in their sources of pleasure . . . that unless there is a corresponding diversity in their modes of life, they neither obtain their fair share of happiness nor grow up to the mental, moral, and æsthetic stature of which their nature is capable " (*ibid.*, p. 125). So far, Mill's psychology is good. One needs, however, to add to his insistence on the value of energetic impulse the fact that in civilized life energy is largely dependent on social inheritance ; it is by education, and by the psychological self-consciousness which results from education, that civilized man learns to substitute steady and carefully economized effort for the casual impulses and casual inertia of the savage. The organized inculcation of an ideal of thoroughness in the use of the intellect may, therefore, enormously

[1] I quote from the edition of the Essay in Dent's Everyman Series.

increase those " great energies guided by vigorous reason,"
which Mill expects to come of themselves, if men will only
let each other alone. But a more serious omission in
Mill's analysis is that he ignores the alternation of the
impulse to lead and the impulse to follow a lead which
marks the instinctive process of co-operation. Of the
impulse to lead, and its value in the field of social and
intellectual progress, he gives a vivid account : " The
initiation of all wise and noble things comes, and must
come, from individuals ; generally at first from some one
individual " (p. 124). But he never seems to suspect
that the impulse to follow the lead may be as natural
for us as the impulse to give the lead, and that scope
for the impulse to follow may also produce " great
energies," and " strong wishes," and " native pleasures."
Obedience is to him, as it was to Hobbes, never a result
of natural impulse, but always a result of conventional
coercion. Referring, for instance, to " some early stages
of society," Mill says, " There has been a time when the
element of spontaneity and individuality was in excess,
and the social principle had a hard struggle for it. The
difficulty then was to induce men of strong bodies or minds
to pay obedience to any rules which required them to
control their impulses " (pp. 118–119). Here " individuality " is an " impulse," and the " social principle " is not.

A still weaker part of Mill's essay is his transition
from psychological analysis to practical advice. Professor
Dicey (who was twenty-four years old when *Mill on
Liberty* was published) says that it " appeared to thousands
of admiring disciples to . . . establish on firm ground the
doctrine that the protection of freedom was the one great
object of wise law and sound policy." [1]   But the object of

[1] Dicey, *Law and Opinion in England*, p. 182.

wise law and sound policy is a good human life. Liberty is one of the conditions of such a life ; but the deliberate invention and organization of expedients for making common action effective is another condition. The medical officer of health in a modern city when he is trying to decrease the death-rate from influenza ; or the city engineer when he is designing a new water-supply or drainage system or "town-plan " ; or the chairman of an education committee when he is considering a scheme for co-ordinating schools and colleges and libraries ; is not helped by Mill's statement that " each individual is the proper guardian of his own health, whether bodily or mental and spiritual " (p. 75). Nor would any one, except perhaps an American cardinal, now dream of acting on Mill's proposal of a scheme of compulsory education in which the state pays the school-fees of the poorer families, but leaves the parents free and unassisted " to obtain the education where and how they pleased " (p. 161).

This defect in the connection between Mill's analysis and his practical advice shows itself not only in the impracticability of his suggestions when he attempts to apply his " one very simple principle . . . that the only purpose for which power can be rightfully exercised over any member of a civilized community, against his will, is to prevent harm to others " (pp. 72–73), but in the large and unconsidered exceptions which he allows to that principle. When the essay appeared, Mill had been for thirty-five years a high official of the East India Company ; and it is with obvious reference to the government of India that he says, " We may leave out of consideration those backward states of society. . . Despotism is a legitimate mode of government in dealing with barbarians. . . . Liberty, as a principle, has no application to any state of things anterior to a time when mankind have become capable of being improved by free and equal discussion. Until then there is nothing for them but implicit obedience to an Akbar or a Charlemagne if they are so fortunate as to find one " (p. 73). He shows no sympathy with any proposal for greater liberty for " young persons below the age which the law may fix as that of manhood or womanhood " (p. 73). Even more significant is his almost casual statement that a man " may rightfully be compelled . . . to bear his fair share in the common defence, or in any other joint work necessary to the interest of the society of which he enjoys the protection " (p. 74). This last exception makes Mill's whole argument almost meaningless. The question of what is " to the interest " of a society depends on our preference as between different ways of living ; Pericles would hold one kind of regulation to be necessary to the interest of society, the Spartan ephors another kind, and Prince Kropotkin a third kind. It is only when Liberty ceases to be " one very simple principle " subject to un-explained exceptions, and is thought of as a careful quantitative and qualitative co-ordination between known psychological facts and actual social expedients that any fertile definition of it becomes possible.

But when *Mill on Liberty* appeared in 1859, the political control of Britain was in the hands of the politically active members of the English middle class, and they were not likely to notice any such insufficiency in Mill's analysis. When an English Liberal in the decades between 1850 and 1870 spoke of our nation's progress, he thought almost exclusively of the growth of our material wealth ; the " leaping and bounding " of our income-tax returns ;

and the scientific discoveries which had accompanied that growth and made it possible. Both seemed to be the result of Liberty as Mill conceived it, and of Liberty only. Our trade had been "free" since 1846; our manufacturers and artisans were free, subject to the mildest of Factory Acts, to use what processes and enter into what contracts they liked; and "great energies guided by vigorous reason" seemed to have been the necessary result. Scientific discovery had come, not from state aid or university organization, but from the free intellectual energy of men like Faraday or Darwin or Wallace. Our free manufacturers had distanced the world, and our free scientists had made the seminal inventions of the time. The need for better technical training than a manufacturer could pick up in his business, or for a larger industrial unit than that of a single firm, or for a wider ideal of effort than the individual self-interest of a manufacturer, was not yet felt; nor did any other provision for the progress of science seem necessary than liberty for the individual inquirer to think what he liked, and say what he liked, and support himself and his family as he could.

The British Liberals of that generation half-unconsciously assumed that political progress would result in the same way and from the same motives as industrial and scientific progress. Hardly any one of them, for instance, seemed to realize that while a business man may perhaps be trusted (as long as the business organization of the world is not too complex) to develop any idea which "occurs" to him, and be immediately rewarded by making a great fortune, the making and development of political and administrative inventions required a concentration of intellectual effort for which neither the

political ideals nor the administrative arrangements of
the time provided sufficient motive or sufficient means.
From 1830 to 1874 we were governed almost continuously
by the Liberal Party, of which Mill was the most important
intellectual leader. But Liberal administration, when the
first energy of the reform struggle of 1832 was spent,
showed a curious combination of national complacency
and national inefficiency; we declared every day that
" the schoolmaster was abroad," and our educational
arrangements remained the laughing-stock of the world ;
we idealized the British workman's home, and watched
new slums growing under our eyes ; we talked ourselves
into a belief that our humiliating adventure in the Crimea
had covered the British flag with glory, and allowed
the Duke of Cambridge to block any proposal for the
reform of our army. British local government was then
" a chaos of areas, a chaos of authorities, and a chaos of
rates " ;[1] but the Liberal ministries after 1835 made no
serious attempt to introduce order into it, and indeed
increased the confusion by piecemeal and inconsistent
legislation which set up new overlapping bodies for health
and roads and education. The accepted Liberal motto
was " Peace, Retrenchment and Reform " ; the British
nation was to secure peace by leaving other nations and
nationalities (with the help of British example and British
good advice) to work out their own salvation. Our salvation at home was to be achieved by a policy of retrenchment, which would take as little of the national income
as possible for state purposes, and leave as much as
possible to be directed by free individual enterprise
towards the creation of individual wealth ; and the whole
policy of Peace abroad and Retrenchment at home was to

[1] M. D. Chalmers, *Local Government* (1883), p. 17.

be maintained by the single process of a gradual extension
of the suffrage. Democracy would be dangerous if it came
at once, but innocuous if it came gradually—if " freedom "
were allowed, as Tennyson said, to " slowly broaden
down from precedent to precedent," and if the borough
and country franchises should be lowered a pound or two
every ten years. " All parties," wrote Cobden in 1859,
" now agree that . . . we must have a measure of parliamentary reform that shall carry us over at least the next
twenty years." [1]

If all British Liberals had really acted on the belief
that Liberty, as defined by Mill, is the only necessary
condition of the good life in modern society, British
Liberalism would have produced the same helpless mal-
administration as did Lamartine's French provisional
government in 1848 ; and would have led as quickly and
as certainly to an authoritarian reaction. That Liberalism
governed Britain as long as it did was due to the fact that
there were always one or two men serving it who attacked
the problem of political organization, not with the expectation of being borne along by a self-acting stream of
progress, but with a deliberate and constructive intellectual effort. Since the political philosophy of the time
was apt to take ratiocination for granted, those who
thought with a conscious effort generally did so because
they were influenced rather by personal example than
by political or psychological theory. The most important
of the nineteenth-century British political inventors were
disciples, at first or second hand, of Jeremy Bentham.[2]

[1] Morley's *Life of Cobden*, p. 585.
[2] See Dicey, *Law and Public Opinion* (1914), pp. 130–131. " In
studying Bentham's intellectual character we are reminded that,
if he was the follower of Hobbes and of Locke, he was the contemporary of Arkwright and of Watt. . . . It is in this inventiveness that he differs from and excels his best-known disciples."

Chadwick had been Bentham's secretary and borrowed from his master's *Constitutional Code* a plan for the structure of local and central government, which he spoilt in the borrowing, but which was at least better than no plan at all. Gibbon Wakefield and Rowland Hill learnt from Bentham the motive and method which enabled Wakefield to turn the British *laissez faire* policy of colonial self-government into something better than a lazy arrangement for "cutting the painter," and Rowland Hill how to invent penny postage. Francis Place invented, with a score of other political contrivances, the system of local party organization which gave a public-spirited voter some voice in the selection and control of his representative. Place was an intimate and devoted friend of Bentham, and he was reflecting the tradition of his master's daily example when he wrote in 1838 to Roebuck that the "power of close, deep, continuous reasoning is the lot of few, and those few have never yet directly governed mankind." [1] Only Mill, Bentham's favourite disciple, and the intellectual autocrat of British Liberalism, invented, as far as I know, nothing in the region of politics. One seems, indeed, to detect a certain softness of fibre, a certain unwillingness to attempt the severest kind of intellectual effort, in the complacency of such passages as that in his *Logic* (1843), "Doubtless the most effectual way of showing how the sciences of Ethics and Politics may be constructed would be to construct them : a task which, it needs scarcely be said, I am not about to undertake." [2]

From the beginning of the dominance in British political thought of the conception of Liberty as the "one very simple principle," there had always existed an articulate

[1] Place to Roebuck, January 24th, 1838 (in British Museum MS. Dept.).   [2] *Logic*, Book VI, chap. i, p. 419.

opposition to it. That opposition drew its intellectual stimulus, to a degree which a mere list of names and dates reveals, from Germany. Early in the nineteenth century Coleridge, because he had read Kant, had given a philosophical content to the British conservatism, which since 1791 had been little but a blind and selfish dread of the principles of the French Revolution. Coleridge was succeeded by Carlyle, who founded his attack on Benthamism and Liberalism on Fichte ; and Carlyle was succeeded by Hegel's followers, Caird and Green. By 1880 it was clear that Mill's undisputed reign at Oxford was over, and Hegelian idealism almost became the official Oxford philosophy. But all these British interpreters of German thought were, like the German thinkers, metaphysicians, concerned to find by metaphysical methods a conception of the state which should form part of a rational solution of the problem of the universe, and should prove indeed that there was no reality in the universe except reason. To the ordinary British politician or statesman the very phraseology of metaphysical idealism was unintelligible ; Mill's plea for Liberty had been psychological, narrow as its psychology was, and not metaphysical, and any criticism of Mill which could influence the main body of British political thought must also be psychological. Such a criticism was attempted by Matthew Arnold in *Friendship's Garland* (1866–70) [1] and *Culture and Anarchy* (1869).[2] He had been sent to Prussia in the early eighteen-sixties to report on Prussian education, and had there learnt to appreciate the extra-

---

[1] Published as letters to the *Pall Mall Gazette* (1866–1870), and as a book in 1871. My references are to the Popular Edition, Smith, Elder (1903).

[2] Republished (1869) from the *Cornhill Magazine*. My references are to the Popular Edition, Smith, Elder (1889).

ordinary achievements both in peace and war possible
to a nation in which " the idea of science governed every
department of human activity " ; [1] while his experience
as school-inspector at home had convinced him of the
inevitable consequences of " so intently pursuing liberty
and publicity as quite to neglect wisdom and virtue ; for
which alone . . . liberty and publicity are worth having." [2]
Arnold makes the Prussian hero of *Friendship's Garland*
say, " We [Prussians] set to work to make ourselves
strong . . . by culture, by forming our faculties of all
kinds, by every man doing the very best he could with
himself, by trusting, with an *Ernst der ins Ganze geht*
[which one may translate " intellectual seriousness and
thoroughness "] to mind and not to claptrap." [3] " Freedom," Arnold says, " like Industry, is a very good horse
to ride, but to ride somewhere," [4] and "somewhere "
means towards " the work of making human life, hampered by a past which it has outgrown, natural and
rational." [5] Therefore he tells his countrymen, " Instead
of every man . . . thinking it bliss to talk at random about
things . . . you should seriously understand that there is
a right way of doing things, and that the bliss is, without
thinking of one's self-consequence, to do them in that
way, or to forward their being done." [6] Englishmen
especially should turn their backs on the " chance medley
of accidents, and intrigues, hot and cold fits, stockjobbing,
newspaper articles, conversations on the railways, conversations on the omnibus, out of which grows the foreign
policy of a self-governing people, when that self is the
British Philistine." [7] If we wished our democracy to

[1] *Friendship's Garland*, p. 10.   [2] *Ibid.*, p. 98.
[3] *Ibid.*, p. 17.   [4] *Ibid.*, p. 141.   [5] *Ibid.*, p. 129.
[6] *Ibid.*, p. 13.   [7] *Ibid.*, p. 88.

survive we must realize, as both the German and the French Liberals did, that the " idea at the bottom of democracy " is not the doctrine that " being able to do what one likes, and say what one likes, is sufficient for salvation," [1] but " the victory of reason and intelligence over blind custom and prejudice." [2] We should, therefore, in so far as we were real democrats, give authority to " our best self or right reason by making the action of the State, or nation in its collective character, the expression of it." [3]

Arnold in 1870 still clung to the hope that the ruling force in German national policy would be a Periclean combination of liberty and thoroughness. In a letter to the *Pall Mall Gazette*, written on August 9th, 1870 (three days after the Battle of Woerth), he makes his Arminius say, " I have no love for the preaching old drill-sergeant who is called King of Prussia, or for the audacious conspirator who pulls his wires. . . . I believe [Germany] will end by getting rid of these gentry ; and that till that time comes the world will never know of what real greatness she is capable." [4] As, during a war infinitely more terrible than that of 1870, I re-read Matthew Arnold's appeal, I myself felt that here was a great opportunity missed by the world. British Liberals might, fifty years ago, have learnt from him and his German teachers a new conception of their own creed ; they might have realized that Liberty only led to " great energies guided by vigorous reason " in a people who, instead of waiting for energy and reason to appear of themselves, were willing to make the organized effort of will necessary to achieve them. And Prussia might have found in Britain, if not a clear and complete realization of political liberty, yet a political tradition

[1] *Friendship's Garland*, p. 11. [2] *Ibid*, p. 8.
[3] *Culture and Anarchy*, p. 84. [4] *Friendship's Garland*, pp. 73–74.

which had already taken many of the practical steps towards such a realization.

That Arnold earned no such place in the history of political thought was, I think, due to two causes. The first was that German Liberalism failed in fact to control German thoroughness; the new empire was formed on the policy, not of Humboldt and Bunsen, but of the "audacious conspirator" and the "preaching old drill-sergeant." But a second reason was that Arnold himself preached *Ernst der ins Ganze geht* better than he practised it. Every advocate of an intellectual method is bound to illustrate his argument by himself using his own method, and is bound to make mistakes in doing so. But Arnold did not give his method a fair chance. He, like Mill, was an official, whose books were written before or after a day of official work, spent, in Arnold's case, in contact with undeveloped or subordinate minds. He, like Mill, consciously avoided the effort of political invention. "Our main business," he says, "at the present moment is not so much to work away at certain crude reforms . . . as to create, through the help of . . . culture . . . a frame of mind out of which the schemes of really fruitful reforms may with time grow" (*Culture and Anarchy*, p. 156). Fruitful political reforms do not grow, but are made. Arnold, again, was more interested in literature than in social theory, and never drove his way through the social prejudices which he acquired at Rugby and Oxford. He thought of his own political work mainly as a fight against the alliance between religious Nonconformity and *a priori* Liberalism, against "Mialism and Millism."[1] Nonconformity represented to Arnold

[1] *Friendship's Garland*, p. 17. Miall was editor of the *Nonconformist*.

the centre-point of the narrowness and vulgarity of the English "narrow and vulgar middle-class." [1] He treats the "Nonconformists' antipathy to Church establishments" as the necessary opposite of "the power of reason and justice," [2] and the Deceased Wife's Sister Bill as the necessary antithesis to "Geist." The policy of Disestablishment and the Deceased Wife's Sister Bill may have been wise or unwise ; but the question whether the permanent endowment of a fixed creed is good, or whether it is better that so important a subject as the propagation of the human race in Britain should be regulated by the House of Commons on sociological grounds or by the House of Lords on grounds of ecclesiastical authority, was matter for inquiry ; and Arnold never convinced the Nonconformists that he had attempted that inquiry with real intellectual seriousness. Every able young Nonconformist in Arnold's time, when he had attained such higher education as the existing Church monopoly allowed, or had succeeded in any profession, knew that he could gain both an easy reputation for " cultur: " and admission to the governing English class, by an insincere or half-sincere acceptance of Anglicanism. To him this was a life-long temptation of the devil, and Arnold's plea in the name of " Sweetness and Light " that he should abandon the " Dissidence of Dissent," and bring himself into " contact with the main current of national life, like the member of an Establishment," [3] seemed only a more than usually snobbish way of presenting that temptation. After the completion of the German victory over France, Arnold wrote, " There are many lessons to be learnt from the present war ; I will tell you what is for *you* the

---

[1] *Friendship's Garland*, p. 17.
[2] *Culture and Anarchy*, p. 125.   [3] *Ibid.*, p. 14.

great lesson to be learnt from it :—obedience." [1] He here ignored the existence of a natural and general instinct to lead, and to assert oneself, as completely as Mill ignored the existence of a corresponding instinct to follow, and to efface oneself. Obedience is a poor word even for one side of that relation between the citizens of a free community in which all govern and all are governed.

In 1874 British Liberalism, after forty-four years of almost uninterrupted power, lost its control over British policy, and lost it largely because its conception of Liberty was inadequate for the solution of any really difficult political problem. Already in 1874 the problem of the relation between the state and the individual citizen was being complicated by the problem of the relation between the state and associations smaller than the state. At the election of that year the Trade Unionists found a clearer recognition of their point of view among most Conservatives than among most Liberals ; and received by the Conservative legislation of 1875 enlarged powers of corporate action. It was the Conservatives who created the powerful County Councils in 1888, and who prepared that further reform of English Local Government which the Liberals passed in 1894. The majority of Liberals were frankly hostile to the grant of liberty of action to an endowed and " established " Church ; but Gladstone was a passionate High Churchman, and his concessions to the Church in the Education Act of 1870 had split the Liberal Party to its centre. Gladstone finally resigned in 1874 because his party refused to follow him in establishing a Catholic university desired by the majority of voters in Ireland and disliked by a majority of voters in the United Kingdom. When Gladstone came back to

[1] *Friendship's Garland*, p. 12 (written Candlemas Day, 1871).

power in 1880, his Government broke up, after five years of confusion and division, because Liberalism provided no guidance in the new imperial and foreign problems which had resulted from the improvement of world-communications. Lord Ripon was sent in 1880 to govern India on the principle of Gladstone's Midlothian speeches ; but he was supported neither by the British officials in India nor by the Cabinet at the British end of the new telegraphic cables. Egypt is on the way to India, and Arabi when he rose in 1881 seemed to some Liberals a patriot " rightly struggling to be free," and to others a rebel against the authority necessary for British safety. The Liberals were willing to bring the citizens of any colony in the Empire (even although, as in Natal, they were a handful of white settlers among an overwhelmingly non-white population) under the formula of " self-government " ; but that formula did not in 1881 solve the problem of the Transvaal Boers. In the " Midlothian campaign " of 1879 Gladstone had said that we had chosen, " I am tempted to say, insanely, to place ourselves in the strange predicament of the free subjects of a monarchy going to coerce the free subjects of a republic, and to compel them to accept a citizenship which they decline and refuse." [1] Yet in 1881 Gladstone's Government fought a Boer force at Majuba Hill, and then concluded a peace which seemed to make the fighting unintelligible. In 1884 Lord Granville told Bismarck that we had no interest in the Cameroons, and a few months later we nearly went to war with Germany because Bismarck had promptly annexed them. Meanwhile the problem of the relation between Liberal principles and private property was slowly developing. Liberalism had assumed that an instructed democracy would under-

[1] Morley's *Life of Gladstone*, Vol. III, p. 27.

stand that the existing inequalities of private property
(except in so far as they were caused by primogeniture
and entail) were due rather to natural law than to the
will of man. In 1890 the Trade Union Congress passed
a series of socialistic resolutions, and henceforth Liberalism
had to compete with a class-conscious Labour Party in
applying the principle of Liberty to a condition of economic
inequality which was now widely thought of as due to
human action in the past, and as modifiable by human
action in the future. The Liberal Government of 1892
to 1895 fell more rapidly than did that of 1880–85 because
their inability to construct an intelligible social or Irish
policy on the principle of Liberty had become still more
clear. Gladstone, for the quarter of a century from 1868
to 1893, was the Liberal Party, and drove his party with
unsurpassed powers of personal work and leadership ;
but Gladstone the orator and financier and " old parliamentary hand " was also Gladstone the author of
Homeric Studies and of *The Impregnable Rock of Holy
Scripture*, the man for whom there had been " a battle
between Eton and education and Eton had won." [1]
Liberty to Gladstone was always the " great and precious
gift of God " without which " human excellence cannot
grow up in a nation " ; [2] but to the end of his life Gladstone
no more understood the psychological processes involved
in the more complex problems of Liberty than he did the
mental processes involved in the composition of the Iliad
and the Pentateuch.

During the years of Liberal eclipse from 1895 to 1905
the practical necessities of an industrial democracy ruling
an overseas Empire ; the increasing power of the Labour

[1] Morley's *Life of Gladstone*, Vol. I, p. 50.
[2] *Ibid.*, Vol. I, p. 84.

Party ; the influence of the Hegelian philosophy of history on a few able Oxford politicians ; and the economic, political and military pressure of German competition, combined to produce a conscious break in the minds of the Liberal leaders with the simple principle of *Mill on Liberty*. In 1906 the Liberal Party came back from the elections with a majority of nearly two to one over all other parties combined. It was no longer the party which Gladstone had led, Mill had inspired, and Matthew Arnold had derided. In 1902 there had appeared a book on Liberalism by Sir Herbert Samuel with an introduction by Mr. Asquith. Mr. Asquith wrote that " it may seem a truism to say that the Liberal Party inscribes among its permanent watchwords the name of Liberty. . . . Freedom of speech, freedom of the press, freedom of association and combination . . . we in these latter days have come to look upon as standing in the same category as the natural right to light and air. . . . But with the growth of experience a more matured opinion has come to recognize that Liberty (in a political sense) is not only a negative but a positive conception. Freedom cannot be predicated in its true meaning either of a man or a society merely because they are no longer under the compulsion of restraints which have the sanction of positive law. To be really free they must be able to make the best use of faculty, opportunity, energy, life." [1] Mr. Asquith here, like Mr. Webb and others, was at that time attempting to use the idea of Liberty mainly as a support for the different though almost equally important idea of equality. He therefore indicates no difference

[1] H. H. Asquith (January, 1902), in an introduction to *Liberalism : its Principles and Proposals*, by Herbert Samuel, pp. ix and x.

between human and non-human hindrances to our faculties.
Nor does he distinguish between Mill's automatic conception of human energy and the conative conception
of Pericles and Matthew Arnold. Sir Herbert Samuel
(whose notes refer to Kant and Green and Bradley, as
well as to Mill and Sidgwick) pushes his analysis much
further, though not so far as Pericles. He sees that the
political idea of Liberty must involve not only Mr. Webb's
" practical opportunity of . . . exercising our faculties,"
but a conscious and organized will to do so. He declares
that " ' advance of the age,' ' evolution of society,' ' the
natural progress of mankind,' these are no more than
phrases, summarizing the results of human effort." [1]

[1] *Liberalism*, by Herbert Samuel, p. 16.

CHAPTER VIII

RIGHTS, HONOUR, AND INDEPENDENCE

THE analysis of Liberty will help us in analysing certain other political principles, of which the most important historically is Natural Right. The term Natural Right acquires a definite and measurable meaning if we consider it, as we considered Liberty, in relation to the psychological fact that obstruction by human action of the normal course of certain instincts, sex, property,[1] family affection, "leadership and following," etc., causes a feeling of painful resentment. When this happens, if we conceive of our position as primarily one of personal helplessness, we say we are " unfree " ; if we conceive of our position as a certain relation to society we say that we are " wronged " ; the two feelings of unfreedom and wrong are different but closely related.

Natural Rights are therefore real things, arising from real and permanent facts in our psychology. But because the instinct which creates them was evolved to meet the needs of a primitive environment, we must remember that in our modern environment it is no more invariably good for us to receive all our natural rights than it is to be completely free. It may be better on any particular occasion to endure the pain involved in the obstruction

[1] For the instinct of property and its relation to modern property systems see my *Human Nature in Politics*, Pt. I, chap. i.

of the instincts which make us claim our rights; or to
"sublimate" those instincts by satisfying them in a
new way; or even to inhibit them by an effort of will,
based on a calculation of results, and leading to a disciplined but unstable habit. All this may sound obvious
enough; but if one considers the use of the term Natural
Right during the centuries when it had its greatest driving
force, one continually finds that confusion and bloodshed
was caused by the fact that there was no common ground
between men who felt a passionate instinctive desire for
their Rights, and men who demanded a rational explanation
and delimitation of them.

In October and November 1647, for instance, a series
of debates on the future government of England took
place in the General Council of the " New Model " army
at Putney, and a short-hand note of them was taken by
William Clarke. Colonel Rainborow, the leader of the
extremists, said in his speech, " Every man born in
England cannot, ought not, neither by the Law of God
nor the law of nature, to bee exempted from the choice
of those who are to make lawes for him to live under,
and for him, for ought I know, to loose his life under "
(p. 305). Ireton made an equally sincere protest that
the idea of natural right, and of the justice and injustice
that followed from it, meant nothing but the casual
opinion of any speaker at any moment. " When I do
hear men speake of laying aside all engagements to consider only that wild or vast notion of what in every man's
conception is just or unjust, I am afraid and do tremble
att the boundlesse and endlesse consequences of itt " [1]
(p. 264). Cromwell told the soldiers that he himself was

[1] Camden Society, *The Clarke Papers*, ed. C. H. Firth (1891),
Vol. I.

an opportunist with no general theory as to the relation of government to Natural Right. He was not " wedded and glued to formes of government . . ." (p. 277). " It is the generall good of them and all the people in the kingdome [we ought to consult]. That's the question, what's for their good, nott what pleases them " (p. 209).

After the Restoration of 1661 the whole progress of English political thought was checked, because there was no chance of an understanding between the followers of Hobbes, who insisted on a psychological basis for political theory but could give no psychological explanation of the passion for Natural Rights, and the followers of Locke, who insisted on the reality of Natural Rights but gave a metaphysical explanation of them. Throughout the years of the French Revolution Jeremy Bentham, the humanitarian and reformer, remained a Tory because of his contempt for the " nonsense upon stilts " of " natural and imprescriptible rights "[1]; and Francis Place, when he set himself after Waterloo to find a rational basis for Radicalism, created a wall of suspicion between himself and the working-class leaders of his time (who thought as their successors still often think in terms of Natural Right, by his contempt for " what are called inherent indefeasible rights, which are made to include whatever particular object may be aimed at." In the American Civil War, both North and South passionately desired those " unalienable Natural Rights " which were asserted in the Declaration of Independence. But the South interpreted those Rights with reference to their strong instincts of property, racial superiority, and corporate freedom ; while the North interpreted them with reference to their metaphysical and religious conception

[1] *Works*, Vol. II, p. 501.

of right and wrong. Both the psychological and the metaphysical argument suffered from the fact that men have continually ignored the difference between that which it is natural to us to claim, and that which it is, in view of the whole circumstances, good for us to receive ; if a claim is natural, men have assumed that its satisfaction is good for us, and if its satisfaction is good for us, they have assumed that the claim is natural. One would say that they have played with two different meanings of the word " right," if it were not that they have never recognized that the two meanings are different.

The long and blood-stained history of the principle of Honour is another instance of the bad results which may follow from the existence of a strong political passion which men name and recognize, but of which they can give no psychological explanation and delimitation. The psychological facts behind the principle of Honour are closely akin to those behind the principles of Liberty and Natural Right. The three feelings of unfreedom, wrong, and dishonour, are all caused by the fact that the normal function of some important instinct has been obstructed by human action ; but while the emotions of unfreedom and wrong are concentrated on our recognition of our helplessness or its social cause, the emotion of dishonour is concentrated on our recognition of the fact that our fellows no longer respect us, and that we can no longer play our part as equal comrades or potential leaders in the co-operative action of our society. A man may feel oppressed or wronged when no one except himself and his oppressor knows what has happened ; he only feels dishonoured when he believes or imagines that others know of it. And, further, he does not feel dishonoured, unless he or others believe that there has been some defect from the normal in his own reaction to the wrong done to him. If he has succeeded in resisting the wrong, or in exacting vengeance on the wrongdoer, or even has fought to the uttermost, though unsuccessfully, his neighbours still respect him ; he and they feel that "his honour has been satisfied." A corresponding feeling of corporate dishonour may affect all the members of a society, if the society as a whole has shown a want of courage in resisting wrong, or has otherwise lost the respect of the members of other societies.[1] The principle of Honour, like those of Liberty and Right, can, in a modern society, be both very useful and very dangerous. If we desire to make it more useful and less dangerous we must consciously learn so to stimulate, satisfy, sublimate, or inhibit the relevant instinct as to lead, here and now, to a good life. We can, for instance, to some extent choose what type of conduct in a man or a society shall be now held by outsiders to constitute dishonour or to satisfy honour. Honour may, fortunately for us, be felt to be satisfied by acts very different from those suggested by our instincts in their primitive environment. In a society where respect for law is inculcated on all, a man who is struck may satisfy honour by prosecuting his opponent without returning his blow ; and we can train ourselves to feel that the " neighbours " to whose contempt or respect we are sensitive, shall be either our own family, or our tribe, or our nation, or even those in all nations who share our outlook on life.

---

[1] The feeling of dishonour is closely akin, not only to the feeling of wrong, but also to the more general and very primitive feeling of shame. A man (and, perhaps a gregarious bird like a rook, or a gregarious mammal like a wolf or a dog) who is a discovered thief, feels a shame that is very like the dishonour felt by a discovered coward.

A fourth principle which can be made enormously more useful by the same kind of psychological analysis is Independence, as the term is used in the phrase, " The Independence of the Judicature." Here the psychological fact behind the principle is not the immediate reaction of feeling in a man whose impulses are obstructed, but the permanent result on his conduct of the obstruction of some impulses and the encouragement of others. We make a judge " independent," not in order to spare him personal humiliation, but in order that certain motives shall not, and certain other motives shall, permanently direct his official conduct. The government or constituent assembly which adopts the principle of Judicial Independence is in the same position as the inexpert members of a firm which has acquired a wall-paper factory, and has to engage a designer. They have themselves neither the knowledge nor the taste, nor the time which would enable them to make their own designs, or to decide which designs will sell or even which designs they themselves after a year or two's experience will like. They therefore choose a man with certain special powers and training, and give him independent responsibility for the firm's patterns. But they desire that he shall not only be capable of making good designs and free from any obstruction in the process, but also that he shall be impelled to do his work by certain positive impulses, conscious or half-conscious, which are much more subtle than the habit of shop-discipline or the fear of dismissal. Therefore, without being themselves quite conscious of what they are doing, they add to the negative fact of independence certain encouragements of these positive impulses. They not only pay him a good salary, but also treat him with personal respect ; they call his working-room " Mr. Jones's studio " ; they ask him and his wife to dinner ; and try to create an atmosphere in which Mr. Jones is encouraged both to give play to his artistic impulses, and half-consciously to co-ordinate those impulses with the general purposes of his friends the masters of the firm. So a President or prime minister knows that if he forces judges to carry out his own decisions he will often prove to be wrong. He therefore chooses judges carefully, and gives them a status negatively free from parliamentary and executive pressure, and positively encouraging to " judicial " impulses.

All this means that the Independence of the Judicature is capable of being made not merely an isolated and simple formula, too sacred to be criticized or modified, but a principle founded on known psychological facts, and capable of development in accordance with new needs. As soon as this is realized, we can freely ask ourselves what are the motives which we desire to encourage in judges, and whether we are taking the right means to encourage them. The administrative methods, for instance, of the United States as to the appointment and position of the federal judicature are based on Alexander Hamilton's eloquent plea in *The Federalist* for the " firmness," " integrity," and " moderation " of the judges. Successive Presidents carry out that tradition by appointing practising lawyers who have earned the respect of their professional colleagues. But there is in America a growing popular demand that judges should not only be firm, and incorruptible, and moderate, but also progressive ; it is felt that a man who is, for instance, entrusted with the tremendous powers of a judge of the Federal Supreme Court, should understand and sympathize with the intellectual and moral tendencies of a generation in which the average adult citizen is not a lawyer, and is at least twenty years younger than the present average judge. An American President may ultimately find it best to appoint somewhat younger men to the supreme court, with a touch in some of them of the qualities which make poets ; and the men selected will, perhaps, though learned in the law, be not necessarily trained as advocates. It may again be found that such men best preserve their elasticity of mind and sympathy during their judicial career if they are brought under other influences as well as those of professional tradition. They might, for instance, be employed from time to time on special inquiries and other quasi-judicial work needing judicial qualities, just as an army engineer officer is sometimes employed on work outside his main duties but likely to increase his fitness for those duties.

In Britain a general reconsideration of the qualities which we require in a judge, and of the means we take to obtain and strengthen those qualities is even more urgently required. The Lord Chancellor, with us, fills a large proportion of the vacancies in the High Court by choosing barristers who have done conspicuous political service to his own party. The judge, when appointed, is so independent of executive or parliamentary control that he is, in practice, never removed except for obvious mental disease. He is well paid, his office is universally respected, and he is trained in that spirit of personal honour which is part of the intensely professional tradition of the English Bar. An English judge must very seldom feel himself consciously tempted to do anything which he consciously believes to be professionally wrong.

But English statesmen are not made to realize that judges need elasticity of mind, or that sensitiveness to impulses wider than professional tradition which we call public spirit. Many Englishmen can, therefore, name cases in which judges have been appointed with the mental and moral characteristics of rather unscrupulous professional advocates, or with the moral blindness of ingrained political partisans. Even less care is sometimes taken to secure the most essential judicial qualities in the provincial (or " County Court ") judges, who do such a large and increasing part of our judicial work. A new analysis of the whole problem might lead to the appointment of English judges by the Minister of Justice, whose creation I have already urged, aided by a permanent " department." English judges might be appointed at a much younger average age than at present, and after experience either as solicitors or barristers or students and teachers of jurisprudence. They might normally begin by being sent to the less important posts, and the best of them might afterwards be promoted to the High Court, which itself might be (in all but appellate work) established in the great provincial cities as freely as in London.

The analysis might be extended to the case of those court officials who do actual judicial work under another name. Important judicial functions are, for instance, at present carried out in England by the " masters," " registrars," " clerks," and other officers of the High Court. These men are appointed by the personal choice of individual judges ; and the evidence which I heard as a member of the " MacDonnell Commission " on the Civil Service in 1915 showed that in this respect the judges are still guided by the traditions of eighteenth-century " patronage " ; and that family and personal reasons in-fluence appointments to permanent, responsible and well-paid posts, to a degree which in any other profession would be held to be inconsistent with common honesty.[1]

A judge, again, is made " independent," not only in order that he may show firmness and integrity, but also because he possesses a body of legal knowledge which it is very difficult for a lay statesman to test. But a modern law-court requires from time to time the presence of other experts whose knowledge and conclusions it is equally difficult for a layman to test. Special knowledge is, for instance, often required by the courts of natural science, of handwriting, of commercial custom, and even of the religious rites of Eastern races. Such special knowledge is usually in England provided by the profoundly unsatisfactory expedient of the " expert witness " ; his evidence is as purely *ex parte* as is the argument of a barrister, but he is generally chosen by the side which pays him because he occupies some responsible public or professional position ; and every attempt is made to suggest to the court that he speaks as an impartial man of science. The court should in all important cases be provided with its own expert assessors (like the naval assessors who sit in the Admiralty Court), and administrative machinery should be invented to secure an absolutely impartial choice of them. The assessor should be required to give his opinion publicly on questions of fact, and should be able to oppose without the risk of loss of employment the opinion of the presiding judge.[2]

[1] See *Appendix to the Sixth Report of the Royal Commission on the Civil Service* (1915), especially questions 44,399–44,408 ; 51,463–51,468 ; 51,509–51,512 ; 57,255–57,259 ; 59,245–59,252 ; 60,242 ; 60,294–60,314. The Commission unanimously recommended that the power of personal appointment by judges should be abolished.

[2] Mr. H. J. Laski suggests to me that as long as judges have the power to decide what sentences are inflicted on convicted criminals

But the principle of "Independence," as soon as we attempt to analyse it, will be found to extend far beyond the law-courts and their officers. Even if we confine ourselves to those public officials whose main duty it is to give responsible answers to technical questions, we are dealing with a body of men which is already large and is steadily increasing. Every government department and every great city employs legal, chemical, engineering, and medical advisers. During the last fifty years people in Britain have come to rely absolutely on the sincerity of all statements of facts made by the members of our central Civil Service, who are appointed as the result of an independent examination, and, like the judges, hold office practically for life.[1] But the experience of other countries, and our own rapid political development during the war, has shown that this position is not nearly so secure as we had assumed. Every government department had during the war its publicity section, and the two great offices of Information and Propaganda employed towards the end of the war huge staffs, and supplied more than half the war news contained in our own journals, and five-sixths of the statements about our actions and intentions which were sent to neutral and hostile countries. Those two departments were wound up after the war; but a large amount of government "publicity work" existed before the war and a much larger amount

they should be required to consult trained and responsible psychological assessors. It would probably be better that all criminal sentences should be "indeterminate"; and that the whole treatment of prisoners after conviction should be controlled by an expert medical and educational department, responsible for all prisons and penal schools and hospitals, and constantly collecting and analysing, both the records of individual offenders, and the results, at home and abroad, of various methods of treatment.

[1] See my *Human Nature in Politics*, Pt. II, chap. iii.

will exist after the war. The officials engaged in this work have special knowledge of facts unknown to their audience, and are responsible for statements based on that knowledge ; it is therefore a political problem of the first magnitude how to apply the principle of Independence to them, and to secure the necessary qualities of " firmness " and " integrity "—not to speak of sympathy with progress. During the later years of the war the British Minister of Information was Lord Beaverbrook, and the Minister of Foreign Propaganda was Lord Northcliffe. On March 11th, 1918, a debate took place in the House of Commons on Lord Beaverbrook's appointment. The speech which saved Mr. Lloyd George's Government from the possibility of defeat was made by Mr. S. L. Hughes, M.P., himself an experienced journalist, who said, " I think that practical and experienced newspaper men are the best men [for the work of propaganda]—I would add, men who are not likely to be hampered in their proceedings by what Dr. Johnson has termed ' needless scrupulosity.' "

In every section of central or local government technical experts are employed not only as referees, but also as administrators. It is, indeed, no easy matter for a minister or town-clerk, or for the expert himself, to be sure in the daily work of an office when an expert should carry out orders without responsibility, and when he ought to claim the rights and responsibilities of his expertise ; and constant friction takes place in all departments and municipal offices (as it takes place in all War Councils and War Offices) between the men who think mainly as administrators and those who think mainly as technicians. The expert, again, must not only direct existing types of work, but also invent new processes,

and in this respect civilians may learn from the ideals
if not from the practice of military organization.   The
military staff works out plans requiring the intimate
interaction of many minds and an atmosphere favourable
to those new ideas which we cannot directly create, but
whose spontaneous appearance we can indirectly encourage.
Attempts are therefore made to give staff officers such
a measure of "independence" as shall strengthen the
motives of interest in the work and desire for distant
results, and shall prevent those motives from being
obstructed by a bullying general, or suppressed by their
own desire for immediate and cheap approval.

The Report of Lord Haldane's "Reconstruction"
Committee of 1915 (Cd. 9230) proposed that throughout
the whole structure of British Government the "staff"
function of inquiry and thought should be separated
from that of executive administration, and that when
the separation had been made the two functions should
be carefully co-ordinated.   The committee pointed out
that "Intelligence" branches already existed in several
of the ministries; and I had opportunities of seeing a
little of the work of some of these branches both before
and during the war.   Those that I saw were remarkable
instances of the difference in the psychological conditions
of thought and of action.   The big halls of a typical
Whitehall Department remind me sometimes of Plato's
Cave of Shadows; but the little untidy rooms where
one found an "Intelligence Branch" seemed to receive
daylight through a cranny in Plato's rock.   Men sat in
easy attitudes and laughed freely; and their talk was
entirely candid and entirely irreverent.   The daylight
from their cranny seemed to shine through things that
in the big rooms were so solid, knighthoods, and salaries,

and official positions and official precedents. Things
also that in the big rooms seemed shadowy, the two-in-
the-morning doubts which one tries to forget during
working hours, the reality of the injury which might
result to unknown human beings from the respectable
official tradition of passing on responsibility from department to department, the feeling that if one squandered
time and was agonizingly sincere with oneself, the solution
of an apparently insoluble problem might yet be found
just below the present level of one's consciousness—all
these things seemed solid matters of fact. It was not
till I had said good-bye, and was walking away through
the passages that I could remember that Plato's *illuminati*
have never by themselves ruled a State, that the ultimate
test of clever talk and wide-ranging thought is the
necessity of turning it into black words on white paper
and seeing that those words are obeyed ; and that in
Government offices, as in army headquarters, the intellectual stimulus of responsibility for truth must be somehow co-ordinated with the more clumsy but often more
powerful intellectual stimulus of responsibility for action.

A thorough analysis of the psychological facts underlying the conceptions of Liberty and Independence might
be further made to influence, not only our policy in
appointing officials and co-ordinating their functions, but
our general conception of modern democracy. In all great
industrialized nations the idea that representative government consists of the irresponsible carrying out by elected
persons of the directions of the electors has definitely
broken down ; and I have already argued that a system
of nation-wide vocational elections managed according to
the same idea would be even less successful. We may
therefore be feeling our way to a conception of democracy

in which the idea of personal responsibility will play a large part. Alexander Hamilton, when arguing (*Federalist* No. 78) for the Independence of the Judicature, refers, with an unaccustomed use of capitals, to the danger that judges might "exercise WILL instead of JUDGMENT." A future democratic representative as he stands before his constituents may realize that besides those simpler desires in himself and in them which Hamilton calls Will he can by conscious effort strengthen the easily daunted impulse of Judgment. The voter who listens to him may learn to distinguish in himself the stirrings of Will and of Judgment. The permanent official and his ministerial superior may learn to recognize that they are both of them servants of a community to whom, as Burke claimed they owe not their "industry" only, but their "judgment," [1] and that though they may both have from time to time to take part in the carrying out of decisions in which their judgment has been overridden, the abandonment of the effort of judgment is a dereliction of duty.

It may even be that some day Hamilton's emphasis on judgment may help us to solve that which is now the most insoluble problem of democracy—the position of the Press. As long as his newspapers pay, and the telephone from his house to the editorial offices is in

---

[1] E. Burke, *Speech at Bristol at the Conclusion of the Poll* (1774). " . . . it ought to be the happiness and glory of a representative to live in the strictest union, the closest correspondence, and the most unreserved communication with his constituents. . . . It is his duty to sacrifice his repose, his pleasures, his satisfactions, to theirs ; and above all, ever, and in all cases, to prefer their interest to his own. But his unbiassed opinion, his mature judgment, his enlightened conscience, he ought not to sacrifice to you, to any man, or to any set of men living. . . . Your representative owes you, not his industry only, but his judgment "

working order, the owner of a group of papers has more absolute irresponsibility in the use of great power than any other living man. If he is to use his power in a way helpful to the community he must aim at the two virtues, veracity and seriousness, i.e. the more obvious virtue of saying only what he believes to be true, and the less obvious virtue of taking trouble to secure that his belief is well founded. But nothing in his position, or in the qualities necessary to reach that position, encourages either of those virtues ; and the anonymous writers whom he hires to carry out his orders have neither the personal independence of artists nor the public responsibility of experts.

I could pursue my argument that the independence of those who carry out any social function is only valuable if it leads to certain positive mental and moral efforts, through the case of the professor, with the *Lehrfreiheit* which he can use or abuse, the doctor, and the plumber. In the end, I should come to the individual trying to regulate his own impulses by his own painfully acquired knowledge of facts, and responsible to his future self for using that knowledge without fear or favour.

CHAPTER IX

WORLD CO-OPERATION

THE change of scale from national co-operation to world co-operation, like the change from group co-operation to national co-operation, involves a change in the form and character of the co-operative process.

In this case also the change is of kind, as well as of degree. If a member of a fairly homogeneous modern nation creates for himself a picture of his fellow-nationals which is near the truth, he is likely to feel, in times of danger or difficulty, an instinctive impulse to co-operate with them. A truthful picture, however, of an alien population often stimulates in us the anti-co-operative instincts of fear and suspicion and hatred, and the instinct of co-operative defence may act as an anti-co-operative force ; the danger-spots of the world are just those regions where markedly different races and cultural types are brought into relations with each other too close for illusion. It can, therefore, be argued that, since contact between different races and cultures stimulates instinctive hatred, mankind shall avoid any attempt to co-operate on a scale larger than that of a homogeneous nation. When, a hundred years ago, the failure of the last serious attempt at world co-operation became obvious, Canning in 1823 wrote to Sir Charles Bagot, " Things are getting back to a wholesome state again.

Every nation for itself, and God for us all." So, in 1920, after six exasperating years of co-operation with Frenchmen, Italians, Russians, Americans, and Japanese, many Englishmen find themselves again longing for a return to the " wholesome state " of national isolation.

But men cannot now exist in their present numbers on the earth without world co-operation. The manufacturing populations of the north-temperate zone require for their food and clothing the vegetable products of the tropics ; and the organization of tropical agriculture and transport requires the energy and science and capital of races who can at present only breed in a cool climate. Metals, again, and coal and oil are scattered irregularly over the land surface of the world, and must be brought from the places where they are found to the places where they can be most effectually used. Improvements in communication and transport are constantly intensifying and complicating this economic process. Cobden dreamt that intensive commercial intercourse could take place without the friction and danger involved in political relations [1] ; but Cobden's dream has proved impossible. Rivalry among nations in the exploitation of the resources of the globe has inevitably led to diplomatic relations, and behind diplomacy there has always been the threat of war.

In November 1918 Mr. Wilson's " fourteen points " seemed to many of us to offer mankind an almost incredibly favourable opportunity of adopting, by a single general decision, a political scheme in the working of which men might gradually learn to base world co-opera-

[1] " At some future election, we may probably see the test of *no foreign politics* applied to those who offer to become the representatives of free constituences." Cobden, *England Ireland and America* (1835), in *Political Works*, Vol. I, p. 43.

tion, not on threats of war, but on a conscious and steadily developing world-policy. That opportunity has passed, and any attempt to bring about " the great experiment of living together in a world made conscious of itself," [1] must now begin from the bottom. Here or there in the world a new thought or a new emotional appeal may give rise to a new institution or habit by which world co-operation may be made more possible ; or a new institution or new educational method may start new thoughts or give new weight to old appeals. The degree of our success in that work will, in the first place, depend on the difficult and halting process which our fathers used to call " the triumph of human reason." We must so strengthen the impulse to think and the habit and art of rational calculation, and so realize the significance of our conclusions, that we may be able to resist or modify or divert some of the strongest of our instincts. In the sixteenth century the invention of new means of world-communication spread syphilis over the globe, and created a danger, which has not yet wholly disappeared, that the human breeding-stock might be destroyed, unless we could so discover the causes and effects of syphilis, and so realize the significance of our discoveries as to bring under new rational control and direction the enormously powerful instinct of sex. Further inventions in world-communications, combined with inventions in military chemistry and transport, have now so increased the destructive power of armies and fleets that the human species is again endangered unless we can so calculate and realize the effects of war as to bring our instincts of hatred and suspicion under the control of reason.

[1] Miss Jane Addams in *The Survey* (November 1915).

Everything, therefore, which helps us to connect cause and effect in human long-range action, helps us to make world co-operation more possible. We may, for instance, by a change of educational emphasis, learn to avoid certain elementary fallacies, which men, who would never use them in their short-range thinking, constantly use when thinking and talking of international relations. The most important of these is the old fallacy of "all and each." If one nation acts selfishly and all other nations act unselfishly, the selfish nation may gain; but if all nations act selfishly, disaster to all must follow. Now that the memory of the war is still fresh, it is easy to see a childish want of logic in Prince von Bülow's statement, in 1913, that British policy was based on "a sound and justifiable egoism . . . which other nations would do well to imitate"; [1] and some of us felt that there was a fault of logic as well as of feeling in Sir Edward Carson's plea in 1916 that our Government ought to wage a world-war "in order that whatever advantage may accrue, shall accrue to this country and empire, and to no one else." [2] Perhaps in the end our political philosophers may even learn to avoid the trick of making plausible generalizations about "The State" which are obviously unsound when made about "states" or "a state." [3]

If we desire to think effectively about world co-operation, we must further learn to bring a new problem-attitude to bear upon each of the political sciences. The background of every political science is history, and it is only in 1920 that Mr. Wells has published the first history

[1] *Imperial Germany*, p. 21.
[2] House of Commons (November 9th, 1916).
[3] See L. T. Hobhouse, *The Metaphysical Theory of the State* (1918), p. 21.

of the world consciously written in the problem-attitude of world co-operation.[1] It is sometimes claimed that international law is by itself a sufficient foundation for world co-operation. We were all thrilled, in 1916, by Lord Grey's statement that we were fighting for "a peace that re-establishes respect for the public law of the world." As I write, the managers of the Republican party in America seem to be arguing that international law, or world-law, as I should like to call it, is a sufficient substitute for world-policy. World-law can never be a substitute for world-policy, and if it is to be an efficient guide and instrument of world-policy it requires, even more urgently than does national law, a fundamental psychological analysis of the idea of law. What, for instance, is the relation of law to custom, and of custom to the process of self-conscious habituation? One of the most important functions of world-law must be the arrangement in thinkable classes of what would otherwise be an unthinkable chaos of facts. But how is the work of classification, when undertaken by lawyers, related to the classification, often of the same subject-matter, undertaken by world congresses of scientists? What is the relation of world-law to national (or as lawyers call it "municipal") law? Is world legislation (the making of

---

[1] A writer in *The Guardian*, with a wide experience of English elementary education, said, "As a matter of fact, the teaching of history and geography with a view to cultivating patriotic virtues is the main principle underlying every syllabus in those subjects" (Letter signed B. D., *The Guardian*, October 14th, 1915). When I was a member of the London School Board I formed the same impression. It is well known that the same principle prevailed, before the war, in the German schools. I believe that an attempt is now being made by the English Board of Education to encourage, under the guidance of Mr. F. S. Marvin, a wider outlook in English school history teaching.

new world-laws or the application of existing world-laws to new conditions) possible without the creation of a supernational political authority ? Is it possible to create an approach towards uniformity in those national laws which deal with points where local differences of rights and customs cause inconvenience in the relations between the citizens of different states ? It is only by a conscious attempt to answer questions like these that we can hope to solve such world-problems as communication by sea and by ocean-canals and air, the spread of disease, or migration and naturalization, credit and currency, the huge debts now owed by states to each other, or the relation between the rights conferred on the United States by a general acceptance of the Monroe Doctrine, and the rights conferred on other powers by a " mandate " under the League of Nations.

The position, again, of mankind on the globe may be seen not only as a problem in the socially inherited expedients of logic and law, but also as a problem in the biological processes of breeding and nutrition. The nineteenth-century biologists lessened rather than increased the possibility of world co-operation. Their statement of the problem made it easy for politicians to claim that any war which they desired was a " biological necessity." [1] But a change in the problem-attitude of biologists, of which one is thankful to believe there are already signs, may make biology one of the main sources of hope for a world co-operation founded on conscious purpose instead of blind struggle. We are only now beginning to acquire the knowledge of the true conditions of improvements in the various human races and the true biological results of intermarriage between races.

[1] Dr. Grueber of Bavaria, *Daily Chronicle* (May 5th, 1915).

Botanists may see their science, not as a section of "national economy," but as a means of enabling the whole human race to co-operate in every region and climate in providing the means of a good life for all its members. Even Malthus's problem of the pressure of population on food-supply will seem less insoluble if it is seen in relation to the possibility of "a world made conscious of itself." The study of geography would receive a new stimulus if school-children and university students and map-makers and travellers could see their science also as the servant of world co-operation, and discuss the effect on mankind as a whole of the cutting of the Panama Canal, or the discovery of a new natural fuel-supply, or the irrigation of a waterless region.

Political "principles" will acquire a new fertility if we learn to think of them in the problem-attitude of world co-operation. Mr. Page, speaking in England as American Ambassador on July 8th, 1917, said of his fellow-countrymen, "Hitherto we have been concerned chiefly with the development and extension of liberty at home. We now enter into a holy crusade to help in its extension in this Old World." [1] It may perhaps be doubted whether the most informing possible description of internal political movements in America during the twentieth century has been "the development and extension of liberty." But President Wilson would certainly have had more influence on world-policy during the Peace Conference at Paris if mankind had had more practice in thinking of Liberty as a world-principle. If the Supreme Council of the Allies could have applied the principle of Liberty to world-problems with the psychological insight with which Pericles applied it to the city-state

[1] *Daily Telegraph* (July 5th, 1917).

of Athens, they might have asked themselves whether
that principle was consistent with the " mandate " given
to Poland over Eastern Galicia, or with the conscious
attempts which have made to break the German national
spirit by wounding the self-respect and lowering the
vitality of the whole German population.

An almost equally important question arises in the
application of the principle of Liberty to those individual
actions of the citizens of any state which concern the
world-policy of their state. If a world-policy is to exist
it must exist in the minds and wills of individual men
and women. Those individuals should obviously be free
to influence the decisions of their nation, but should they
also be free to oppose or condemn the national decisions
when once formed ? Professor Hearnshaw pleaded in
his *Freedom in Service* (1916) that in order to make the
principle of Liberty secure, " the individual must be
brought to recognize that politically he has no separate
existence, and must learn to limit his operations to his
proper share in the constitution and determination of the
general will. . . . The State must be supreme." [1] Was he
right ? In every nation the national policy as to pass-
ports, copyright, postal facilities, marriage, immigration,
and a hundred other questions affecting freedom of individual intercourse with foreigners will depend on the
national acceptance or rejection of Professor Hearnshaw's
argument that the individual citizen has " no separate
existence," and therefore no moral relation, as an individual,
to the rest of mankind. On that decision within each
nation will also depend the world-question whether the
development of conscious world-policy shall be carried
by the free interaction of millions of human minds and

[1] *Freedom in Service*, by Professor F. J. C. Hearnshaw, pp. 95–96.

wills across the frontiers of states, or by the efforts of a
few tired statesmen and officials aided by the confused
voices of national parties and national newspapers. I
have already said that the relation of the newspaper-
press to internal national policy is a still unsolved
problem of political science.[1] That is still more true of
world politics ; we have learnt that international crises
under modern European conditions are apt to bring into
supreme power statesmen who have impressed their
personalities on hundreds of millions of mankind, and
who are therefore likely to be more sensitive, more vain,
and more suspicious than their fellows. If a newspaper
proprietor, who has made his wealth by his skill in
manipulating men, gets personal access to such a statesman, he can surround him with a refreshing and exhilarating
atmosphere of quick understanding and cynical amuse-
ment, and with the subtle flattery of the newspapers
which the statesman reads. A few weeks of this process
may divert to world destruction national energies, which
might have been used for world co-operation. In the
election of December 1918 Mr. Lloyd George made it
impossible for him to use at Paris the power of Britain
for the promotion of reconciliation and goodwill in
Europe. Because of what he then said and did children
a century hence in every European country who might
have lived in health will be crippled or killed by disease ;
youths and girls who might have entered into the kingdom
of knowledge will toil in ignorance; nations who might
have been friends will hate and fear each other. After
the election, Lord Northcliffe's *Weekly Dispatch* announced
that, " Those on the inside of the election are warmly
congratulating Lord Beaverbrook on the success of his

[1] See *ante*, p. 197.

handling of it and of the Prime Minister. It was largely due to him that the first flabby election appeals—including the address of the Prime Minister himself—were brought into line with the Eight Points of the Northcliffe Press, on which the election was practically fought. Lord Beaverbrook has been offered high office, but he is understood to have declined it, partly for reasons of health and also because he wishes to exercise his great journalistic talent in developing his *Sunday Express*, to which the *Weekly Dispatch* offers a very hearty welcome." [1] When I read this paragraph I felt, as an Athenian spectator must have felt who watched the tragedies of Œdipus or Agamemnon, how small and pardonable are those weaknesses of mankind which can set in motion such an avalanche of human suffering. But world co-operation cannot be achieved unless we learn to think even of the power of the modern press not as an irony of fate, but as a thing which the human mind has contrived and the human mind can alter.

During the war hundreds of thousands of young Britons and Americans consciously fought for the " principle of Nationality," the principle, that is to say, that every body of human beings who feel themselves to share the emotion of nationality should become an independent state. Before we can calculate the effect on world co-operation of a universal adoption of this principle, we must ask ourselves how far the emotion of nationality is an unchangeable fact of biological inheritance, and how far it can be controlled by rational choice. We can do so best by taking a marginal case. Cardiff is a city with a mixed Welsh and English population. Cannot and does not a young Welsh professor at Cardiff choose whether he

[1] *Weekly Dispatch* (December 29th, 1918).

shall feel and act primarily as a Welshman, or primarily as a scientist, or as a human being, or as a citizen of the British Empire? Every day Jews in New York, Germans in Wisconsin, Poles in Pittsburg, and Scandinavians in Dakota decide in what language they shall talk to their children, what songs they shall sing and to what newspapers they shall subscribe.[1] In such decisions the " principle of Nationality," because it is an absolute and not a quantitative idea, gives them no help ; and the same defect of thought has brought upon once prosperous territories of Eastern Europe war, which does not know whether it is national war or civil war, and pestilence and famine.

Has the principle of Equality any meaning in the problem of world co-operation? The fact that men had not reached any answer to that question was one of the main reasons of the helplessness of the European Socialist parties at the crisis of August 1914, and of their confusion in the presence of aggressive Russian Sovietism since the war. A nation whose citizens approximate to economic equality with each other, is, it may be argued, more likely to be capable of world co-operation than a nation divided into permanent factions of rich and poor, or " whites " and " reds." But does the principle of Equality mean that North Americans, who are able and willing to work harder and more effectively than South Americans, should aim at economic equality between the two civilizations? Should there be economic equality between Russia and Italy, or England and India? One may feel that some quantitative economic relation between differing populations is both conceivable

[1] See W. B. Pillsbury, *Psychology of Nationality and Internationalism*, especially chap. v.

14

and desirable, but at the same time that every factor
in that relation should be represented by a quantitative
symbol infinitely more complex than that of equality.

Any serious effort, again, to make world co-operation
possible will require us to approach from a new angle
the invention and criticism of both national and supernational institutions. Does the fact that the hereditary
British House of Lords can hang up any legislation at
any moment for two years help or hinder the British
nation in co-operating with other nations? The United
States Senate can pass by a bare majority any amendment
to a treaty negotiated by the executive ; but the treaty,
when amended, must drop unless it obtains a two-thirds
majority. How does that arrangement work in world-
politics, or how does the arrangement work by which
the American Federal Government is sometimes constitu-
tionally unable to enforce on one of its constituent
states a foreign treaty which only the Federal Government
is empowered to make? Many of the internal problems
of the British Empire are conveniently solved by the
existence of " self-governing " Dominions with armies
and navies and treaty-making powers of their own. But
other nations often consider that relation to be one in
which Spenlow benefits by the uncontrollable acts of
Jorkins, and Jorkins by the uncontrollable acts of
Spenlow. In the " Annex to the Covenant of the League
of Nations," the British Empire stands as one of the
" original members " ; followed by the " indented "
names of Canada, Australia, South Africa, New Zealand,
and India. What does that indentation mean, and
where, if anywhere, does Great Britain appear in the
list? The indented states are to meet with Great Britain
in 1921 to make a new constitution for the British Empire.

Will any one, except perhaps Mr. Smuts, then realize that they are making a constitution not only for the Empire, but also for a section of the League of Nations ?

The British Empire contains a quarter of the human race, and constitutes a laboratory for the exploration of many of the most difficult problems of world co-operation. Shall we be able to use our imperial experience in the development of world co-operation ? Shall we be able so to improve the relations of India and South Africa to the Empire as to assist in improving the relations of India or South Africa, or China, or Syria to the rest of mankind ?

Every nation appoints diplomats and consuls and foreign office secretaries whose work often affects other populations even more directly than their own nationals. When the war broke out, I was a member of a Royal Commission which was then inquiring into the British Foreign Service. We had, I believe, in our minds no very clear recognition of the fact that we were discussing the appointment of servants of mankind as well as servants of a nation. One of our witnesses, who had himself been a diplomatic attaché, described to us " the type of man who is fit for this international career called diplomacy." " All of this type of man," he said, " speaking metaphorically, speak the same language ; they have the same habits of thought and more or less the same points of view, and if anybody with a different language, and, roughly speaking, a different point of view, came in, I think he would be treated by the whole diplomatic circle more or less with suspicion." [2] This type was then secured in Britain by appointing to the diplomatic service only

[1] Mr. Ian Malcolm, M.P., *Appendix to Fifth Report of the Royal Commission on the Civil Service*, question 42, 519.

young men of good family, educated in certain expensive schools, whose fathers gave them a large private allowance. The habits of thought and speech of these men were those of a polite duellist, and were exactly the least likely to enable them to care for the interests of other nations as well as of their own. When it was proposed in 1917 that British Labour delegates should be permitted to go to Stockholm, Lord Hugh Cecil protested. " Labour," he said, " is quite unfit mentally and by training to deal with the questions that will come under discussion, in fact, I would as soon send a child of three up in an aeroplane as let the Labour Party send delegates to Stockholm." [1] Every one, of course, in the complexity of modern civilization, is intellectually unfit to settle any question on his own sole responsibility. The flying officer does not start until a mechanic has assured him that his machine is ready, and a meteorologist has assured him that the weather will be favourable. Our dependence on expert knowledge is more clear in foreign politics than elsewhere, because the ordinary voter cannot even know the names of the cities and provinces whose fate he must decide. But knowledge is not the only factor in human action ; a Labour representative, Mr. Henderson, or Mr. Clynes, or Miss Bondfield, of unusual natural and trained good will and sympathy, might, with proper expert assistance, have made, from the point of view of mankind as a whole, a much more useful representative of Britain at Stockholm than the most experienced of our professional diplomats.[2] World

[1] *Manchester Guardian* (August 17th, 1917).
[2] Sir H. H. Johnston has always protested against joint international administration of dependent territory, on the ground that, " The world has not yet developed an international conscience." The development of that conscience may perhaps be made a little

co-operation does, however, require that we should think out, more clearly than in other political activities, the relation of good will to knowledge. When Mr. Wilson went to Versailles, none of us realized that the degree to which America would be able to help mankind at a supreme crisis would mainly depend neither on the good-will of Mr. Wilson and his assistants, nor on Mr. Wilson's tenacity of purpose and power of speech, but on the degree of his ability to carry on " team-work " with a body of responsible experts, and on the existence of a tradition in American diplomacy which would force him to recognize that such " team-work " was necessary.

In the invention of supernational institutions, there has been during the last twenty years a clearer recognition of the need of fundamental brain-work than in the adaptation of national principles and institutions to supernational purposes. In every nation there have been a few men who have worked at the invention of international courts and councils and assemblies almost as hard as if they were trying to invent a new valve for a petrol-engine. But most of the work still remains to be done. Nations will not surrender their individual interests to the larger interests of mankind, unless they feel that in the formation of a common decision their individual interests have been fairly considered. If all nations were of the same size, and were equally interested in all questions, such fair consideration might be represented by a majority vote among national representatives. But nations vary from hundreds of millions to two or three millions, and, so far,

more possible in the future if officials, when learning the language chosen for world-intercourse, study great literature as well as non-literary text-books, and so acquire emotional as well as intellectual associations with the words which they will use.

the only method of international co-operation which has been agreed to is that of theoretical equality, involving the practical dominance of the stronger powers over the weaker, not by voting, but by the constant threat of force.[1] Now, if one looks up the old codes of law which represent the submission of hitherto independent families and tribes to courts and governments covering new and larger areas, one finds that their most important sections are certain numerical tables, looking rather like the tables of weights and measures in a child's arithmetic book. The earl, or bishop, or freeman, or churl, was to count, when testifying, as " twelve-handed," or " six-handed," or " two-handed," and his relations were to receive so or so many shillings wehrgeld for his death.[2] Before the acceptance of such numerical tables men who desired peace had to trust to the fact that the strong and dominant individuals and groups who might break away unless their strength and dominance were recognized would stay because they felt that they could get control by the clumsy and dangerous process of instinctive " leadership and obedience." The real making of the German Empire as an instrument of peaceful co-operation among the German states came when Bismarck at Versailles induced the German princes to agree to a table of voting-power on the *Bundesrat*, in which all the subtle factors of Prussian dominance and Bavarian and Saxon particularism were represented by the figures 17 for Prussia, 6 for Bavaria, and 4 for Saxony. The fact that such a table has never yet been agreed to in international organization was the main cause of the failure of the

[1] An excellent description of the actual working of a European Congress is given in the *Life of Disraeli*, Vol. VI.
[2] See e.g. Stubbs, *Select Charters* (8th ed, 1895), p. 65.

Hague Conference of 1907. Germany was determined never to be outvoted on any point by any majority, and the numerous independent republics of South and Central America cared more for their theoretical equality with Germany or the United States or the British Empire, than for the advantages to be gained from effective international co-operation. In the Postal Congress established in 1874 the votes of all nations are equal; but the great nations accept a position in which they can be outvoted by the small, only because they do not expect that the small nations will insist on their full rights. In the drawing up of the Treaty of Versailles, international co-operation was made possible by the very rough expedient of giving the " Big Four " or " Big Three " equal votes, and the smaller allies no votes at all. The Covenant of the League of Nations recognizes the inequality of nations by distinguishing between " The Principal Allied and Associated Powers," who are always to be on the Council; other Great Powers who may be asked to join the Council; and the smaller Powers, from among whom four representatives shall be chosen by the Assembly to sit on the Council. But since, in all important matters, the proceedings of the Council, and, in nearly all important matters, the proceedings of the Assembly, require unanimity, the whole proceedings of the League have hitherto, like those of the Supreme Council of the Allies, been carried out on the old diplomatic principle of unanimity secured by threats of war or disruption on the part of individual Powers. It may be that the real beginning of a world-constitution in which voting minorities will be prepared to give way to voting majorities, may come from arrangements for dealing with particular problems, the control of a waterway, or precautions against an epidemic, or the formation of a court for sea-law, in which unequal voting power (not always the same for different problems) is given to different nations.

As I write, it seems probable that the League of Nations created by the Treaty of Versailles will come to an end. America and Russia do not seem likely to join; France will exercise her veto on the membership of Germany; and at any moment the French or Italian Parliament may refuse to vote its share in the expenses of the secretariat. But if the League, in spite of its weakness, still continues to exist, it may help in the invention of expedients and habits which will be useful if ever mankind come to desire a more effective organ of world co-operation. For that reason, one hopes that the men whom the nations send to Geneva will realize that they are creating a political type which may prove to be more permanent than its first embodiment. A choice, for instance, in League administration between various national "rules of public business," an attempted solution in the Geneva offices of the enormously difficult intellectual and emotional problem of language, a question of etiquette, or a decision to found a national or an international club, may all be factors in making men remember the League of 1918 either as an organization which, within the limits allowed to it, succeeded, or as a failure whose repetition must be avoided.

The uncertainty, again, of the League's immediate future ought not to prevent any nation which has adopted a policy of world co-operation from sending to Geneva the men and women who are working at the collection and analysis of the statistics of disease, the psychology and geography of industry and commerce, or the international survey of the heavens. Mr. J. M.

Keynes has told us how even in the nightmare of Paris during the spring of 1919 he became "a European in his cares and outlook." [1] Scientists as well as diplomats may learn at Geneva to become world-men and world-women in their cares and outlook.

[1] *The Economic Consequences of the Peace*, p. 3.

CHAPTER X

CONSTITUTIONAL MONARCHY

I SHALL not in this chapter pay much attention to
" absolute " or " personal " monarchy. Serious thinkers
have in the past argued for that form of government.
At the cultural stage of medieval Europe the absolute
monarch stimulated the same instinct of personal obedience
as did the " old man " of the early human or pre-human
group, and so enabled co-operation to take place among
people who would otherwise have been helpless against
an organized enemy ; and the fact that he was selected
by primogeniture helped to save his subjects from those
periodical struggles between rival leaders which must
have been one of the main difficulties of primitive society.
But mankind are now apparently agreed in rejecting
hereditary personal monarchy as a practical means of
controlling the internal and external problems of a modern
industrial nation. We have found that the complexity
and range of modern government require the interaction
of many minds and wills, under conditions inconsistent
with the life-long dominance of one man or woman.
And the same complexity and range require that any one
who takes a direct and leading part in the government
of a great community or association of communities shall
be above that average of health and intelligence and
character which alone, at the present stage of eugenic

art, can be secured by hereditary succession. The recently published letters and telegrams and minutes of the Russian Czar and Czaritsa and the German Kaiser, before and after August 1914, disclose a danger which no great modern nation is likely voluntarily to incur again. Even in the minor instance of the British House of Lords, the expedient of personal hereditary power only survives because British statesmen are not agreed on any substitute for it.

Nor shall I pay much attention to the forms of elective monarchy which have been tried in the Holy Roman Empire, in Poland, and in France under the Napoleons. Elective monarchy has been generally found either to lead to hereditary monarchy, or to involve most of the dangers of hereditary power without its advantage of security in succession. The chief importance of the idea of elective monarchy may, indeed, in the future be found in its influence on the position of the President of the United States. The only form of monarchy which I shall here consider is the Constitutional Monarchy which exists in the British Empire, and in a few countries, such as Italy, Belgium, Norway, Sweden, and Greece, which have for the most part deliberately imitated the British example.

British constitutional monarchy originated in the deadlock reached during the seventeenth and eighteenth centuries between the British Parliament and the British Crown. It was defended by eighteenth and early nineteenth century constitutional writers as a " balance of power " between two independent forces, a compromise which left to the monarch real but " limited " authority.[1]

---

[1] See *Blackstone's Commentaries*, Vol. I, chap. vii, " One of the principal bulwarks of civil liberty, or, in other words of the British

It was "limited" monarchy in this sense which was accepted by the Kaiser when in April 1917 he promised "to hold the just balance between the people and the monarchy." But such a "limited" monarchy is not what most British constitutional writers since 1832 have meant by "constitutional" monarchy. Our monarchy is now generally described not as a means of "checking and balancing" parliamentary government, but as a means of making parliamentary government both absolute and secure. "The constitutional King," said Sir George Cornewall Lewis, "is King, in order that no one else may be King." [1] The appropriate stimulus, the argument runs, of the human instinct of obedience is a person. In a republican government the person who will stimulate the instinct of obedience will be the President or prime minister, and he will thereby be enabled to resist a parliamentary majority. Constitutional monarchy, on the other hand, concentrates the instinctive passion of obedience on a person so chosen, trained, and situated, that all his actions are the actions of a parliamentary ministry. The Constitutional monarchy becomes a "crowned republic," or rather a crowned parliamentary majority.

The clearest statement of this argument is given in the chapters on Monarchy in Walter Bagehot's *English Constitution*,[2] in which he bases it on that psychological analysis which he used with all the gusto of a scientific

constitution, [is] the limitation of the sovereign's prerogative by bounds so certain and notorious, that it is impossible he should ever exceed them, without the consent of the people."

[1] Quoted by Sir Herbert Samuel, *Liberalism* (1902), p. 294.

[2] Originally written as a series of articles in the *Fortnightly Review*, published as a book in 1867, and republished with a new introduction in 1872. I quote from Nelson's edition in the *Library of Notable Books*.

pioneer who was also a born man of letters. He insists, not only on the reality and force of the instinct to obey (which, as a Lamarckian, he ascribes to the biological inheritance of acquired habit) but also on the quantitative biological limitations of human imagination and knowledge. " The French people," he says, " were asked : will you be governed by Louis Napoleon, or will you be governed by an assembly ? The French people said : We will be governed by the one man we can imagine, and not by the many people we cannot imagine " (pp. 106–107). " So long as the human heart is strong and the human reason weak, royalty will be strong because it appeals to diffused feeling, and republics weak because they appeal to the understanding " (p. 112). Again and again, Bagehot employs the parallel of magic and the mystery religions : " That which is mystical in its claims, that which is occult in its mode of action . . . is the sort of thing . . . which . . . comes home to the mass of men." (pp. 75–79). " The monarchy by its religious sanction now confirms all our political order. . . . It gives now a vast strength to the entire constitution, by enlisting on its behalf the credulous obedience of enormous masses " (p. 117). Bagehot (as he wrote in his new introduction of 1872) was " exceedingly afraid of the ignorant multitude of the new constituencies " created by that parliamentary reform which was contemplated when the book was written, and carried out in 1867. Britain was " a community in which primitive barbarism lay as a recognized basis to acquired civilization " (p. 111). " Those who doubt should go out into their kitchens " (p. 77). " The real question is," he says, " will they defer to wealth and rank and to the higher qualities of which these are the rough symbols and the common accompaniments ? " The continued deference of the masses to the classes could only be secured if the psychological analysis of British monarchy were confined to the *Fortnightly Review* and to literary treatises on the constitution. " Its mystery is its life. We must not let daylight upon magic " (p. 134).[1]

Bagehot wrote before the British people had become conscious that a new Empire has taken the place of that which we lost in 1783. But since Disraeli's premiership of 1874-80 and the Jubilee of 1887, Bagehot's psychological argument has constantly been used to prove the vital importance of the constitutional monarchy to the maintenance of the imperial connection. Mr. H. A. L. Fisher in his *Republican Tradition in Europe* (1911), says, " The taste for ritual, for playthings, for make-believe, is deeply rooted in human nature," that the colonists are " fascinated by the pomp of an ancient and dignified institution which they have no means of reproducing in their several communities " (p. 277). In similar language Mr. and Mrs. Webb wrote in 1920 that the King's " duty as a King is not the exercise of governmental power in any of its aspects, but . . . the performance of a whole series of rites and ceremonies, which lend the charm of historic continuity to the political institutions of the British race, and go far . . . to maintain the bond of union between the races and creeds of the Commonwealth of Nations that still styles itself the British Empire." [2]

[1] On the other hand, I have heard socialists argue, rather unconvincingly, as a reason for maintaining the monarchy, that the credulous loyalty of the property-owning classes may be useful to a socialist government.

[2] S. and B. Webb, *A Constitution for the Socialist Commonwealth of Great Britain* (1920), pp. 61, 62.

In the general discussion of the constitution of the empire which arose out of the Imperial Conference of 1917, the Crown was continually spoken of as " the great symbol of the unity of the Empire," or the " glittering emblem of our Imperial unity." The *Westminster Gazette* (June 20, 1917) once more used Bagehot's argument. " The King, as Emperor of India and titular head of the Empire, has the immense advantage of commanding allegiance without impinging upon government ; whereas an elective President would necessarily have defined powers and responsibilities which, in regard to the Empire, would either have to be openly and frankly nothing, or to encroach at some point or other upon the spheres of the self-governing Dominions."

Such being the generally accepted theory of British Constitutional monarchy, how in fact does that institution work ? The relation between a British monarch and his ministers at any given moment is a secret which is amazingly well kept, and which only becomes known about a generation after the events ; but in so far as the facts of nineteenth-century history are now known, they indicate that at no time in that century did the institution work as the theory required that it should work. No British monarch during the nineteenth century accepted the view of his position laid down in the constitutional treatises. Queen Victoria, for instance, was during her life believed by the public to be an exceptionally " constitutional " monarch ; but the publication of her letters for the period 1837–1861, of Disraeli's life for 1868–1880, and many other sources, now show that neither she, nor her husband, nor the Duke of Cambridge as Commander-in-Chief, nor Baron Stockmar, nor any other of her personal advisers, ever acted on the belief

that she was the figure-head of a " crowned republic."
Sir Sidney Lee, who has studied many unpublished documents, gives a typical description of Queen Victoria's
action in his account of the Denmark question in 1862–
1864. " She appealed," he says, " to the Cabinet to
aid her against the Prime Minister. She invited, too,
in the service of peace the private support of the leader
of the opposition, Lord Derby. She hinted that if
Parliament did not adopt a pacific and neutral policy she
would have to resort to a dissolution and let the country
decide between her and her Ministers." [1] Lord Esher,
who knew her well, said in an interesting lecture
(*Times*, March 6, 1909), " She never seemed to doubt
that the country was *hers*, that the Ministers were *her*
Ministers. . . . Ministers and Parliaments existed to
assist *her* to govern. . . . This outlook, with its pathetic
earnestness, and at times almost tragic persistence, was
the source of the Queen's influence, and sometimes the
cause of her few mistakes." At the end of the lecture
he says, " We owe to Queen Victoria the reinstatement
of the Monarchical principle in the eyes of all grave and
earnest men." Sometimes, as in the enormously important
case of the threatened war with the United States over
the Mason and Slidell incident in 1861, the Queen and
her personal advisers were in the right, and her ministers
were either persuaded by her at the time that they were
in the wrong, or came afterwards to acknowledge that
it was so. Most students would, however, now say that
she was more often in the wrong, especially when, as in
her determined opposition to the unity of Italy, she was
influenced by the Coburg family tradition. Very little is
now known about the political activities of Edward VII

[1] *Life of Queen Victoria*, p. 350.

or George V, but certain comments in the newspapers on British action during the war in respect of the Czar of Russia, the King of Greece, and the royal telegram to Marshal Pilsudski at the time of the Polish offensive of 1920, indicated that complaints may have been made of a court policy in foreign affairs sometimes separable from that of the Prime Minister.[1]

It may be contended that as against a united cabinet a British court policy must always be helpless. But cabinets are seldom united, and in any case the process of wearing down the determination of a strong-willed monarch involved during Queen Victoria's reign an almost incredible expenditure of time and temper. Even Disraeli once complained that the Queen wrote to him every day and telegraphed every hour.[2] When it was suggested that Lord Derby should succeed Disraeli as Premier in 1876 (a change which would have gone far to save us from the results of " backing the wrong horse " in the Near East) Lord Derby gave as his first reason for refusing that " he could never manage Her Majesty." [3]

Disraeli himself always believed that the monarchy

[1] See, e.g., *Evening Standard* (October 25th, 1918), and *Westminster Gazette* (July 22nd, 1920). M. Venezelos, *New Europe* (March 29th, 1917), p. 326, complained that the Allied Powers had expressly stipulated that his movement " should not be anti-dynastic."

[2] Childers, who was Secretary for War during the dispatch of the Egyptian expedition of 1882, mentions that in one day he received seventeen letters from the Queen or her private secretary (*Life of Hugh C. E. Childers*, Vol. II, p. 104).

[3] *Life of Disraeli*, Vol. V, p. 495. Gladstone in a letter to Bright (November 28th, 1879) which was intended to explain his position as to the acceptance of the premiership, gave, as a possible reason against acceptance, " Nothing could be so painful, I may almost say so odious to me, as to force myself, or be forced, upon the Queen," who notoriously detested him (*Life* by Morley, Vol. II, p. 599).

should be "real," always protested against the "Venetian Oligarchy" of parliamentary absolutism, and looked on the "management" of the Queen as one of the most important as well as the most amusing of his duties.[1] Liberal Ministers, on the other hand, constantly declared that the personal prerogative of the monarch did not exist, and constantly compromised with it.[2]

But even the power of a united cabinet, supported by a united parliamentary majority, to override the will of the monarch depends on the validity of the two "conventions of the constitution" which forbid the monarch to retain a ministry that has lost the confidence of the House of Commons, and require the monarch to assent to any law that has passed both Houses. No British monarch has retained in office a ministry against a definitely hostile vote of the House of Commons since 1784, or had refused to assent to a law passed by parliament since 1707. But, since the law-courts would probably recognize the legal right of the monarch to do both of these things, the only reliable safeguard against a breach of either convention is an agreement of all political parties that no minister should accept responsibility for any act which is (in the sense of either convention) "unconstitutional," and that, in particular, no War Minister should make himself responsible for a refusal of the army

[1] After Disraeli's victory at the election of 1874, Lady Ely wrote to him from Court, "My dear mistress will be very happy to see you again. . . . I think you understand her so well, *besides* appreciating her noble fine qualities (the italics are mine). (*Disraeli's Life*, Vol. V, p. 286).

[2] E.g. Gladstone, *Gleanings of Past Years*, Vol. I, p. 233. "It would be an evil and perilous day for the Monarchy were the prospective possessor of the Crown to assume or claim for himself final or preponderating, or even independent power in any one department of the State."

to carry out a parliamentary policy. If one of the great British parties declares that it is not bound by such an agreement, both conventions would, *ipso facto*, come to an end.

Now one of the effects of the severe social and political struggle which followed in Britain the Liberal victory of 1906 was that the Conservative Party denied, in a formal declaration of its leader, its acceptance of the convention which forbids the monarch to veto laws which have passed through their legally necessary stages in parliament. Mr. Bonar Law, speaking as leader of his party at Edinburgh on January 24th, 1913, said, " Suppose the Home Rule Bill, which involves as you know the use of British troops to drive loyal men out of our community —suppose that Bill had passed through all its stages and was waiting for the Sovereign to decide whether or not it would become law. What then would be the position of the Sovereign of this country ? Whatever he did, half of his people would think he had failed in his duty. If he refused to give his assent to it the whole Radical Party would be yelping at his heels on the ground that it was withheld in an unconstitutional way ; if he did give his assent to it, then one-half of his people would say he was giving his assent to a vital measure of which half the people did not approve, and that in such circumstances the assent ought not to be given." [1] That speech destroyed one of the two main conventions of our constitution. It made it certain that in any future political crisis in which the monarch personally sympathized with the view of a socially and politically powerful minority, his possible refusal to assent to a law " which had passed through all its stages," would in future be a vital element in the calculations of all statesmen.

[1] *Times* (January 25th, 1913).

Lord Halsbury, though not, like Mr. Bonar Law, the responsible leader of his party, held in 1913 an important position as having been Lord Chancellor for seventeen years, and as having during that period filled vacancies among the judges who would have to interpret the constitution with lawyers whose political opinions were as far as possible identical with his own. He said on November 5th, 1913, " It was said that the King's veto was abolished two hundred or three hundred years ago. . . . It is all nonsense to talk about the King's veto being abolished. He did not assent to that argument. He was of opinon—and he apologized for saying so—that it was part of the British constitution that if something was to become law and to bind their liberties that something must be assented to by the King, Lords, and Commons " (*Times*, November 6th, 1913). Lord Halsbury would probably say that it was the Liberals who destroyed the constitutional convention when they passed the Parliament Act (by a threat to create Peers) in 1911. But the important thing is not the moral responsibility of this party or that, but the fact that the convention that the King may not on his own judgment veto legislation is no longer generally accepted, and therefore no longer exists.[1]

[1] The effect of the belief that this convention is no longer valid was seen in the Home Rule crisis of July 20th, 1914, when the consideration of the " Amending Bill " was suddenly postponed, and a conference of party leaders called by the King was substituted. The *Daily News* (July 21st, 1914), said that " it is stated by those who have the best means of knowing the King's mind that he now intends to withhold his assent from the Home Rule Bill unless an amending Bill is presented to him along with it." The parliamentary correspondent of the *Daily News* said (July 21st) that " in the gallery of peers sat . . . Lord Stamfordham, the private secretary of the King, whose day it was." Lord Courtney

Mr. Bonar Law in his speech of January 24th, 1913, gave, as the first reason in his argument that the King should reject the Home Rule Bill, the fact that the Bill involved " the use of British troops to drive loyal men out of our community." Since the Restoration of Charles II it has been held by most British Statesmen that the obedience of the army to the civil power is best secured by the concentration of the instincts and habits of military loyalty and discipline on the person of the monarch. Some observers of the process by which the new armies of 1914–1916 were formed claimed a real effectiveness for this policy. Mr. " Ian Hay," the clever author of *The First Hundred Thousand*, ends his description of the conversion of a typical radical private into an enthusiastic devotee of the monarchy with the words, " And yet there are people who tell us that the formal ' O.H.M.S.' (On His Majesty's Service) is a mere relic of antiquity." [1] When, as I have already described,[2] the officers of the Curragh camp declared themselves in 1914 unwilling to march into Ulster, the Liberal ministry seems to have decided to use the personal interposition of the King for the restoration of military discipline. It will not be known to more than perhaps forty people for the next twenty years what really happened in Buckingham Palace on March 23, 1914—how the " terms of peace " were drawn up, and under what circumstances they were

in the House of Lords, July 20th, said, " I am afraid this step will be viewed by the world at large as something like a supersession of Parliament." The ministry accepted responsibility for the King's action ; but one may doubt whether if the convention against the royal veto on legislation had been intact, the postponement would have taken place.

[1] *The First Hundred Thousand*, p. 24.
[2] See Chapter VI, p. 135.

repudiated by the Cabinet at the cost of the resignation
of the Secretary for War and the military members of
the Army Council.   One guesses that the King may have
shown a high degree of personal good sense ; and that
if George V had been born with the temperament of
George III, or with that of the German Kaiser, the
injury done to the British Constitution both then and
throughout the long crisis of 1906–1914 might have been
very much greater than it was.   But the whole incident
made it clear that while in future it may be possible for
us to argue either that unrestricted parliamentary government is the best constitution for our modern needs, or
that a " balance " between the power of parliament and
the personal power of the monarchy is better, yet there
is one argument which it will be impossible for us to
use—that our existing constitution makes parliamentary
government in a serious crisis both absolute and secure.[1]
Not only have responsible leaders denied the supposed
restrictions on royal power, but in times of national
excitement less responsible politicians will always be
found ready to appeal to the personal loyalty of the army
for the monarch as a means of opposing a parliamentary

---

[1] Colonel Repington, long known as military member of the
Times staff, says in his published diary (*The First World War*,
1920), " Had a talk with Carson about the Ulster business. He
told me how near we were to an explosion, that the government
had determined to arrest the chief leaders, that he had arranged
to send one word, H.X., over the wire to Belfast, and this was to
be the signal for the seizure of the Customs throughout Ulster.
He called to see the King, and told Stamfordham [Lord Stamfordham, private secretary to the King] exactly what was going to
happen, and the arrest of the leaders was promptly stopped."
If Colonel Repington accurately reports Sir Edward Carson, the
question whether the King did or did not stop the Liberal plans
for dealing with the Ulster rebellion is not much more important
than the fact that Sir Edward Carson acted on the expectation
that he would do so, and on the belief that he had done so.

majority. During the war the newspaper most read by British soldiers was Mr. Horatio Bottomley's *John Bull*, and Mr. Bottomley thought it good policy on March 4th, 1916, to issue over his own name a flaming appeal headed, " Let's have a Dictator ! Suspend the constitution— Let the King be King." [1]

If one looks away from Britain to the states which have copied the British political model, one finds that " constitutional " monarchy has not in times of crisis remained " constitutional." In Italy, Holland, Roumania, Bulgaria, Sweden, and Norway, during the war, no actual conflict took place between crown and parliament, but in all these countries, except perhaps Norway, the personal power of the crown seems to have been strengthened by conditions arising out of the war. In Bulgaria the King seems to have been practically his own Prime Minister, and in Greece a King whose constitutional position was obviously copied from that of the British crown was able with the support of army officers appointed by himself to oppose, for years, M. Venezelos and a large majority of the Chamber.

Outside the British Empire, indeed, the experience of the war seems to have produced a wide-spread disbelief in the likelihood of the sincere maintenance of the convention of constitutional monarchy by a monarch who feels himself strong enough to disregard it, and a general preference by opponents of personal government for a republic rather than a constitutional monarchy. Mr. Fisher could write in 1911 in his *Republican Tradition*

---

[1] It was interesting, on the other hand, to notice that during September 1920 many writers in the Liberal papers urged the King, in the question of the hunger-strike of the Mayor of Cork, to use against the Cabinet the prerogative of mercy.

in Europe, "There can be little question that, since 1870, the cause of republicanism has made no substantial progress in Europe. France is still the only great European Republic. . . ." (p. 270), and again, "The accepted formula of political progress seems, if we are to be guided by the recent examples of Russia and Turkey, to be constitutional monarchy rather than republicanism" (p. 284). In 1920, outside the British Empire, not more than perhaps a fifth of the inhabitants of the globe are living under monarchical institutions of any kind, and all movements towards monarchical restoration seem to aim not at constitutional monarchy but at absolute monarchy based on military power. In 1917 a well-known writer in the *Manchester Guardian* asked whether we thought that the Russian progressives would be able to "launch into the Russian world our weird metaphysics of limited monarchy."[1]

But obvious as are the difficulties and dangers in the practical working of the British expedient of constitutional monarchy, our ultimate verdict on that expedient must depend, I believe, mainly upon our estimate of its central idea—the monarchy as a symbol by means of which the instinct of personal obedience can be used to support an impersonal government. This problem is really one of the relative advantages and disadvantages of two kinds of symbols. As long as man, or any other animal, is dealing only with objects coming directly within the range of his senses, and directly stimulating his instincts, no symbolism is required. But when man entered into relation with things too large or too distant for direct perception, he had to represent these things to himself and others by symbols, which were usually

[1] Letter signed H. (*Manchester Guardian*, March 22nd, 1917).

either words or pictures or tangible specimens of the things. If an Italian, for instance, in the reign of Augustus bought a field, he might receive from the seller either a clod of earth from the field, or a written or oral contract of sale. The clod of earth had, as a symbol, the advantage that it directly stimulated in a stupid or ignorant man the instinct of ownership; though it had the disadvantage that it might behave like a clod as well as like a symbol, might, for instance, turn itself into mud or dust. A verbal contract involved a severer initial effort of imagination; but, when once the effort had been made, it was easier to turn the contract-symbol than the clod-symbol into the detailed knowledge of the relationship of the purchaser to the land which constituted in both cases the " meaning " of the symbol; and unless he understood that meaning the purchaser was not likely to act wisely. Primitive man, in propitiating the gods, used the scapegoat as a symbol of the herd, and the priest-king as a symbol of the tribe; but the connotative words " herd " and " tribe," when he learnt to use them, were, even though they made a less direct and vivid appeal to his instincts, more effective instruments for the daily work of pasturage and government.

Now Bagehot's constitutional monarch represents the same psychological expedient as the clod or the scapegoat, and is, in fact, the direct descendant of the symbolic priest-king. Mr. Balfour, speaking on July 22nd 1910, said that the President of a federal British Republic would " represent the abstraction of a constitution and not the personal head of an empire." If Mr. Balfour had been careful to compare like things to like, he would have said that the words " British Commonwealth " would be an abstraction of a community, and that a constitutional

monarch is a specimen of the community used as a symbol
for it. The first advantage of the monarch as symbol
is that, like other specimen-symbols, he requires no effort
of the imagination; the words "British Commonwealth" have to be explained to a child of six, and the
sight of the King has not. The second advantage is
that the sight of him directly and easily stimulates
instinctive love and loyalty. But one disadvantage of
the monarch as symbol is that he may behave as a
human being as well as a symbol; he may be insane
like George III, or self-willed like Victoria. And another
disadvantage is that a man who only knows that he has
seen and loves the King has not such a useful working
idea of his relation to his government as has a man who
has learnt the meaning of the words British Commonwealth.

I am here, of course, oversimplifying the psychological
facts; for many of those who consciously know the
monarch to be a symbol may yet feel personal loyalty
to him as a symbolic person; Disraeli saw political facts
as clearly as any statesman of his time, and yet he could
work himself up into a passion of quasi-personal loyalty
for Queen Victoria. But these more complicated states
of mind are apt (like "eating caviare upon principle" [1])
to lose much of the driving force of simple instinctive
reaction, and may be destroyed by a sudden sense of
absurdity. Carlyle's hero in *Sartor Resartus* only laughed
once in his life—at the idea of men's conscious loyalty
to a "cast-metal King." It is more important that
such complicated states of mind are apt to encourage
among intelligent people an evasion of the real difficulties
in any constitutional relation.

All these advantages and disadvantages may be clearly

[1] See my *Human Nature in Politics*, p. 183.

seen in the use of the British monarch as a "symbol of unity" for the British empire. The crowds of Sydney and Ottawa were moved in 1920 to enthusiastic affection by the sight of the Prince of Wales, who was both a symbol of the empire, and an unusually attractive specimen of it. But at the Imperial Conference of 1921 the premiers of Great Britain and the Dominions and the representatives of India will have to turn both their specimen-symbols and their word-symbols of the empire into the best "meanings" they can, and then take action which will affect a quarter of the human beings on the globe. They will have to decide whether the Imperial connection shall be (in the phrase of the *Westminster Gazette*) "openly and frankly nothing," or "an encroachment at some point or another" upon the independence of its parts, with no third alternative. Hitherto the constitutional monarchy has enabled them to avoid the painful choice between eating their cake and having it. Now that the choice has to be made, I think that our imperial statesmen and their constituents would have been in a better condition to make it, if the word-symbol "British Commonwealth" had been in more general use, and if we had been less insistent in using the monarch as a sacred and all-sufficing specimen-symbol.

Sometimes, of course, insistence on the supreme importance of the Crown as "the keystone of the imperial arch" is caused by a belief that time is a safer guide than thought. I have the greatest possible admiration for the keenness and objectivity of Mr. Smuts' mind; but I always feel that beneath his real enthusiasm for the Crown as an institution lies an expectation that the Crown will hide from statesmen and voters in Great Britain the development of the Empire on lines which they might refuse consciously to accept. And when British Ministers echo his words, I sometimes feel that they also are expecting that, if we put off the necessity of decision, imperial development will take place on lines different to those desired by Mr. Smuts. Time, however, on this question is running out.

But it is in world co-operation rather than imperial co-operation that the advantage of verbal abstraction over the symbolic specimen is greatest. I have already argued that the possibility of world-peace founded on world-purpose depends mainly on our ability to calculate the effects of world-war, and to derive a sufficiently powerful impulse from our calculations. In world co-operation, as in imperial co-operation, and in the internal co-operation of single nations, the practical wisdom of our decisions largely depends on the truth of those pictures of our fellows which we use both for our conscious and for our subconscious thought. A Middlesbrough iron-moulder will be more likely to vote for a kind and wise policy in British India if he thinks of India, not as " the brightest jewel in the British Crown," but as three hundred million human beings for whose fate he has his share of personal responsibility, who are troubled each week, more keenly than he is troubled, about food and clothing and housing, and who sometimes feel, though less often than he feels, the vague stirrings of political and social hope. And because the racial and cultural types of mankind are unlike as well as like each other, and a true realization of unlikeness may stimulate the instinct of hatred, world-peace also depends on the voter's ability to think of all the eighteen hundred millions of mankind as a part of that universe for which, as a whole, he feels pity or hope but seldom hatred. It will be better still if he conceives, as the average civilized man can now be taught to conceive, of our social heritage of civilization as a possession to which all races can contribute, and from which all can draw. It is easier to train a recruit or a boy-scout to cheer for King and Country than to make him understand that a man who believes that his national culture is of value to mankind may do well to face death rather than allow it to be destroyed. But in the longer processes of history it is the soldiers who, as Cromwell said, " know what they are fighting for and love what they know " that will do the most lasting service to the world, and will, when they fight, leave least bitterness behind. It is a real hindrance to such a conception of the relation of men to mankind when the citizens of one state think, whether truly or falsely, of other states not as communities of men like themselves, but as the obedient subjects of a different monarch.

We cannot use a symbol which deceives our own people without the danger that it may deceive others. If the German liberals of 1849 had succeeded in making a German Federal Republic, French and British liberals would have found it much easier to popularize in Britain the idea of a Europe inhabited by human beings who could all help or hurt each other. And the German social-democrats and progressives might have had more influence over German foreign policy before the war if so many Germans had not thought of Britain as an embodiment of the personal " encircling-policy " of Edward VII. Kant and Mazzini tried to analyse the moral and intellectual conditions of permanent peace, and they both stipulated that the European nations should think of themselves and be thought of by others as alike in that they were republics. A real understanding between

Britain and America is made difficult because so many Americans are still able at Presidential elections to hate Britain as a brutal monarchy; and the sympathy of mind and feeling between British and Chinese democrats which is one of the splendid possibilities of civilization would be made more possible if the " weird metaphysics " of our constitution were out of the way.

No British writer can ignore the strength of the British political tradition that any institution whose discussion arouses passion, and which is working without obvious and immediate bad results should be left undiscussed. But the whole of this book is meaningless if the effort required to make our own working conception of the world resemble as near as may be the facts is not as worth while in politics as it is in the natural sciences. Especially is it true that " democracy," in Sir Arthur Steel-Maitland's words, " will only be equal to its task if it can see through make-believes to reality." [1]

British democrats should therefore, I believe, at least insist on knowing what the personal prerogative power of the Crown at this moment is. " The Queen," said Bagehot, " has a hundred . . . powers, which waver between reality and desuetude, and which would cause a protracted and very interesting legal argument if she tried to exercise them. Some good lawyer ought to write a careful book to say which of these powers really are usable and which are obsolete." [2] We should not have to wait till those powers are tested, as they were in March 1914, by an actual crisis. Suggestions, again, are often made which would strengthen either the personal prerogative or the prerogative atmosphere, as

[1] *Times* (November 21st, 1916).
[2] *English Constitution*, p. 133.

when Sir Sidney Low urged (*Times*, February 17th, 1916) that "Windsor should be the seat of the proposed Imperial Parliament." In the British War Office and Foreign Office steps are daily being taken which either strengthen or weaken the tradition that the army and the diplomatic corps have a different relation to the person of the monarch than have other forms of government service.

And, even if any public agitation of the question can be postponed without loss, the task of invention cannot. Extraordinarily little thought has been given to the question of non-monarchical executive government. No one has even begun to compare the working of the various republican institutions which have been set up since the war. It ought to be possible to invent some form that would work more smoothly in internal politics than either the plebiscitary presidency of the United States or the particular kind of parliamentary presidency which is found in France, and which could be applied to the new problem of the British Empire. Meanwhile if the new republics all over the world desire to make use of the primitive instinct of personal loyalty they can do so more safely by the expedient of personification than by the older expedient of a symbolic person. The third French Republic has proved enormously more stable than its predecessors because the ordinary Frenchman directs his affections rather to the personification of *La République* than to the person of the President. And at this moment of the world's history anything which increases the prestige of the idea of majority rule against the disruptive forces of racial or class or military minorities, will be a help to human progress.

CHAPTER XI

SCIENCE

IN the preceding chapters I have discussed particular forms of thought, and particular social and political expedients, with a constant fear that they will prove to be inadequate, even when taken all together, to preserve us against worse disasters than those from which we are now suffering. In the next two chapters I shall discuss two conceptions of the universe—two " world-outlooks," if one may so translate the German word *Weltanschauungen*, on behalf of both of which it is claimed that they can so penetrate and illuminate our particular forms of thought and action as to make a good life possible for all mankind. The first of these " world-outlooks " is Science, the general conception of cause and effect which underlies " scientific method " in thought but which has never been embodied in a formal creed or an organized institution. The second is the tradition embodied in the organization of the Church.

The idea of Science is, as Mr. William Archer has said, the Apollo of the modern world, " Destroyer and Healer in one " (*Daily News*, October 7th, 1918). Since the first conscious use of scientific method the world-outlook of science has given mankind a constantly growing sense of power in dealing with their environment. It is because we assume that the same effects always follow the same

causes in our environment, that we have learnt to make
world war, and may some day learn to make world peace.
The conception of an immutable relation of cause and
effect has inevitably extended from our idea of our environment to our idea of ourselves and our conduct, and our
growing knowledge of human psychology offers us in this
region also a new sense of power. But it is a serious
misfortune for mankind that the idea of causation in
conduct leads straight to the old dilemma of necessity
and free will. When a man thinks of the whole universe
as a finite interrelated unity he willingly submits to the
conception of universal necessity ; but when he thinks
of his own behaviour, or that of his neighbours', as facts
separable from the rest of the universe, he often finds
himself possessed with a passionate conviction that the
human will is somehow " free " ; that the issues of his
own struggles against temptation or his own choice of
means and ends are not predetermined ; and that his
neighbours, when they do things for which he blames or
praises them, could have acted differently. The argument that his own volition, and his own sense of freedom
in exercising it, are as immutably the results of ante-
cedent causes as anything else in the universe seems to
him in such a mood to be a mere verbal trap.

When I ask myself what is the truth behind these two
opposite convictions, I find myself guessing that to an
intellect higher than or different from our own it may be
evident that everything that happens is both free and
caused. Somewhere in Mars, or on the other side of the
Milky Way, or in the universe of Einstein, there may be
a being who would find it hard to realize our difficulty
in seeing that force and life, the flow of a river between its
banks, and the dart of a fish upstream, are manifestations

16

of the same thing ; and that, if one must use human words, it is nearer the truth to say that everything is alive than that everything is dead. But just as the rhinoceros, by the structure of its spinal column, is prevented from seeing, and therefore from imagining its own tail,[1] so man, owing either to his ignorance or to some fact in his cerebral or cellular or atomic structure, is prevented from seeing more than one side at a time of the problem of free will and causation. Yet, if the rhinoceros ever evolved something like human intelligence while retaining the general outline of its present anatomy, one can imagine that a future rhinoceros might ultimately, by observation of his neighbours' tails and introspection as to the kinetic sensations accompanying the stimulation of his own tail-muscles, come to believe if not to realize that he himself had a tail. And mankind in like manner may ultimately form a conception of human motive which will enable us to believe if not to realize that freedom and causation are two sides of one shield. Perhaps we may get help in this respect from the spread into common thought of new conceptions of infinity. The conception of determinism is closely related to the idea of the universe as finite ; but we can all try now to conceive not only of space as infinite, but also of the atoms, whose finite number and indivisible simplicity used to fix a narrow limit to the complexity of the universe, as being, perhaps, each of them an infinitely complex individual.[2]

[1] See Professor F. Wood Jones's admirable *Arboreal Man* (1916), p. 167. " A tapir . . . can see but little of its body, and can examine with its tactile nose only a very limited portion of it. . . . An arboreal animal gains a precise knowledge of its own body ; it can realize its form, and it has, to a certain extent, a working idea of the alterations in its form which are the outcomes of the movements of its several parts."

[2] I owe this suggestion of the possible effect of the idea of the

In early human thought, the problem of free will and determinism tended to take religious forms. In the Greek tragedies the will of man, though conscious of itself, is as helpless against fate as a withered leaf against the wind. From Augustine till the middle of the seventeenth century, men discussed free will as a problem in the interpretation of the Christian dogma of the omniscience of God; since God is omniscient, he must know all that we shall do, as well as all that we have done or are doing. It was, however, so difficult to harmonize predestinarianism with the Christian ethical conceptions of sin and holiness, that no one could prophesy how any rigorously logical predestinarian thinker would in fact behave. He might become a persecutor like Calvin, or a lunatic like Cowper.

In 1667 Milton, in his *Paradise Lost*, told how the fallen angels " reasoned high, of . . .Fixed fate, free will, foreknowledge absolute, and found no end, in wandering mazes lost." But in 1651 Hobbes had published his *Leviathan*, and the Royal Society was founded in 1660. Since the middle of the seventeenth century, the application of determinism to human conduct has mainly used arguments drawn, not from divine foreknowledge, but from the observed uniformities of physics or astronomy. In his *De Homine* (1658) Hobbes writes that " every one is compelled to seek what for him is good and avoid what for him is bad . . . by a necessity not less than that which compels the stone to fall downward." [1] Already in Hobbes one can trace that which was to

infinite complexity and individuality of the atom upon the psychological reaction of the idea of determinism to Mr. James Harvey Robinson.

[1] *De Homine*, quoted by Halévy, *La Formation du Radicalisme Philosophique*, Vol. I, p. 277.

prove the main practical danger of determinist sociology.
There are certain simple facts in human behaviour which
it is much easier to compare to the behaviour of a falling
stone than other and more complex facts. These primitive instinctive processes seem to us to be much more
inevitable in their action than the processes which involve
doubt and choice. When Horace says, "Expel nature
with a pitchfork, and she will always return," it is hard
for us not to feel that the instincts which he calls nature
are more predetermined than the conscious decision
which he calls the pitchfork. Hobbes' own list of effective political motives contained little but fear in the
governed and the desire of power in the governor. Every
other motive seemed to him to be unscientific, and therefore, by the subconscious process of psychological logic,
either non-existent or existing illegitimately. Helvetius
in 1758 uses a conception of human motive even simpler
than that of Hobbes; "If the physical universe," he
says, "is subject to the laws of motion, the moral universe
is not less subject to the laws of interest,"[1] and by
"interest" he means nothing more than the desire for
pleasure and the avoidance of pain. Bentham took his
philosophy of motive in the main from Helvetius,[2] and
Bentham's political ideas, as distinguished from his legal
ideas, reached the British public mainly through James
Mill. James Mill in the *Essay on Government* (1829),
which was widely accepted as "the gospel of scientific
radicalism," wrote that "the positions we have already
established with regard to human nature, and which we

[1] Helvetius, *De l'Esprit*, Discours II, chap. ii.
[2] "What Bacon was to the physical world Helvetius was to
the moral" (Bentham in the fragment quoted by Halévy, *La
Formation du Radicalisme Philosophique*, Vol. I, p. 290).

assume as foundations are these, That the actions of men are governed by their desires, That their desires are directed to pleasure and the relief of pain as ends and to wealth and power as the principal means, That to the desire of those means there is no limit " (p. 7).

Every student of the history of economic thought is familiar with the effect during the first half of the nineteenth century of this tendency on " the classical " English economists ; and on those whom their ideas reached at first or second hand. Ricardo, writing in 1817 on the effects of non-deterrent Poor Laws, said : " The principle of gravitation is not more certain than the tendency of such laws to change wealth and power into misery and weakness " ; [1] and, in spite of occasional attempts to protect himself from oversimplification in his reasoning, Ricardo ordinarily assumes that men will be inevitably guided by simple economic motives. Macculloch definitely denied the usefulness of any other motive. " It is," he wrote in the last paragraph of his *Principles of Political Economy* (1825), " by the spontaneous and unconstrained but well protected efforts of individuals to improve their condition, and to rise in the world, and by these efforts only, that nations become rich and powerful." [2] And having denied their usefulness, he proceeded to ignore in his economic analysis their existence.

But the statesmen and employers who looked to the economists for guidance had not only to think, but also to take practical decisions by which the lives of men and women and children were affected. While so doing they

---

[1] *Principles of Political Economy* (1817), p. 114.
[2] It is noteworthy that in the fourth edition (1849) the words " and by these efforts only " are omitted.

discovered in themselves comparatively complex and variable motives, such as love or pity, which were much less easily assumed to be analogous to physical laws like gravitation than were the simple and apparently uniform attractive and repulsive " economic " forces of pleasure and pain. What was the relation of these more complex motives to the " laws of political economy " ? The statesman or manufacturer was apt to act on the half-conscious assumption that economic " laws " were rules of conduct which the economists commanded (with all the authority of " Science " behind them) mankind to obey ; but which any man was free at his own risk to disobey. A hard-hearted manufacturer, therefore, deliberately attempted to inhibit his own feelings of pity, and justified himself for brutal exploitation of women and children by saying that he was " obeying the laws of political economy " ; while a kind-hearted statesman pleaded for a policy of mercy with the feeling that he was a rebel against law. When in 1834 Lord Althorpe asked the House of Commons to maintain the Poor Law with modifications, instead of abolishing it as some of the more logical economists desired, he said, " He was of opinion that a well-regulated system of Poor Laws would be of great benefit to the country. He was aware that he was now expressing an opinion contrary to the more strict principles of political economy. Indeed those principles went further, for they even prohibited the exercise of private charity. . . . But as long as we were accessible not only to the feelings of religion but to the dictates of humanity, we must be convinced that the support of those who were really helpless and really unable to provide for themselves, was not only justified but a sacred duty imposed on those who had the ability to assist the dis-

tressed " (April 17th, 1834). Sir James Macintosh in
1832, during the debate on the first effective Factory
Act, said that he " was anxious to avow himself a political
economist, but at the same time . . . he would not allow
even the principles of political economy to be acces-
sory to the infliction of torture " (February 1st, 1832).
To men and women like Archbishop Whately, or Harriet
Martineau, or even Ricardo, this simplification of human
motive had the further half-conscious attraction that it
created a world which was, like the cricket news or chess
column in the newspaper, far easier to think about than
the world of concrete happenings to concrete and complex
human beings.

From the publication of Ricardo's *Principles* in 1817,
until the revolutionary year 1848, most people thought of
the conception of scientific determinism, and the simplification of human motive which was associated with it,
as supporting the position of the propertied classes in
Europe. But already in 1813 Robert Owen's *New View
of Society* had shown that the conception could be used
to support a scheme of revolutionary philanthropy, and
from 1820 to 1830 Hodgskin and the other English pre-
cursors of Marx turned Ricardo's economic analysis
from a middle-class argument for capitalism into a working-
class argument for revolution. Marx himself and Lassalle
based the " scientific ·socialism " which became the
" gospel of the working classes " on the same simplified
determinism. A Marxist believer in the materialist
explanation of history could henceforward agree with
the disciples of the " classical " economists in reducing
all motive to the simple desire for pecuniary gain. When
certain German socialist deputies visited Brussels in
September 1914 to remonstrate with the Belgian socialists

for resisting the German invasion, Dr. Koster, editor of the Socialist *Hamburger Echo*, is said to have argued, " You ought to have let us pass ; you would have been handsomely compensated by our government." The Belgians asked whether no weight should be given to national honour, international treaties, and the rights of free peoples. " National honour," Dr. Koster is said to have replied, " that is mere middle-class idealism with which socialists have nothing to do . . . does not historical materialism teach us that the development of the proletariat is intimately bound up with the economic prosperity of the nation ? " A Belgian said that the only thing they seemed to possess in common was a stomach ; but that on the Belgian side there was a heart as well.[1]

Darwin's demonstration that human instincts could be brought within the conception of biological evolution increased, both in Germany and elsewhere, this tendency to simplify human motive. The word *Realpolitiker*, for instance, means a man who believes that the political relation between human beings should be conceived of scientifically in the simple terms of " the struggle for life " ; that any motives which do not lead up to that struggle are unscientific and illegitimate ; and that therefore it is his duty, if he feels love or pity for his neighbours, or a desire to take their good into his consideration, to ignore or if necessary to inhibit that feeling and desire.[2]

Bergson originally offered his " élan vital " as a means of

[1] W. S. Sanders, *Pan-German Socialism*, pp. 22–23. I have heard M. Vandervelde give a similar account of this interview.

[2] General Lord Rawlinson, who has since been made Commander-in-Chief in India, is reported (*Daily News*, May 5th, 1920) to have said, " I am much afraid that war is a law of nature. From the very microbes in your blood to the great contests between nations the whole thing is a struggle for existence."

avoiding the dilemma of determinism, by conceiving of uncalculated human impulse as outside that sphere of causation in which rational logic must work. But the syndicalists in France before the war, and the Bolsheviks in Russia during and after the war, associated Bergsonism with Marx's "materialist explanation of history," and treated it as one more reason why they should ignore in their own conduct any but the simplest motives. Mr. Julius West, for instance, who spoke Russian, and had often talked with the chiefs of the Petrograd Soviet, wrote (May 5th, 1918) in the *New Statesman* about the current use of the Russian word "*stikhiyny*," which means, he says, "elemental," perhaps "intuitive." "One finds Bolshevik leaders justifying most of the things for which they are responsible by the statement that they result from elemental forces. Revolution . . . is a matter of these forces rather than of deliberate organization." [1] And any one who has had much intercourse with those British or American artisans who have formed their habits of thought on popular expositions of Marxianism, must have met men and women, who if they were in power would feel themselves bound to show the same kind of scientifically conscientious ruthlessness as Lenin or Trotsky.

In the United States the number of serious students of sociology and politics is very much larger than in England ; and a general acquaintance with the technical

[1] In a wireless statement (published in the *Daily News*, September 16th, 1920) Lenin says, "Executions seem to have aroused Dittmann's indignation, but in such circumstances as indicated it is natural that revolutionary workers execute Mensheviks, a fact which, of course, cannot very well appeal to him." I do not know what Russian word is here translated "natural." The final phrase may indicate a vague feeling in Lenin's mind that it is difficult to draw from his own philosophy a generally applicable rule of human conduct.

terms of those sciences is much more widely spread. In
the universities, in the newspapers, and in ordinary conversation, psychological terms are used where an Englishman would not expect them. This fact appears sometimes to produce the incidental, and, as it appears to me,
undesirable effect of increasing the feeling of helplessness
in the individual citizen when faced by great movements
of opinion among tens of millions of his fellow citizens.
That feeling often seems to paralyze the personal initiative
without which democracy is the worst possible form of
government, and to be heightened by forms of thought
which treat the impulses of the majority as more capable
of scientific treatment than the impulses of the individual.
I have been shown by an able academic thinker a plotted
curve illustrating a certain tendency, and on saying that
such a curve should be a stimulus to individual action
in opposition to the tendency, have been told that I am
apparently a believer in the obsolete " great man theory,"
and " preaching theory " ; and I have known American
progressives who received an appeal for a protest against
what they themselves believed to be gross oppression to
be satisfied to answer that it was " a case of mass-
psychology." The British Labour Party in its eloquent
manifesto *Labour and the New Social Order* pleads for the
application of " scientific method " to politics ; " In the
still undeveloped Science of Society, the Labour Party
stands for increased study, for the scientific investigation
of each succeeding problem, for the deliberate organization
of research, and for a much more rapid dissemination among
the whole people of all the science that exists."[1] Admirable

---

[1] *Labour and the New Social Order* (1918). Mr. Sidney Webb
in a letter (as Labour candidate) to the electors of London University, said that the policy of his party " calls for knowledge
and the scientific method and sustained and disinterested thought."

as that plea is, it will not have its full effect unless the members of the Labour Party learn to avoid the habit of separating the facts of human motive into those which are " scientific " and those which are not ; and they are not likely to do so unless they receive more help than they do at present from professed students. The students of the physical sciences often seem indeed to deny that the moral sciences have any right to the common name.[1] A physiological psychologist so able as Professor J. B. Watson, rejoices in the fact that " It is possible to write a psychology . . . and . . . never to use the terms consciousness, mental states, mind, content, will, imagery, and the like " ;[2] as if things that one does not mention will cease to exist. On the other hand, the metaphysical philosophers who associate human will with divine purpose sometimes, while insisting that the human will exists,

---

[1] In 1916 a number of the most distinguished British scientists published a manifesto on the neglect of " what is called science " or " physical science," and explained that " By these terms we mean the ascertained facts and principles of mechanics, chemistry, physics, biology, geography and geology." The manifesto urged that these subjects should be given " a preponderating or at least an equal share of marks " in the examination for the Civil Service. No reference was made to the sciences of economics, psychology, history, and jurisprudence, which are directly related to the art of administration. At the conference held to advocate the manifesto, all the speakers confined themselves to a comparison between the educational value of the laboratory sciences and of Greek and Latin literature (*The Neglect of Science*, Harrison & Son, 1916). Sir William Ramsay in his evidence before the Royal Commission on the Civil Service (January 10th, 1913), said that the Civil Service as a whole " can be divided into two classes—the scientific and technically trained persons and the administrators . . . administrators might be very largely dispensed with because the scientific persons are capable of the amount of administration necessary to administer their departments " (question 22, 578).

[2] *Behaviour* (1914), p. 9.

deny to the psychologists the right to think about it Mr. Ernest Barker, for instance, argues against " those English sociologists like McDougall and Graham Wallas who seek to find in psychology the key to social phenomena. . . . To analyse the processes of social instinct that lie in the dim background of a society now united in the pursuit of a common moral object is not to explain the real nature or the real cause of such a society." The " pursuit of a common moral object " is not, apparently, part of the legitimate subject-matter of psychological science.

CHAPTER XII

THE CHURCH

In August 1920 the Archbishop of Canterbury issued, on behalf of the Lambeth Conference of two hundred and fifty-two British and American bishops of the Anglican Communion, a letter " to all men and women of good will," and especially to those " beyond the frontiers of the Christian Society . . . who have been watching, in deep concern, the wasting of the moral resources of the world during these recent years. . . . We bespeak their considerate attention. To them the future of the Christian Church can never be unimportant . . . the strengthening of the individual and the cementing of society are the very things which the world, on the morrow of the supreme catastrophe of the war, clearly needs for the re-ordering of its life." [1] In the Encyclical Letter issued from the Conference, the Archbishop says that " the sense of nationality seems to be a natural instinct," but that " the love which Christ pours into the hearts that are His, makes men cease to hate each other because they belong to different nations." [1]

Dr. Gore (then Bishop of Oxford) made in 1915 a similar appeal on behalf of that sacramental conception of Christianity which is now the most powerful force in the Anglican, as it has always been the dominant force in

[1] *The Church Times* (August 13th, 1920).

the Roman Communion.　" The central idea of the Bible is that the knowledge and worship of God is to express itself in a visible and tangible human fellowship, and in the New Testament it is apparent that this fellowship must be Catholic, that is, must be supernatural.　The very idea of the Sacraments, which are social ceremonies of incorporation and sharing together, is to identify the idea of personal union with God with the idea of fellowship in the community. . . . The religious idea of the Catholic Church (which if it is to be truly Christian must be fundamentally independent of national organization) is to be the handmaid of such an organization of nations as shall subordinate the nation to humanity. . . . A nation can re-construct itself, if it will, with a conscious corporate aim and effect . . . but its efforts and its aspirations must be such as culminate in the worship not of a national God . . . but of the only true God, who has no preferences for nation over nation, but wills that all should realize themselves in mutual service, and has founded a Catholic Church to show to men of good will the true path of human progress." [1]

No " man of good will " can read these eloquent words without sympathy with the hope that a religion which emphasizes the reality of human volition and sees that volition in relation to the good which is in the whole universe may strengthen the weak forces which make for world peace and a conscious world purpose.　But the " considerate attention " for which the Archbishop pleads requires that we should ask what influence organized Christianity and especially Catholic and Anglican Christianity, did in fact exercise throughout " the supreme catastrophe of the war."　The war is still so recent, and

[1] Sermon in Birmingham, *Church Times* (October 8th, 1915).

the disruptive forces which it loosed are still so active, that it is difficult to find any incident in the war on which the moral judgment of mankind is now agreed. Perhaps the German invasion of Belgium in 1914 comes nearest to such an incident ; or the initiation of unlimited submarine warfare in 1917. On the treatment of Serbia by Austria in 1914 there is not so complete an agreement ; but here too the judgment of mankind may be said to have fairly declared itself. What influence on those events was exercised by the Catholic and Lutheran Churches in Germany, and the Catholic Church in Austria ? During the war I read the little evidence on this point which was available, and since the war I have asked every German or other observer whom I have met and who could give me first-hand information. The evidence seems to point unmistakably to an inverse statistical correlation between membership of those churches, and an attitude of protest against the national wrong-doing. Thousands of men and women were imprisoned in Germany and Austria for protesting, but I have not heard that any of them (except where, as with the Poles in Posen, and the Czechs in Bohemia, membership of a rival nationality was in question) were members of any recognized Christian body. And those political parties which were most closely identified with the Churches were most eager in supporting the actions now condemned.[1] Many observers since the

[1] Innumerable cases of this were published during the war. I may quote as an instance a resolution of the clericalist Centre Party in the Bavarian Diet, welcoming the appointment of Hindenburg as Chief of the General Staff as a proof that " all the weapons of Germany will be employed without reserve, and against all our enemies with equal relentlessness " (*Westminster Gazette,* September 29th, 1916). Bethmann-Hollweg told the Reichstag committee in 1919 that at the confidential conference of January 30th, 1917 (to consider President Wilson's suggestions of peace)

war have regretted the French "Carthaginian" policy with regard to Germany and the ruthless nationalist ambitions of Poland; but such evidence as I have seen seems to indicate that in each case the anti-humanitarian policy was supported by the Catholic Church, and only opposed by persons who were not members of that Church.

No one can, I think, accuse the Church of England of going, as the Lutheran and Catholic Churches in Germany and Austria and Poland and France seem to have gone, beyond the average of public opinion in advocating those incidents of the war and peace which have most deeply injured good will among mankind. In the advocacy of a League of Nations the Anglican Church in Britain and America has an honourable record; the Archbishop of Canterbury spoke at the important meeting of the League of Nations Society on May 14th, 1917, and on December 5th, 1918, was one of the signatories to an "appeal to Christians" on behalf of the League, issued by the official heads of all British Churches except the Roman Catholics, in which it is stated that the League is "now accepted by the consent both of leaders and of public opinion." [1] But future historians will, I think, say that

---

"All the Conservatives were for the submarine war, and against the very moderate peace terms we offered. The Centralists joined the Conservative ranks, and begged us not to stick to those terms if it really came to peace negotiations" (*New York Sun*, November 18th, 1919). Edward Bernstein said (*New Statesman*, March 20th, 1920), "The war was, in a degree, the work of the Austrian Catholic clergy, whose organ, the Vienna *Reichpost*, did very much to create the atmosphere which bred it in the Hapsburg Empire." On the other hand, the majority-socialist and anti-clerical *Vorwärtz* had the courage in 1917 to say, "There is such a thing as right, and Belgium has a right to her independent life" (*Daily Telegraph*, September 20th, 1917).

[1] *Daily News* (December 5th, 1918).

the official pronouncements of the Anglican Church did not go beyond public opinion at those moments of the war and peace when a courageous humanitarianism would have had most effect. The policy of the British Government during the election of December 1918, and, in consequence, during the peace negotiations of the following months, will, some day be generally thought of as a disaster to mankind. After the signature of the Armistice, and before that policy had been declared, Professor Deissman of Berlin forwarded, through the Archbishop of Upsala, an appeal " to the Christian leaders whom I know in the belligerent countries, to use all their influence so that the approaching peace may not contain the seed of new universal catastrophes "; and the Archbishop sent his reply to the English newspapers. It was a moment when a single word of kindness or even pity might have done incalculable good. But Lord Northcliffe's *Evening News*, which published the Archbishop's reply in full, rightly headed it as " a stern rebuke "; it sets out " the savagery which the German high command has displayed in carrying on the war," states that " the position would have been different had there been on the part of Christian circles in Germany any public protest against the gross wrongs, or any repudiation of their perpetrators," and, in a passage which the *Evening News* quotes as " the note which marks the reply," says, " righteousness must be vindicated even though the vindication involves sternness." [1]

---

[1] *Evening News* (November 27th, 1918). One has to be cautious in judging a church or party by its newspapers. But those who know the Church of England will agree that the *Church Times* is an unusually representative, as well as unusually able organ of the Anglo-Catholic, and the *Guardian* of the moderate High Church, parties. On October 17th, 1918, the editor of the *Guardian* wrote that " the Church must preach and the Allied Governments

17

In 1918 the Archbishop of York visited the United States, and preached at the Good Friday service in Trinity Church, New York, on the " seven words from the Cross." On May 11th, 1918, Lord Northcliffe's *Daily Mail*, in an article headed " On Loving the Hun," accused the Archbishop of inviting his hearers (while preaching from the words " Father forgive them ") " to think kindly, not only of the soldiers and peoples of Germany and Austria, but also of their rulers." The Archbishop replied, in a letter printed in the *Daily Mail* May 27th, 1918, " I did not choose the subject. Obviously it could not be avoided " ; and explained that he had said that a prayer for the forgiveness of our enemies " could not be a prayer that they should be let off." The *Mail* cabled to their New York correspondent, and appended to the Archbishop's letter the correspondent's reply—that there was no mistake about the words, which he had taken down in longhand, but that " they were spoken in a purely religious sense, and that there was nothing pacifist about them." " No practical man," wrote Canon Temple in 1915, " dreams of turning to the Church to find the way out from the intolerable situation into which the nations have drifted." [1]

must practise a righteous hardness of hearts," and as late as May 29th, 1919, the editor of the *Church Times* urged that the Allies " should insist on the strictest compliance with the Peace terms, and for every attempt to wriggle out of their obligations should impose still severer terms." As far as I know, no protest was made from the side of the Church against such headings as " Fewer little Huns," given by the editor of Lord Northcliffe's *Evening News* (March 3rd, 1919) to a paragraph calling attention to the high death-rate and low birth-rate of infants in Berlin, or against the head-line in Lord Northcliffe's *Daily Mail* (November 16th, 1918) referring to Solf's appeal to Wilson for economic aid, as " Hun Food Snivel."

[1] *Church and Nation* (1915), pp. 25, 26.

Future historians may also say that a great opportunity
was lost by the want of humanitarian imagination and
sympathy both among Irish Catholics and among British
statesmen, at the time of the Irish rising in 1916. But on
May 3rd, 1916, after the rising, the Anglican Archbishop
of Dublin wrote to the *Times* mentioning a rumour, " that
the officials at Dublin Castle are anxious to dispense
with martial law," and urging that " this is not the time
for amnesties and pardons ; it is the time for punishment
swift and stern." [1] Similarly, during the discussion of
the Dyer incident at Amritsar the Archbishop of Simla
wrote to the *Daily Mail* that " if the present tendency to
make a scapegoat of the white soldier amid a coloured
race succeeds, the military authorities in the future may
hesitate to act, and that hesitation will have consequences
which no white man cares to contemplate." [2]

There are many causes of this apparent contradiction
between the official claims and the actual influence of the
national Churches.[3]   In the case of the Church of England,
one cause is, I think, the absence of a consistent and helpful metaphysical " world-outlook."   To a Christian the old
paralyzing dilemma of will and fate must take a theological
form ; and the official leaders of the Church of England
do not seem even to attempt the solution of that dilemma
with sufficient intellectual seriousness.   The war raised,

----

[1] *Times* (May 5th, 1916).   [2] *Daily Mail* (May 26th, 1920).
[3] It may, of course, be argued, that no failure of Christianity
can be proof against the validity of its message.   Dr. Gore, for
instance, writes (in No. 1 of the S.P.C.K. *War-time Tracts for the
Workers*), " Christianity has not failed, we have only to try it."
But what the Archbishop of Canterbury asks for in his message
to " men and women of good will " is " considerate attention "
to " our work."   If a religion which has existed for two thousand
years and has been officially held by most powerful nations in the
world for fifteen hundred years, has not been tried, it has failed.

as did the earthquake of Lisbon in 1755, the question
whether God is omnipotent, or benevolent, or both, or
neither ? The leaders of the Church of England gave
us many answers. The Bishop of London was frankly
Manichean, " You have no right to blame God ; it's the
work of the Devil.   God is hindered at every moment by
the Devil and all his works ; you cannot therefore blame
our great and glorious God for the defeat of his design." [1]
The Bishop of Chichester told us not that God's design
has been defeated by the Devil, but that the apparent
failure of his design is due to our taking too short a view
of it. " May it not be that God has allowed this war,
with all its sorrow and suffering and misery and cruelty,
in order that we may hear His voice to which we have been
so long growing more and more deaf, and hearing we
may live a life worth living ? " [2] The Bishop of Chelms-
ford seems to have formed on this point a theology of his
own. " Why," he is reported to have asked, " did God
not interfere in the war ? " " It seemed as if God Himself were sitting on the fence." " How could we get Him
to come down on our side, and give us a mighty victory ? "
The bishop's answer seemed to be that God is bound by
his own nature to interfere in war on the side of the more

[1] Sermon at St. Giles's, Cripplegate (February 3rd, 1916), reported
in the *Christian World Pulpit* (February 16th, 1916).

[2] *The Guardian* (July 20th, 1916). So, the Anglican Bishop of
Edinburgh said in June 1916, " The unexpected hindrances that
we found in Gallipoli and Mesopotamia . . . are designed to
awaken a spirit of dependence on God " (*The Christian World
Pulpit*, June 28th, 1916). The very able High Church leader,
the late Dr. J. N. Figgis, put the same thought somewhat differently,
" God . . . acts precisely like a wise human parent. You may
have boons, gifts, pleasures that you are willing, and indeed desirous
to give to your children, but you will teach them that they are
not to have them unless they ask properly " (*The Christian World
Pulpit*, September 13th, 1916).

moral nation. By abandoning such moral offences as
" strikes, slackness in work, dishonesty in contracts, and
drink " we shall " get God out of His dilemma and make
it possible for Him to come and give us victory." [1] All
these views seemed rather to be forced from the bishops
by the need of meeting objections, than held with a confi-
dent sense of illumination. And none of the bishops
seemed to attempt, as the theologians of all parties in the
sixteenth and seventeenth centuries attempted, to think
out with logical thoroughness the implications of their
metaphysical beliefs.

Closely connected with the metaphysical problem of
divine omnipotence and benevolence is the problem of the
efficacy of prayer. On this point I read, during the war,
very many Anglican ecclesiastical pronouncements, and
always with the same feeling of the absence either of clear
conviction or serious intellectual effort. At the opening
of the war the prevalent ecclesiastical view seemed to be
that the more we pray the more likely is God to give us
the victory.[2] Throughout the war this doctrine remained
articulate. The Editor of the *Guardian* on February 2nd,
1916, stated that " for times of war the *locus classicus*
obviously occurs in the Old Testament " and quoted
Cowper—

> When Moses stood with arms spread wide,
> Success was found on Israel's side ;
> But when through weariness they failed,
> That moment Amalek prevailed.

---

[1] *Church Times* (February 18th, 1916). The Editor of the
Church Times on this occasion blames the bishop for his reckless
choice of words.

[2] The Bishop of London used his great influence to encourage
the formation of " prayer chains " which should make it certain
that prayer should go on without a break for twenty-four hours.
See *Church Times* (August 14th, 1914, and December 18th, 1914).

Admiral Sir David Beatty was often praised for the letter to the Society for the Promotion of Christian Knowledge in which he said, " Until religious revival takes place at home just so long will the war continue. When she [England] can look out on the future with humbler eyes and a prayer on her lips, then we can begin to count the days before the end." [1] The Anglican Bishop of Edinburgh put forward a curious Gnostic theory that " the spiritual forces that are liberated by our prayers " are helpless in respect to such obvious and calculable military factors as " equipments and munitions," but powerful in regard to such " unknown and unexpected factors " as " the wind, the rain, the light, the health and temperament of the general." [2]

But, as the war went on, the moral and metaphysical difficulties involved in the popular Old Testament conception that prayers by their mere urgency influence the result of battles made themselves felt. The Dean of St. Paul's excited some resentment in February 1916 by quoting the saying of Christ which forbids Christians to " use vain repetitions as the heathen do," and by arguing

[1] Quoted in *Public Opinion* (February 11th, 1916).

[2] Sermon reported in the *Christian World Pulpit* (June 28th, 1916). " Not only our righteous cause but our armies and our fleet and those of our Allies depend upon our prayers at least as much as they do on the equipment and munitions with which we supply them. Can we not learn—shall we not learn—that prayer reaches places where the wit of man can never find a way ? Is it not true that the more we know of engagements and battles the more we find out how much they depend on some unknown and unexpected factor—the wind, the rain, the light, the health and temperament of the general who is acting—elements quite beyond the power of guns and men and valour and strategy ? And does not the Word of God teach us again and again that it is just these very factors that are so susceptible to the spiritual forces that are liberated by our prayers ? "

that we should not " pester the Deity." [1] In 1916 the
phrase generally used on the subject by the more responsible ecclesiastical authorities was that by humbling
ourselves before God we should show ourselves " worthy
of victory." [2] Yet the new phrase seemed to me itself
to cover a certain deficiency in intellectual thoroughness.
It seemed to suggest that prayer would in fact lead to
victory without definitely saying so. There is a more
definite note in the Kaiser's address to his troops in
December 1916, " The act is in God's hands as is our
whole struggle. He will decide upon it, and we will leave
it to Him. We must not argue with His orderings. We
will be grateful to Him that we have thus far the honour
to be His instrument in the divine judgment that has come
upon our enemies. Let the decision fall as it will. The
hewing will proceed further till the adversary has enough "
(*Westminster Gazette*, December 19th, 1916).

But the current psychology of the Church of England
seemed to me during the war to be a more important
cause of practical weakness than its metaphysic. Recent
analysis of the subconscious in man, combined with
inquiries into primitive religion, have turned the attention
of all students to the origin of the impulses and emotions
which are stimulated by sacramental ritual. The psychology of the subconscious may indeed ultimately be

[1] See letters in the *Times* from Sir H. Craik and Dean Inge
(February 16th and 17th, 1916).
[2] See e.g. New Year's message from the Bishop of Winchester
at Worcester in the *Guardian* of January 6th, 1916. See also
a sermon by Canon Rees (July 22nd, 1915). The circular addressed
to me by my own Vicar before the National Mission (July 1916)
stated that " we have no right to look for the restoration of peace
unless we are trying to make ourselves worthy of it—indeed it is
possible that God is awaiting our true conversion to Him to end
the war."

found to have influenced thought about Christianity more
than the astronomy of Copernicus, or the philosophy of
Descartes, or the biology of Darwin. Some of the ablest
High Church ecclesiastics base on recent psychological
discoveries a claim both for the practical efficiency and
the speculative truth of Catholic sacramentalism. Dr.
Chandler, for instance, the Bishop of Bloemfontein, who
had watched the primitive rites of the South African
Kaffirs, wrote in 1911 a comparison of the " Dionysiac "
element in primitive religion with the intellectual element
in English Moderate Churchmanship. " In the worship
of Dionysius we recognize a passionate hunger for life
and immortality, a real religion which springs from real
human yearnings and intuitions, and which smacks of the
soil of its origin in its strange union of the playful and
grotesque with a fierce and savage ecstacy. Compared
to Dionysius, Apollo is a mere bloodless creation of poetical
imagination, a statue that can never come to life. The
worship of Apollo corresponds to a cold and stately service
of Matins as rendered in an English cathedral ; that of
Dionysius combines the profundity of a solemn Eucharist
with the orgies of the Salvation Army (p. 15). . . . The
primitive instinct of religion seized upon sacrifice as the
one essential rite in which it could find a natural and
adequate satisfaction for itself (p. 33). . . . It is very
obvious how the force of these primitive rites is expressed
in Christianity by the doctrine of the sacrifice of Christ,
God and Man, a sacrifice which effects reconciliation or
atonement, and the merits of which are applied to
individuals by the communion with God which is secured
in the Eucharistic feast (p. 34). . . . If we value the
natural and primitive instincts of religion, which we have
recognized to be the foundation of revealed truth, then a

revelation which thus marvellously justifies and perfects them must gain thereby, to say the least, a very strong claim on our consideration (p. 35). [1]

Mr. C. E. Osborne, Rector of Wallsend-on-Tyne,[2] one of the ablest of the leaders of the Anglo-Catholic movement, is even more explicit. He says, " In all ages communion of the worshippers . . with the God and with one another is effected and expressed by means of a sacred feast, the ' eating with the God,' or ' eating the God,' in Hebrew language the ' eating bread before Yahve.' The Eucharist in some form or other is as old as religion and as world-wide. Only as religions become philosophies do they cease to be sacramental. Mohammedanism is, of course, an exception, but it is a comparatively modern religion. Buddhism is in essence a philosophy. All naïve original religions, not smelling of the lamp, not children of the brain, but springing as it were direct from the soil, have been sacramental religions. The fact that of all religious services, the Eucharist or Mass is that which draws and holds great bodies of worshippers in Christendom, and among those worshippers large numbers of men (as conspicuously in Russia as in the West) . . . is immensely significant . . . the instinctive common-sense of the humanity of the common people even when baptized into so spiritual a religion as Christianity, remains incorrigibly sacramental, wedded to the concrete, as far as it has any religious sense. It cannot grasp an academic religion." [3] In the great struggle now going on

[1] *Faith and Experience : an Analysis of the Factors of Religious Knowledge.* By Arthur Chandler, Bishop of Bloemfontein. London (1911).

[2] Author of *Religion in Europe and the World Crisis* (1916).

[3] *Church Times* (March 31st, 1916). Sermon on *Sacraments and Common Sense.*

between Mohammedan monotheism and primitive paganism in Africa Mr. Osborne would obviously be on the side of paganism.

The arguments of writers like Bishop Chandler and Mr. Osborne seem often to involve one of two assumptions ; either that for the purpose of sacramental apologetic the reality of the sacramental emotion is a sufficient proof of its supernatural origin ; or that in dealing with non-rational facts one need not argue rationally—since " He who drives fat oxen should himself be fat." On the other hand, Dr. Inge, the Dean of St. Paul's, who is himself a mystic of a more intellectualist type, admits that primitive rites satisfy instinctive cravings, but seems to argue that the calculated adoption of an irrational mental attitude by a modern church in the modern world, must result in intellectual superficiality and moral weakness. Describing the state of English society before the war, he says, " The greater part of our lives so far as we are masters of our time, was taken up with playing at emotions which were once serious things in the days of primitive man, but which now only survive as irrational promptings to do things for which civilization provides no outlet. The life of the savage is mainly taken up with fighting, which he regards as a semi-religious exercise, and dresses up in his best finery to perform it, in hunting for his daily food, and in deprecating the malevolence of unknown spiritual powers by sacrifices, incantations, and queer ritual. All these things we have been diligently playing at, in order, if we knew it, to gain what Aristotle calls ' a purgation of the emotions,' a relief from vague inarticulate desires. . . . Instead of hunting we massacre harmless birds and animals bred for the purpose. And is not too much of our religion in its most fashionable forms a sort of playing at the sombre superstitions of the savage, carefully disguised in decent æsthetic forms ? And all this make-believe is so utterly futile and barren. It soothes the savage nature in us, and makes us superficially at peace with ourselves ; but how lamentably superficial it all is, and how entirely out of connection with all the realities of life." [1]

The Dean's argument was pushed still further in a quite extraordinarily touching and penetrating sermon (which I wish that I could quote in full) by the late Canon H. Scott Holland on June 4th, 1916. Referring to " our new discovery of the range and survey of the subconscious " he says, " We have for the first time become distinctly aware of that dim underworld that lies below the level of our actual vision, and yet plays so vital a part in colouring each thought and action. . . . From below and from beneath the level of conscious life there surges up out of the depth of nature a strange multitudinous movement going far back into the regions of vegetable and animal life through which we emerge into daylight. . . . Our Christianity is not in the least afraid to acknowledge how deep our roots go down into the hidden soil of the underworld. But none of this avails to cancel the compensating truth which is, that, small as is the space which consciousness illumines, nevertheless in that illuminated spot lies the key to our whole position. There, in it, is laid out the arena on which the spiritual battle is lost and won. . . . It is on this supreme importance of consciousness that the faith of Jesus Christ lays all its emphasis. There are religions, as we know, which tend in the other direction. They invite man to communion

[1] Sermon by the Dean of St. Paul's in the Temple Church, *The Guardian* (October 8th, 1914).

with the Divine by swooning back into those inarticulate and unreasoning abysses of emotion in which personal and individual consciousness is lost. But the Jew has passed on the word to the Christian Church that truth has not to be sought in chants or ecstasy, but in the reasonable spirit of prophecy. . . . Thought and will must come out into the open and make their venture. 'For judgment am I come into the world'; to force a decisive choice upon the indeterminate elusive soul. The stress of life comes to its climax in that decision." [1] If Canon Scott Holland were still alive, I should ask him whether he is sure that if the growing generation of young wide-minded men and women follow his advice, if their "thought and will come out into the open and make their venture," that venture will necessarily lead to catholic orthodoxy. He himself had gone far from the naïve apologetic of Archbishop Whately, "If you admit . . . Paul's epistles to be genuine, and not the work of a fool, or a madman, or an imposter, he must have been inspired because he says so." [2] But meanwhile to many young Anglican

[1] The Commonwealth (July 1916). Part of this sermon is printed in The Philosophy of Faith (H. Scott Holland, 1920), and I have corrected two misprints from it. The Commonwealth version is later and much better.

[2] Life, Vol. I, p. 424 (1839). Canon Scott Holland may have indicated one side of his own intellectual position when he said in the same sermon, "We know that to recover confidence we shall have to go down to the very ground of our life and test and sift and prove what it is that will stand unshaken in the day of the Lord . . . the platitudes on which we have confidently rested break from under us. . . . Men are . . . ignorant of what they themselves intend . . . they cannot commit themselves . . . they are evidently taking stock of themselves. . . . They have got to do a lot of thinking before they know where they stand. . . . Such is our mood surely. . . . And then [the Church] believes that there will come at last the Hour of Speech : the hour of the conscious and free Word." If so, it may be that death came on him before his thinking was completed.

priests the leadership of Bishop Chandler and Mr. Osborne, the policy of " The Mass for the Masses," [1] will make an irresistible appeal. The rites which he will use as a " Catholic " are of tried efficacy, and his daily experience indicates to him that the more intellectualist forms of worship developed in the English Church during the seventeenth and eighteenth centuries are losing their power to attract. The letters and sermons in the *Church Times* reveal an agonizing sense of futility produced by what Dr. Dearmer calls " the dismal turning of the Hanoverian prayer wheel," [2] the recitation of the morning and evening services of the Prayer Book to inattentive congregations in churches half-empty on Sundays and nearly empty on week-days. " Men," writes one clergyman, " who have faced death in the trenches . . . will never be content to sit in a hypnotic trance while prayers, psalms, and lessons, are read over to them [3]; " and another writes, " I suppose no one except the priest of a country parish can realize the absolute indifference to religion which prevails. Such ' religion ' as may exist to the English rustic is really a sort of pantheism. God is either rather a disagreeable man responsible for all their troubles, or a negligible quantity. People know nothing about the Sacraments and care less. The proportion of communicants is infinitesimal." [4] With the bored indifference of the Anglican " parade service " the Anglo-Catholic Army Chaplains contrasted the fervour of the Breton soldier at the Roman Mass, and the religious

[1] This phrase is often used, see e.g. the reference to it by the Bishop of Carlisle, *Hibbret Journal* (January 1917), p. 239.

[2] *Church Times* (January 19th, 1917).

[3] Letter signed R. B. Nevitt, *Church Times* (April 14th, 1916).

[4] *Church Times* (April 28th, 1916). Letter signed " A Parish Priest."

ecstasy which they read of as existing throughout the whole Russian Army. " The remedy," declared Father Bull (one of the most important of the Anglo-Catholic leaders), " was to make the Eucharist the parade service. Experience proved that when men saw the Sacraments they desired them." [1] Priests, indeed, from the stone ages onward, have stood before armies, not to repeat familiar and indifferent words, but to do medicine for victory, and to deepen thereby the instinctive sense of comradeship which men, like all other gregarious animals, feel when assembled to resist their enemies. The only objection to the claim of sacramental Christianity to be both an efficient war instrument and an efficient world religion is that implied in M. Barbusse's account of the airman flying above the lines in France and seeing the Mass performed simultaneously at French and German altars for the success of both armies.[2] But to me that objection is unanswerable.

The main defect, indeed, of sacramental emotion as a basis for religion is its want of connection with any general ethical scheme. Primitive religion, we are told by anthropologists, was not ethical ; it mainly originated in the " early science " of magic, i.e. in the performance, not necessarily accompanied by any strong emotion,[3] of rites considered necessary for the success of the crops and the health of the tribe and of its herds. Only those

[1] *Church Times* (February 25th, 1916). Speech by Fr. Paul Bull at a meeting of the English Church Union.

[2] *Le Feu*, p. 282 (translation by W. Fitzwater Wray).

[3] See B. Malinowski, *Journal of the Anthropological Institute* (July–December 1916), pp. 380 and 382, on the *ioba* or ceremonial hunting away of the spirits in the Trobiand Islands. " There is no doubt that the *ioba* . . . is a matter of importance. It would never on any account be omitted . . . but in its performance it has no traces of sanctity or even seriousness."

rites now survive which are accompanied by strong emotional effects. But the emotions produced by them do not point to any clear line of conduct. They may strengthen any ethical impulse which happens to be already current in the group which practises them, but they add nothing of their own ; we are told, for instance, that Spanish brigands take the Sacrament as a means of success in their occupation. In a highly industrialized society like that of England the current morality generally, though not always, indicates socially useful conduct in the customary " short-range " relations of a man with his neighbours. When practised by men and women of naturally humane instincts who have been influenced by the recorded sayings of Jesus they produce from time to time lives which it would be an impertinence to praise. But experience shows that sacramental religion does not of itself and by itself offer any clear guide in the " long-range " ethical problems which involve different social or racial groups with different ethical customs, or in new problems which have not yet become questions of custom. Yet it is in respect to new and long-range problems that our biologically inherited instincts are now least helpful, and the socially inherited world-outlook which religion claims to provide is most important. The Archdeacon of London [1] spoke in 1917 of the thousands who were " living or trying to live up to the standard life of a weekly communicant." What is that " standard life " in respect to those international or industrial relations on which the very existence of modern civilization depends ? The *Church Times* in 1914 quoted " the scandal of German militarism " as a proof of the ill effects of German modernism, and as showing " how the paths diverging

[1] *Church Times* (September 14th, 1917).

from the Catholic belief have led to the rejection of the old ethical standard." [1] But when, in the matter of militarism, did that "old ethical standard" actually prevail among the body of faithful Catholics ? Was it in the days of Constantine, or Hildebrand, or Simon de Montfort, or Bossuet ?

On the other hand, the duty of performing accurately the rite is always clear ; and sacramental religions therefore tend to exalt ritual above a rational calculation of the effects of conduct. If Europe, for instance, is to recover permanently from the disaster of the war, the problem of human reproduction is at least as important as the problem of nutrition ; and every politician knows that clear thought and wise action on that subject will be hindered by the organized opposition of the clergy of the Church of England. Marriage is one of the Catholic sacraments, and almost the whole Catholic party believe, on sacramental grounds, that a marriage once consummated should be indissoluble. At present the law (created by decisions of the courts but unchangeable without an Act of Parliament) is that if a man after marriage contracts syphilis and infects his wife, so that she is henceforward incapable of bearing healthy children, she may divorce him, marry again, and bear legitimate but unhealthy children. If he contracts syphilis, but does not infect his wife, she may get a separation from him, but may not divorce him and may not bear healthy and legitimate children.[2]

Sacramentalism, in spite of its obvious efficiency in stimulating emotion, has the further disadvantage of

[1] *Church Times* (November 6th, 1914).
[2] The *Guardian* calls the whole theory of eugenics "the ethics of the farmyard applied to humanity" (March 2nd, 1916).

strengthening the most dangerous tendencies of the Church considered as a guild of organized producers. Ordination is a Catholic sacrament, which gives supernatural authority to the claim of the properly ordained clergy to a monopoly in the exercise of spiritual authority. It is therefore possible to find in the Church more clearly than anywhere else the typical faults of the guild outlook, the hatred of the schismatic blackleg, the fear of the shock to mental habit caused by the inventiveness of the heretic, the insistence that the guildsman alone shall fix, on a basis which constantly tends to narrow itself, the terms of entry to the guild. The clergyman's profession is on one side that of a teacher, and his teaching impulse is, like that of other teachers, naturally intermittent ; but he claims supernatural authority for his guild dislike of the idea of an intermittent exercise of his office : " Once a priest always a priest."

From the beginning of the eighteenth century to the recent rapid growth of the High Church party the corporate feeling of the Anglican clergy has been that rather of the social class of " gentlemen," consisting mainly of laymen, than that of a supernaturally privileged guild of ecclesiastics. This is no longer true, and is becoming, especially among the urban clergy, every year less true. One of the causes and effects of this combination of a growing professionalism in the Church with a growing emphasis on the subconscious mind as against the conscious reason, is an acknowledged lowering of the standard both of natural ability and of acquired education among those who become clergymen. The report of the Archbishops' Committee on the Teaching Office of the Church (1919) says (p. 8), " There has been a tendency to contrast the intellectual with the spiritual. . . . The result has been a depreciation and a fear of the honest operation of the intellect . . . fewer able men seek ordination." [1] At the same time some of the more extreme sacramentalists disparage the English tradition that an Anglican priest should always be a highly educated man. " Priests," says the Editor of the *Church Times* (April 7th, 1916), " may be found in abundance among men of less education than has recently been demanded in candidates for Holy Orders. . . . Men of little education can minister the sacraments and do much of the routine work required. . . . If the English people, like the Russians, were in the habit of frequenting the sacraments, and seeking the ministration of the priesthood as a matter of course, the problem would be simplified," and again, " It is most desirable that people shall be taught that we make our confession to a priest because he is a priest with supernatural powers, not because he is a man whom we like or trust. . . . Cases are not unknown of people refusing even to go to confession when their usual confessor is absent. It . . . helps one to understand what some one . . . meant when he said that if he had daughters he would send them to make their first confession to a drunken priest in order that they might understand that it was not the personality of the man that mattered but his priesthood." [2]

[1] Bishop Welldon (Dean of Manchester and late Headmaster of Harrow School) argued in 1915 against a large increase of the episcopate because " the Church does not attract so many men of high intellectuality into Holy Orders as of yore " (*Guardian*, October 21st, 1915). See also the *Church Times* (May 23rd, 1919) on the " Post Ordination Studies of the Clergy," which says, " The intellectual status of the clergy, so far from advancing *pari passu* with that of the people, has now for many years been declining not merely relatively but absolutely. . . . The ideal of a learned clergy would seem to have been forgotten."

[2] Leader in *Church Times* (May 12th, 1916).

One effect of the growth of sacramental guild-feeling will be a change in the position of the Anglican Church as a political force. The Church will be more independent than it has been of the Conservative Party, and will probably take a political line like that of the Church in France under the Third Republic, and in Germany and Italy and, perhaps, Russia since the war. The change will be quickened if, as seems now almost certain, the "establishment" of the Church—the *concordat* which secures for the state the appointment of bishops and the ultimate control of Church discipline—breaks down, as similar arrangements have broken down in the rest of the world. Many Anglo-Catholics openly call for disestablishment.[1] Cabinets and Premiers are no longer predominantly Anglican, and the powers of self-government given to the Church of England by the Enabling Act of 1920 will undoubtedly strengthen the demand for a real independence. If the clergy secure the right of appointing the bishops that fact will undoubtedly strengthen the sacramental party, and will tend to the exclusion of other parties. The process of disestablishment will also be accompanied by a greater or less measure of disendowment, which will leave the clergy with a burning sense of injustice and sacrilege. Judging from continental instances, the Church will then become a disruptive rather than a conservative force ; it will tend to ally itself with the anti-democratic guild-feeling in the

[1] See an able article in the *New Statesman* of August 28th, 1920, describing the Anglo-Catholic Conference at the Albert Hall : "Several speakers, including two of the most respected missionary bishops, denounced the establishment in terms which might have been thought fifty years ago a little strong at a Liberation Society meeting, and their denunciation was greated with roars of applause from an audience which packed the great Hall."

Trade Unions,[1] and with any anti-parliamentary party
in the army or elsewhere which is in favour of the restoration of personal monarchy. The Coronation Service still
bears traces of the medieval claim that the authority of
the monarch is a delegation from the sacramental authority
of the Church ; and the Editor of the *Church Times*
(January 28th, 1916) argued that " the eagerness with which
the public mind entered some years ago into the conception
of the Coronation Service affords reason for thinking that
the nation would rally round the venerable throne as the
centre of its regulated life. Parliamentary institutions
do not appear to have an important future. Something
more efficient, but also making more appeal to the imagination and the religious sense is needed." In the next
number (February 4th, 1914) the editor glorified Charles I,
and deprecated the idea, " that it was the King's duty
to obey Parliament rather than his conscience." Such
things in times of social peace may be negligible, but
in times of social strain, when perhaps a moderate socialist
government is in power, opposed by a syndicalist minority
and by the whole of the classes which furnish professional
officers to the army, they may become important. But
while a self-governing sacramental Church with a grievance
will always be ready to weaken the parliamentary state,
it will do so not in the interests of the responsibility and
initiative of the individual citizen, but in the interests
either of the Church as a corporation, or of the nation
as an ideal personality. Dr. Melville Scott expressed a
wide-spread clerical feeling when he wrote to the *Guardian*

[1] See e.g. S. G. Hobson, *National Guilds*, p. 259, " the Church
which, by the way, is a guild." In October 1920 Canon William
Temple said that " Guild Socialism was the system he would vote
for if he had the chance to-morrow " (*Church Times*, Oct. 15th,
1920).

(September 21st, 1916), " The War has put the individual in his proper place." During the war I was surprised to see how completely British Catholics (whether Anglican of Roman) accepted that subordination of the individual to the nation which was the main count in our case against Prussian political thought. The Editor of the *Church Times* wrote on September 3rd, 1915, " A French priest in France can be purely patriotic in his catholicity ; he is bound to pray for his country, to act for it, and in case of need even to fight for it. A German priest in Germany, whatever he may think privately of his country's policy, is tied to the same patriotic course. In either case the larger duty is fulfilled by a careful performance of the smaller, just as the catholicity of a Christian man is expressed by loyal adherence to his own bishop." [1] Father Bernard Vaughan, who was the most popular and effective controversialist among British Roman Catholics, wrote at the beginning of 1916 to the *Daily Graphic* in favour of the " cry," " Keep on killing Germans." When asked by a correspondent, " Do your Jesuit Fathers of the German province accept your advice to keep on killing Germans ? " he answered, " If they did, all I would say to them would be, ' You would be shot for it, and it serves you right '." [2]

The chief point on which a sacramental and independent Church will concentrate its efforts will be the securing of as much control as possible in schools and colleges supported by the community, and the maintenance in the schools so controlled of that general mental attitude which is called in current educational controversy the

[1] An ex-Army chaplain wrote on July 20th, 1916, in the *Guardian* that for a chaplain " a *robust* [the italics are mine] belief in the national cause is absolutely vital. His opinions on the rightfulness or otherwise of war are quite immaterial."

[2] Quoted in the *Evening News* (February 10th, 1916).

" atmosphere." " What is wanting," says the *Church Times*, " in English Christianity is the supernatural atmosphere and temper " (May 5th, 1916). A *Church Times* article on " The State of Religion " (March 24th, 1916) complains also that " there is no atmosphere of the supernatural," and urges that " the whole scheme of religious knowledge," falsely so called, should be drastically reformed," that the children in Church schools " from their earliest youth should be brought into touch with the supernatural by being present week by week at the Holy Eucharist, that they should be definitely and thoroughly instructed in the sacramental system as a whole." " To teach the doctrine of the Mass," says the Editor of the *Church Times* (January 11th, 1916), " without insisting on attendance at Mass is as futile as to attempt to teach horsemanship by lectures in a classroom. The truth of the Real Presence is grasped easily and naturally in the presence of the Sacrament ; without this it remains something vague and obscure and unrelated to life and practice." The existing religious lessons do not produce " a robust loyalty to the Catholic Church." From the outbreak of the war till the Russian revolution of 1917 British sacramentalists were never tired of pointing to Russia as an instance of a nation in which this " atmosphere of the supernatural " actually prevailed. We have seen since then, in the published letters of the Czaritsa, in the accounts of the influence of Rasputin, and in the whole social history of Russia, what are the dangers to national life involved in that deliberate return to the world-outlook of the stone ages which the *Church Times* advocates and the late M. Podiedonostseff achieved.[1]

[1] It is disquieting to see how easily the " atmosphere of the supernatural " penetrates the minds even of highly educated

No one, however, in any modern industrialized society is likely to be as successful as was M. Podiedonostseff in agricultural Russia. What is likely is that in English " Church schools " and American " parochial schools " a minority of the community will be brought up (with increasing precautions, as the intellectual difficulties of orthodoxy increase) in the same atmosphere of the supernatural, and will show in later life the same " robust loyalty to the Church " at elections, as do the more religious-minded products of the Catholic schools in Paris, or the Flemish children whom I saw waiting their turn to kiss the glass cylinder containing the Holy Blood at Bruges. Meanwhile, the general fear of a recrudescence of religious controversy may, in the case of Britain, tend to maintain such compromises as the wooden " Cowper Temple " Bible lessons in the municipal elementary schools, and the numbing conventional Anglicanism of the secondary endowed " public schools." [1] It is difficult enough to teach boys and girls to watch for and welcome that

Englishmen living in contact with primitive thought. The Bishop of Bunbury (ex-Bishop of Melanesia) speaking for the Melanesian Mission said, " It should be an inducement to young men to go out to Melanesia that they had opportunities there . . . which never occurred at home. They lived in fact in the atmosphere of the Acts of the Apostles, the natives having converse with spirits and performing acts that could not be explained, and the missionary seemed to be endowed with special power to deal with these manifestations of an evil power " (Church Times, June 11th, 1920). In a letter in the Church Times of April 17th, 1919, the writer says, " When I was Town Major of a village near Doullens last June I saw the box palm of the previous Palm Sunday being used by an old lady to sprinkle with holy water the door-posts of her house and barns in view of an approaching storm. What a pity it is that we cannot be more simple in our religion."

[1] " Our disingenuous Anglican compromise is like a cold in the English head, and the higher education in England is a training in evasion " (H. G. Wells in Daily News, January 5th, 1917).

feeling of vague discomfort which, if resolutely followed up, is the precursor of creative thought.[1] But if, in the case of the most important of all subjects, they are either definitely warned against that feeling as " doubt," or are discouraged, by the silent example of their teachers, from the venture of thought and will for which Canon Scott Holland pleaded, the difficulty is enormously increased.

What, then, ought " men and women of good will " who are " beyond the frontiers of the Christian Society " to do in answer to the Archbishop's appeal ? There are, I think, two courses open to them. The first is that for which Disraeli so ably argued. " If," he said in 1861, in an obviously sincere letter to his old friend Mrs. Brydges Willyams, " the Church were to fall, philosophy would not profit : we should only be handed over to a narrow-minded and ignorant fanaticism," [2] by which he means what he called in 1870 (in the General Preface to his novels) " the medieval superstitions, which are generally only the embodiments of pagan ceremonies and creeds." To a man holding this view, the control of the Church by the state is essential, and the Church so controlled becomes the best guardian of rational intellectual freedom and social coherence. It is to this argument that the

---

[1] See *ante*, Chapter II.

[2] *Life*, Vol. IV, p. 360. It is interesting to see the form which this argument took in an almost contemporary public pronouncement. " Man is a being born to believe. And if no Church comes forward with its title-deeds of truth, sustained by the tradition of sacred ages and by the conviction of countless generations, to guide him, he will find altars and idols in his own heart and his own imagination. . . . There are no tenets however extravagant, and no practices however objectionable, which will not in time develop under such a state of affairs " (Speech at Oxford, *Life*, Vol. IV, p. 371).

Church of England officially appealed in 1918, when asking for subscriptions to a " Central Fund." " By beginning in the earliest years to form the character of the people, religious education saves the nation from uncountable evils and dangers. Even as a mere investment the cost of the work would be well worth the Nation's while, through its citizens to defray. The ideal of service, the obligations of self-support and thrift, of temperance, soberness and chastity firmly established in the minds of the young, enrich society." [1] To Disraeli's view there are two obvious objections. The control of the Church by the state is doomed, and the disestablished Church, endowed or disendowed, will apparently be directed in the near future by those forces which Disraeli called " ignorant fanaticism." And Disraeli's attitude involves, on the part of those who adopt it, a degree of personal evasion and reticence in which Disraeli himself delighted, but the effect of which on most men is bad. Disraeli said that he held " the religion of all sensible men," but that " sensible men never tell " what it is. Those who are determined never to tell their beliefs seldom take the trouble to think them out, and at this moment I am sure that the " good form " and " good sense " which in England, and still more in America, prevents so large a proportion of educated men and women from deciding whether they accept or reject the supernatural claims of Christian orthodoxy have a real tendency to sterilize the intellectual life of our nations.

The second course open to " those beyond the frontiers of the Christian Society " is the personal effort of clear thought and frank speech on religious questions. To-

[1] Official appeal beginning, " The Church of England appeals." *Observer* (November 24th, 1918).

wards the end of the nineteenth century some one said that " the great events of the twentieth century will be events in the region of the intellect." So far that prophecy has been grimly falsified ; but the twentieth century is still young, and the prophecy may still be fulfilled. Again, as in the fifth century before Christ, or the sixteenth or eighteenth centuries after Christ, men and women may find themselves stimulated by their own intellectual needs, and by the example of their fellows, to think and speak on the whole relation of man to the universe. If such a period of intellectual energy occurs, it will, I believe, reveal the fact that much of the religion of Christendom, and particularly of the English-speaking peoples, is in a position of unstable equilibrium. The particular combination of the tradition of a great teacher with elements drawn from ancient mythology and contemporary East Mediterranean religion and philosophy, which was formulated at Nicæa in 325 A.D., may now prove to be no more firmly rooted than was the Græco-Roman state religion—in spite of its temples and priesthoods and its intimate connection with men's habits of thought and speech and feeling and education—when Lucian attacked it in the second century A.D. It is true that there is evidence which persuades many observers that Christian orthodoxy will maintain or even increase its authority by shedding its mythology and absorbing non-Christian ideas. But a time comes when a religion loses its power of retaining its vitality in a new form ; there were indications of a corresponding transformation of the state religion in the times of Marcus Aurelius and Porphyry, but the transformed faith soon died out. I myself think it more probable that the children or grandchildren of most of those who reject the main dogmas of

Christian orthodoxy will cease to call themselves Christians ; and that Christian tradition will come to be represented in the Western nations by a minority of born mystics and their followers.

If that happens what world-outlook will take the place now occupied by Christianity in our social heritage, and in what way will it affect the life of mankind ? To that question no one, I believe, can give a simple answer. New religions of the type of Buddhism and Christianity and Mohammedanism and Bahaism, where a supernatural mythology forms itself round the facts of a religious teacher's life, will appear, but are not likely, in the presence of the modern newspaper reporter and photographer, and the atmosphere of modern science, to spread over the world. Something more like the " philosophies " of Zeno and Epicurus in the Roman Empire may have a better chance. If our educational systems are not starved by war and the consequences of war, they may so develop that whole populations will have access to the outlines of agreed knowledge and to the emotional appeal of great literature. Differences in mental training may follow differences of individual nature, and not differences of hereditary class or caste. If so, Bagehot's assumption that political authority must be based on " the credulous obedience of enormous masses," and the corresponding assumption underlying the phrase, " the Mass for the Masses " may seem less convincing than they do now, and many social and professional and racial hindrances to the free exchange of thought may be broken down. A book of sayings by some countryman of Confucius or Laotze, who has known Western civilization and has accepted it without dread and without illusion as an instrument of the good life, may then seem true, not only

in Pekin and the cities of the Yangtze valley, but to many
thoughtful men and women in New York and London,
and Moscow and Milan. Artisans and teachers and
societies of college students may begin to use some term
like " The Path," for an ethical plan based on a common
world-outlook and making a common emotional appeal.
It may be that there will be several such competing
" philosophies," existing side by side with many new and
old " religions."   No attempt, such as was made in Czarist
Russia, to enforce religious uniformity within any nation
by state persecution is now probable.

But meanwhile, in the national educational systems,
in the celebration of great events, in the use of periodical
days of leisure and of reflection, and in many sides of the
development of the arts of music and painting and literature,
the need will still be felt for means by which emotions
common to the great majorities of whole populations can
be expressed. On November 11th, 1918, as I came back
from telling the news of the armistice to a family of Belgian
exiles who had wept with joy, I passed the buildings of a
big endowed school. The boys were assembled in the hall,
and were apparently singing all the doggerel verses of
" God Save the King."   I listened, trying to imagine the
hymns that were being sung before other national flags
in all the schools of the Allies ; and a conviction swept
through me that the special task of our generation might
be so to work and think as to be able to hand on to the
boys and girls who fifty years hence, at some other turning
point of world-history, may gather in the schools, the
heritage of a world-outlook deeper and wider and more
helpful than that of modern Christendom.

INDEX